THE MAKING OF JUDGE DREDD

From HOLLYWOOD PICTURES ANDREW G. VAJNA Presents An EDWARD R. PRESSMAN / CINERGI Production In Association With CHARLES M. LIPPINCOTT A DANNY CANNON Film

SYLVESTER STALLONE "JUDGE DREDD" ARMAND ASSANTE DIANE LANE ROB SCHNEIDER JOAN CHEN JURGEN PROCHNOW and MAX VON SYDOW Music by ALAN SILVESTRI

Special Visual Effects by MASS.ILLUSION Film Editors ALEX MACKIE HARRY KERAMIDAS Production Designer NIGEL PHELPS Director of Photography ADRIAN BIDDLE, B.S.C. Executive Producers ANDREW G. VAJNA EDWARD R. PRESSMAN

Based on the JUDGE DREDD Characters, Owned by FLEETWAY PUBLICATIONS LIMITED and Created by JOHN WAGNER and CARLOS EZQUERRA Written by WILLIAM WISHER and STEVEN E. DE SOUZA Produced by CHARLES M. LIPPINCOTT BEAU E. L. MARKS

THE MAKING OF JUDGE DREDD

JANE KILLICK

WITH DAVID CHUTE AND CHARLES M. LIPPINCOTT

BOXTREE

First published in 1995 by Boxtree Ltd, Broadwall House, 21 Broadwall, London SE1 9PL

10 9 8 7 6 5 4 3 2 1

Designed by Dan Newman
from a concept by Nigel Davies

Reproduction by Jade Reprographics Limited

Printed and bound in Great Britain by
Cambus Litho Limited

ISBN: 0 7522 0641 9

A CIP catalogue entry for this book is available from the British Library.

Acknowledgements

The Publishers would like to thank the following: Erick Feitshans at Cinergi and Liliana Bolton and Mike Lake for making this book possible; Richard Blanshard for all the stills and behind-the-scenes photographs; Daniel Karp and William McCoy for the post-production photographs; Terry O'Neill for his photographs of Sylvester Stallone; Chris Halls for allowing us access to his Mean Machine material; Alex Rutherford for the graphics; Steve McManus at Fleetway and all the *2000 AD* artists featured in this book; Storyboard Artists Robbie Consing, Dennis Rich and John Greaves; Nigel Phelps, Matt Codd and Simon Merton for all their help sourcing the artwork; Diane Pearlman at Mass.Illusion; Peter Acton; Bernie Morris and the *Judge Dredd* cast and crew who made us feel so welcome at Shepperton; and finally, to all the other people, too numerous to mention, who made invaluable contributions to this book.

CONTENTS

2000 AD... AND ALL THAT

LEVEL 1

MEET the TOUGHEST LAWMAN of THEM ALL...

Judge Dredd's first appearance in 2000 AD, *way back in 1977*

Nowadays, the British comic book has a deservedly high reputation among fans around the world. In addition to Judge Dredd and his *2000 AD* cronies, trend-setting writers like Alan Moore (*Watchmen*) and Neil Gaiman (*Sandman*), and newer cult objects such as *Tank Girl*, have given British comics a distinct cachet. But in the past, Britain's comics rivaled its food as its least popular commercial product.

Many successful British comic books have been humor anthology offerings like the classic and clean cut weeklies *Dandy and Beano*. In recent years, *Beano* has been superseded by the raunchy, wildly successful *Viz*, a sort of bad-taste version of *Mad* whose clueless standard-bearers include characters like Johnny Fartpants and Buster Gonad and his Unfeasibly Large Testicles.

American-style superheroes were few and far between in England. The most familiar British super-guy, Marvelman, a 50s spin-off from the litigation-plagued American creation, Captain Marvel, was revived by Alan Moore in the late seventies, in edgy postmodern style. (The name was eventually changed to *Miracleman*, after Marvel Comics threatened a proprietary lawsuit over the use of the word "Marvel".) Moore's version was a surpassingly passionate look at the life of an ordinary man who happened to be *afflicted* with superhuman abilities.

Judge Dredd wasn't cut from the same cloth as the muscle-bound American superhero. Home-court fans like the young Danny Cannon approved of the fact that "he didn't wear a cape, that he was tough, that he was *cool*." The merciless future cop Joseph Dredd, *2000 AD*'s most popular character, might have seemed a long-shot candidate for youth cult status. Although he was introduced in 1977, at the height of the British punk movement, he always looked a lot more like one of *them*. Sneering "Freeze, creep" at his cringing criminal prey, he was openly modeled upon Clint Eastwood's authoritarian shamus Dirty Harry Callahan – "fascist overtones and all," in the words of John Wagner, Dredd's first writer and, with artist Carlos Ezquerra, his official co-creator.

The Angel Gang: Mean, Link, Pa and Junior with Fink in the foreground. Mean Machine, left, would bulk up considerably for the movie

The British pop culture scholar Martin Barker talks about "the role of future fantasy in thinking about increasingly disempowered readers." His article "Seeing How Far You Can See: On Being a 'Fan' of *2000 AD*" considers why high-intensity action fantasies like *Judge Dredd*, *Robocop* and *The Terminator* tend to be most popular with kids who

Carlos Ezquerra's work from Prog 32: a slim and young-looking Dredd

Above: *Dredd dispenses his usual form of justice*

Above right: *Dredd as profiled by Bolland – good strong jaw, but never enough forehead*

are either tough or crave toughness – kids who, if they thought it through, would realize that they are a lot more like the "perps" the robo-protagonist blows away.

Nevertheless, Dredd was a pop icon for English punks, mods and skinheads right from the start, a popular T-shirt emblem and the subject of several pop songs, including "I Am the Law," by the Human League, and two tunes, "Mutants in Mega City One" and "Mutant Blues," by The Fink Brothers (aka Madness).

Throughout the 1980s and into the '90s, Joe Dredd was the most popular pop hero in Britain. When future *Judge Dredd* movie director Danny Cannon was living in suburban Luton, England as a teenage rock fan, he says his first conscious wish was "to be [new wave rock star] Paul Weller" when he grew up. Never a fan of the form, the only comic book he read regularly was *2000 AD,* a weekly anthology title specializing in hard-edged, sarcastic science fiction. And he was not alone.

In 1977, a British comics newcomer named Pat Mills was appointed editor of *2000 AD,* a new science fiction adventure comic weekly for publisher IPC Magazines, Ltd, launched several months prior to the *Star Wars* premiere. Mills came up with the cool-sounding moniker Judge Dredd, although his first thought was to make the character a steely occult investigator. Meanwhile, freelance comics writer John Wagner was polishing his pitch for a series about the toughest cop in a post-apocalyptic city of the future, a law enforcement officer who was also judge, jury and summary executioner. "You have been judged, and the sentence is death" became the title's first must-quote catch-phrase.

Wagner wrote the very first Judge Dredd script, and the Spanish artist Carlos Ezquerra was called in to illustrate. It was Ezquerra who designed, to order and virtually on the spot, the costume, the gun, and the fat-wheeled Lawmaster motorcycle that have become part and parcel of Dredd's physical image. It was decided pretty early on that Dredd would never remove his face-concealing, eagle-crested helmet, his impenetrable carapace functioning as a graphic

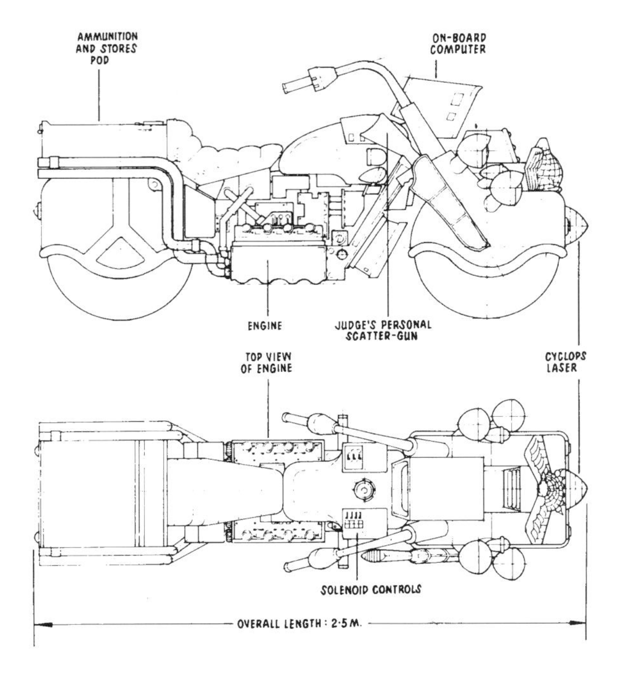

Blueprints for the Judges' Lawmaster bike and Lawgiver gun

representation of his unswerving, almost inhuman, devotion to the letter of the Law.

A grim and grisly twenty-first-century New York was the first projected setting for Dredd's adventures. But in just the second instalment of exploits, Dredd's turf was extended significantly. "By 2099," intoned the narrator of the second story, " the Great Eastern cities of America had swollen into a vast mega-city, stretching from Montreal in the North to Georgia in the South."

Dredd never took his helmet off – or at least, when he did, his face was never seen. After being shot in the head, he appeared bandaged, left*; in Prog 8, editorial concern for the readers took over,* above right*. And in Prog 52,* above*, he used 22nd-century technology to disguise himself*

Mega-City One has more than its fair share of odd inhabitants: from the mutant subterranean Troggies to super-intelligent apes, left. *Mutie the Pig, however, turned out to be a rogue Judge in a mask –* top right. *Even the "normal" inhabitants go to great lengths to stand out from the masses: Eric Plunket,* above, *changed his name to Aaron A. Aardvark to be first in the vid-phone book – and as a result was the first to be killed by the lunatic Chief Judge Cal. Check out the kneepads – high fashion in Mega-City One*

MEGA-CITY ONE

Judge Dredd changed appearance and shoe size depending on who was drawing him. Mike McMahon, left*; Ian Gibson,* below right*; Brian Bolland,* bottom right*; and Massimo Bellardinelli,* below

A lot of attention was lavished upon the details of life in Mega-City One, and especially upon its varied and endlessly eccentric population. An underclass of mutants, "fatties," and predatory thugs was a menacing fact of life. The stories created not just a city but a constantly expanding fictional universe. Piece by piece, the awareness of Dredd readers was expanded to include the sister metropolis Mega-City Two, on the West Coast of the US, Mega-City Three in Texas City, a colony on the moon, the encircling wasteland known as the Cursed Earth, and a prison colony on Titan, the largest moon of Saturn.

Nevertheless, the depictions of the city itself in the comic book are not particularly consistent. Its architecture seems to change from one story to the next. Over the years, a wide variety of artists depicted the character and his surroundings, and in ways that surprisingly often were freely interpretative rather than literal. Even the central character seemed to be

dealt with as an indistinct legendary figure that could be safely re-imagined by each new storyteller.

If the firm, clear lines and precise detailing of Brian Bolland's familiar Dredd (the definitive version, in the opinion of many fans) seemed to stress his unyielding iron spine, the freer drawing styles of Carlos Ezquerra and Simon Bisley hint at some spiky psychosis lurking just beneath the surface. Is there a consciousness of chaos at the heart of this rigidly overcontrolled and controlling character, spurring him to escalating extremes of overcompensation?

Still, Judge Dredd was the sort of fictional character that starts simply and grows into his complexity along the way. He was an immediate success with the reading public, and quickly replaced the rather stodgy holdover Dan Dare as *2000 AD*'s favorite cover boy.

The issues of 2000 AD were called "Progs" (for "Programs"). Apparently it wasn't until his first really lengthy serialized story, "Robot Wars," began to appear, in Progs 10–17, that Dredd's popularity grew to superstar levels. The Robot Wars, in which mankind's metal menials rose up to smite "The Fleshy Ones," became a cornerstone of Judge mythology. For the movie, a panoramic bas-relief depicting the rebellion was designed and sculpted in plaster as a

Ron Smith always drew a neat and detailed Dredd, above

The "Robot Wars" serial started with a bombshell – Dredd's resignation

Simon Bisley's heavy metal Dredd, right

Above: *Dredd tells it like it is in the Cursed Earth*

Below: *the Council of Five, with the Chief Judge in the center, meet to discuss disciplining Dredd … over his expenses*

decorative frieze running all the way around the Judges' Council Chamber.

Key episodes came thick and fast in the character's early days. Brian Bolland made his debut in Prog 41, and the "Cursed Earth Saga," in Progs 61–85, established the series's reputation for mixing sarcastic satire with blood and guts. In fact, portions of this epic adventure, which was reprinted in two graphic novels, have never been published in the States, because the sequence "Burger Wars" tweaked an overly sensitive American corporate fast food giant. As former Eagle Comics editor Nick Landau has remarked, "The Cursed Earth is where Judge Dredd really falls into place."

As a point of interest, many of the narrative elements that are central to the Judge Dredd movie have been at least implicit in the comic book from the beginning. The paramilitary powers bestowed upon the cops, in this hellishly overpopulated city that is always teetering on the verge of social chaos, is one of the most resonant, and potentially controversial, aspects of the Dredd legend in both versions. The Judges also seem to wield the civic political power, centered upon a ruling Council of Judges, presided over by a lordly Chief Judge whose power is close to absolute. The concept is a ringingly old-fashioned depiction of an oligarchy, explicitly modeled upon the governmental structures of ancient Rome.

Some of the screenwriters and directors who were approached to work on the movie apparently balked because they couldn't stomach the character's politics. But the writers and artists of the comic book had already confronted the moral ambiguities of Dredd's position head on.

In Progs 89–108, in the story "The Day the Law Died," Dredd is framed for murder and becomes an outcast, wandering the Cursed Earth, because he resists the "illegal" rise of a demented Chief Judge

Below: *Dredd gets a taste of his own justice*

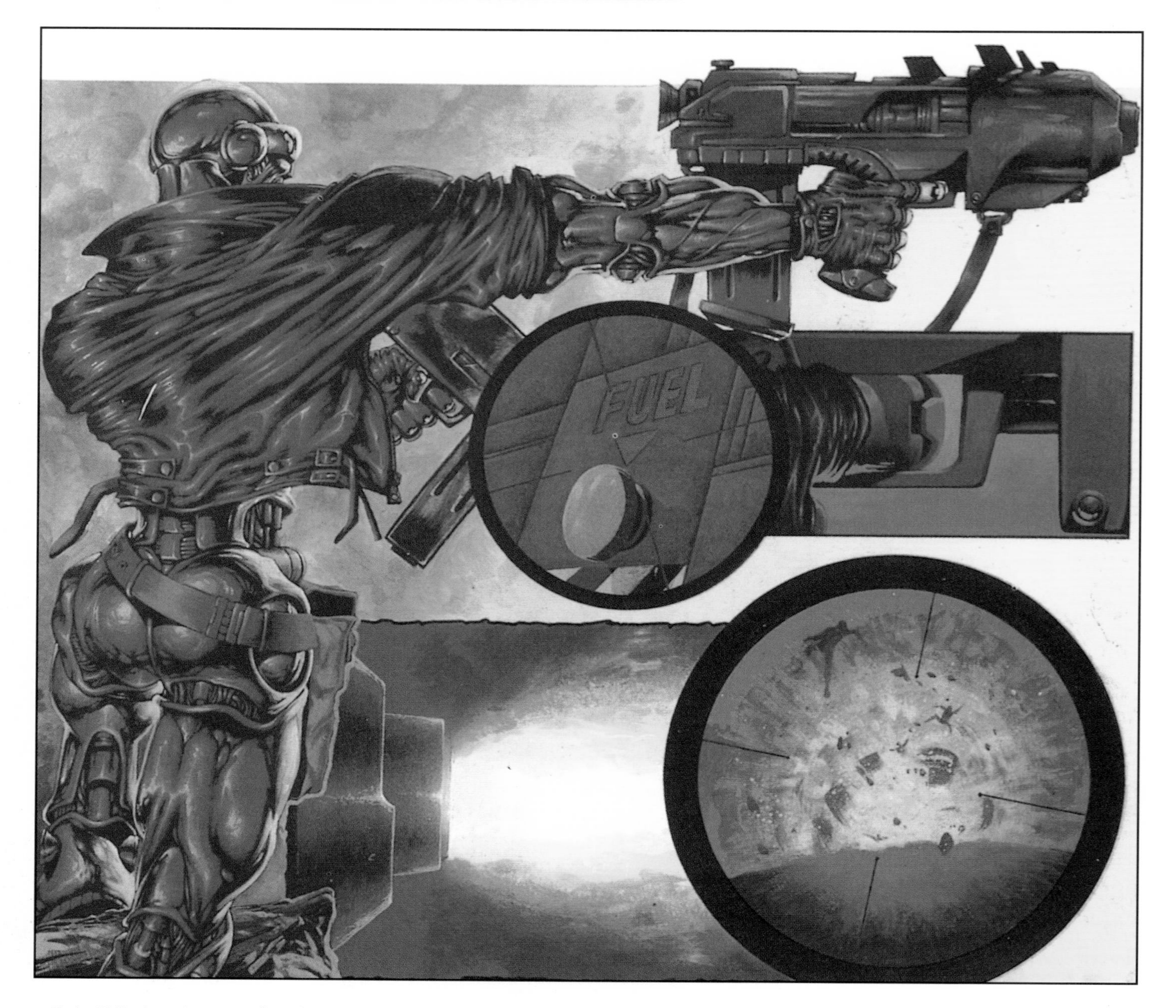

Kevin Walker's work on 2000 AD *included another steel-jawed dispenser of brutal justice – Joe Pineapples, the ABC Warriors' deadly sniper*

based upon the mad Roman emperor Caligula. This storyline, which supplied key plot elements for the Dredd movie, is itself enough to indicate that the creators of the Judge system were well aware of its troublesome contradictions.

"[Dredd] is extreme," John Wagner has admitted. "Wishy-washy characters do not go down well, but someone who is extremely bad or good is automatically more interesting. Dredd scores twice here because he is both good and bad: the stern upholder of the law, never wavering from his code, and yet making judgments that are, by today's standards, terrifying."

Very little was ever revealed in the stories about Joseph Dredd the human being. In Prog 30 we learn that he was trained for fifteen years, from the age of five, to become a Judge – a training period so all encompassing that it becomes a form of indoctrination or brainwashing. In Prog 34 his birthdate is given as 2066, so his median age is around forty. "I AM THE LAW," he says, on many occasions. Perhaps there is no human being behind the omnipresent helmet; perhaps his sense of himself as an agent of the Law is, by now, the only form of self-awareness he has left.

The movie's screenplay is based upon the closest

Dredd (finally) hits the screen, with Sylvester Stallone donning the helmet

thing to a classic comic book "origin story"("The Return of Rico," Prog 30) that exists for this character. Fans of the comic stories should have a leg up, then, when it comes to sorting out the picture's pivotal puzzle, although there are plenty of new twists and turns added along the way.

Obviously, most of those comics fans are British, and it has really been only in recent years that Dredd has developed a small fan following in the US. Set in the States and modeled upon an American movie character, Judge Dredd himself seems to owe little to his British origins. The occasionally biting tone of the *2000 AD* stories, however, has a distinct tang of ironic British wit.

Kevin Walker, the only artist from the Dredd comics hired to work on the Los Angeles pre-production of the film (as a conceptual and design illustrator), recalled the first Dredd story he ever worked on: "The main thing was that Dredd himself was scarcely in it. He was the subject of the story, but the main participant was a rat who was the pet of a villain Dredd had killed in an earlier story, and it got its revenge by – how to put this? – taking a dump on the seat of Dredd's Lawmaster motorbike. That was the whole story! It was one of Alan Grant's crude one-line jokes, specifically designed to just look at the world of Dredd from an oblique angle."

But the complexity of tone that helped keep the comic book interesting also created unique problems when it came to adapting Judge Dredd for cinema screens. In the end, it would take almost ten years to get from the first gleam in producer Charles Lippincott's eye to a screenplay by William Wisher, "green-lighted" by Cinergi's Andy Vajna, with the young Brit Danny Cannon at the helm.

Always the toughest of tough nuts, Dredd would prove to be exceedingly hard to crack.

The black and shiny Judges form a ceremonial arch for Chief Judge Fargo as he takes the Long Walk into the Cursed Earth

LEVEL
1

JUDGE DREDD IN [DEVELOPMENT] HELL

Even in an industry in which projects routinely take years to come to fruition, *Judge Dredd* took a very Long Walk indeed from page to screen. As might be expected, a variety of factors contributed to the delays, including a drawn out tussle over the movie rights with another producer, and the release of a successful SF action picture with admitted "similarities" to *Dredd* which necessitated some quick rewrites.

But all of the parties involved seem to acknowledge that the major conundrum was the material itself, especially the thorny personality of Joseph Dredd. This was a potentially expensive science fiction picture with a complex attitude toward a hero who was not all that easy to like – a rigid law enforcer whose depredations are viewed alternatively with dismay and wicked delight. Very few people seemed to be able to hold those two ideas in their heads at the same time.

Screenwriters who tried to crack the Dredd puzzle during the early years of development seemed to be pretty evenly split. One group consisted of those who simply hated the bloody SOB, for political as well as visceral reasons, and wanted to build a harsh critique

Dredd enthusiasts either loathed the character for his totalitarian tendencies or loved him so much they couldn't bear to see any deviations from the comic book, left. Drawing by Carlos Ezquerra

LEVEL
2

BLAMM!
BADDOW!
BADDOW!
BADDOW!
AAAGHH!

There was no way a sympathetic hero could be made from a comic book character who would skin suspects alive, above

of Dredd's ferocious tactics into the story. Another group comprised the so-called "fan-boys," who loved Dredd a tad too much, and couldn't bear to see a single rivet on his leather codpiece shifted a quarter inch from its position as "established" in the comic book.

Despite the PC reservations of some potential screenwriters and directors, producer Charles M. Lippincott, who first fell in love with the cinematic possibilities of *Dredd* around 1978, and optioned the property from IPC Publishers Ltd after a full year of frustrating negotiations, rejects the notion that Dredd is a fascist. "The original fascists," he says, "were a middle-class movement, not a populist or a workers' movement. It was all about putting the middle class in the driver's seat – 'the good people,' the voters, the property owners. In that sense, Newt Gingrich is much closer to true, Mussolini-style fascism than Judge Dredd is. At the start, at least, Dredd is an unthinking person, a soldier, who has been thoroughly indoctrinated and follows the letter of the Law. He believes in the Law because he knows nothing else. But to me he's like the grunt who shipped out for Vietnam just taking the rightness of it for granted and is now just playing out his string. Or the white cop in the inner city. Or the British soldier in Northern Ireland. Can you hate those people? Can we really just write them off as Nazis? I think their situation is more interesting than that.

"In the comics an infrequent but fascinating theme is Judge Dredd having doubts and experiencing internal conflicts about his absolute devotion to the letter of the Law. And the Dredd of the movie, too, is an unthinking good soldier who finally begins to

Charles M. Lippincott, producer, left

think and ask questions. He doesn't get to the point of replacing the prevailing belief system with something else, but he mitigates its harshness. I'm not sure how much more we can realistically expect from such a person, at least as a first step. For him even the flat acknowledgment that the Law is not infallible and doesn't cover every human possibility is a gigantic change; it reconfigures his entire world view.

"Now, I don't know how many moviegoers will take this away from the story," Lippincott continues, "but for me *Judge Dredd* is very much a cautionary tale. It shows us where we will end up if we keep going in the direction of Enforcement Before Prevention and Three Strikes You're Out. It will come to this if we don't get our act together."

> ***"How do you take something that's literally two-dimensional and make it three-dimensional? And Dredd presents additional problems because in a way there's almost too much material, too many ways to go with it"***
>
> **Charles Lippincott, Producer**

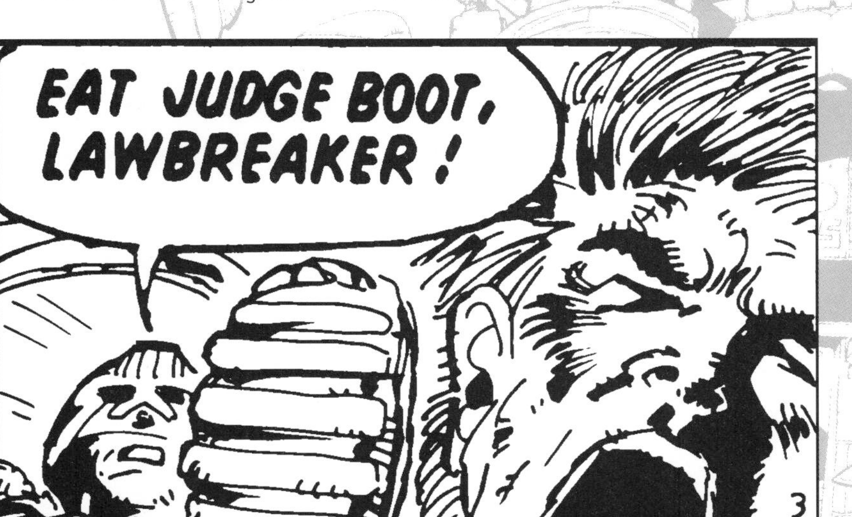

Translating a two-dimensional character to the screen was never going to be easy, however cool he was in the action sequences, below

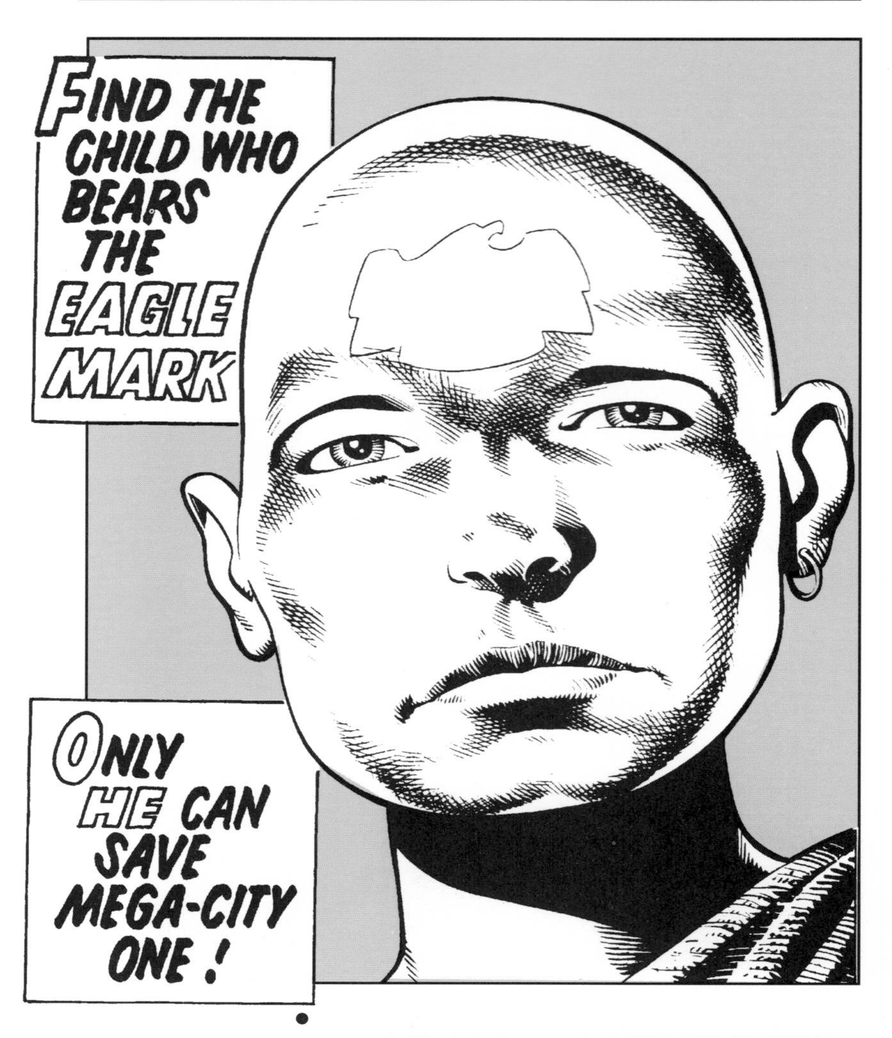

One of the problems with the 2000 AD material was that there were simply too many interesting storylines to follow. The search for the Judge Child, above, took seven months and saw Dredd traveling the universe in a spaceship, meeting no end of aliens

At first glance, however, as Lippincott admits, it wasn't the thought-provoking political subtext that got him going on Dredd. "I just thought it was a colorful and exciting take on a *Dirty Harry*-style cop hero in the future. It was one of the best comic book concepts I had ever seen outside of the United States."

In 1980, Dredd's guardians at Britain's IPC Publishing Ltd didn't even bother to respond to Lippincott's queries about the movie rights. He was a pioneering publicity specialist well known in Hollywood as the young marketing whiz who had masterminded the campaign and licensing for the *Star Wars* film, and who had worked effectively with Alfred Hitchcock on his last film, *Family Plot*, and with Ridley Scott on *Alien*. A passionate researcher, Lippincott produced dozens of epic memos during the development and production of *Dredd* on subjects as diverse as the Jungian deep structure of the quest legend and the historical differences between movies that sell a lot of toys and those

There was no budget on earth that could film Dredd in chains with thousands of mutants as drawn by Ron Smith, below

Another long and complex plot line in 2000 AD *involved the rise of the lunatic Chief Judge Cal,* above, *drawn by Ron Smith*

that don't. Lippincott is, above all, a chap who does his homework.

But in 1980 the British rights holders of *Judge Dredd* had no way of knowing all this. Lippincott was an unknown quantity to them. Besides which, the rights were already spoken for. It wasn't until 1983, when a young British documentarist allowed his claim to lapse, that IPC began to negotiate with Lippincott in deadly earnest. They hired the lawyers that George Lucas had used for his work in England and spent the better part of a year haggling over every conceivable detail.

But the deal was finally made, for an amount that Lippincott found fairly terrifying. Overextended already, he knew he would need a more formidably endowed financial partner to help get the development process rolling for real.

"*Dredd* was actually sort of a tough sell," he recalls. "Most studios don't make big SF movies, unless there's an exceptional filmmaker like Cameron or Spielberg attached. Contemporary action is easier for them because it is star oriented. And comic books aren't generally popular with studios, either. Warner Brothers owns DC Comics, which publishes Batman, so that's a special case. I can understand their anxiety. It's hard trying to find a way to handle a comic book character. How do you take something that's literally two-dimensional and make it three-dimensional? And Dredd presents additional problems because in a way there's almost too much material, too many ways to go with it."

As former Lippincott development executive Susan Nicoletti recalls, Lippincott initially made some efforts of his own to develop a *Dredd* screenplay. "In 1983, when I started working with Charley, one of the projects that we were really targeting was Judge Dredd. And in 1985 we started talking to comic book

writers and fans. Jan Strnad, I think was the first writer. The first comic book fan was Ed Neumeier, who was a fan of *Dredd*. Charley was in Ed's office and saw either *Dredd* comic books or *Dredd* posters, and it turned out that Ed had tried to buy the rights, but couldn't because, you know, we had them. And of course he went on to co-write *RoboCop*, which borrowed liberally, to say the least, from *Dredd*."

But it didn't take very long, or very many fruitless visits to the offices of studio production executives, to confirm Lippincott's feeling that *Dredd* would have trouble finding a home there, at least during the development phase.

Lippincott turned to Executive Producer Edward R. Pressman, whose considerable reputation with critics and industry analysts alike is based upon the split-level structure of his firm's activities. He is well known for his strong ongoing relationships with challenging filmmakers like Oliver Stone and David Byrne. He's very much a part of the cutting-edge creative wing of the Hollywood community. But Pressman has also pursued another, parallel course as a producer, turning out high profile commercial

Equipment from 2000 AD *underwent drastic changes – witness the flying Lawmaster,* below. *In the comic book this could only be used in the low gravity of the Moon, where Dredd spent time as governor*

> ***"There was an essential strength to the property that separated it from other comic books that I saw. Like* Conan *it seemed so logical and distinct, I never doubted its viability as a movie or that it would be worth the effort – even when it seemed that it was going to take forever."***
>
> **Ed Pressman, Executive Producer**

Fergie made it to the screen, albeit in a slightly cleaner and more eloquent form than he was in 2000 AD, *below*

Mean Machine, below right

pictures like *Conan the Barbarian* and *Masters of the Universe*.

"After the success of *Conan*," Pressman observed, "I'd been looking for another character that could lend itself to film in the way that Conan did. The success of that film and the benefits that it brought to our company really were the underpinnings of the productivity that we've been able to have over the last fifteen years. Films like *Homicide*, or *Bad Lieutenant*, or *Good Morning Babylon*, or *Walker* could not have sustained this company's operations."

Former Pressman Senior Vice President for Production Caldecott "Cottie" Chubb was instrumental in the development of the Dredd script in its Pressman period. "My recollection," Chubb says, "is that Charley [Lippincott] brought Ed the material and made him, Ed, his partner. They were each responsible for half the money, although in the end I think Ed was responsible for most of the money, and he probably used that as a negotiating lever later on."

"My first awareness of Dredd as a character," Pressman recalls, "was when Charley brought it to me in 1986. It had a long history and there was a constituency that was very passionate about it. There was an essential strength to the property that

separated it from other comic books that I saw. Like *Conan* it seemed so logical and distinct, I never doubted its viability as a movie or that it would be worth the effort – even when it seemed that it was going to take forever. After all, Conan took eight years from the time I first was introduced to the material to the time we actually had the film on the screen. It was a very complicated legal process with a lot of public domain problems. But it just seemed to present a whole gestalt cinematic world and a strong central character that was distinct from all other heroes, a genre that was fresh. *Dredd* was the first project I'd come across that seemed to have the same strength." Not that the two title characters were ever

Fergie and the Angel Gang, above

Crumley and Hunter's first draft screenplay included 2000 AD's *scavenging Angel Gang, outlaws who live in the Cursed Earth,* left. *Drawn by Matt Codd*

Evidence of the Angel Gang's cannibalism as depicted in the film, above

The mutants of 2000 AD, *right by Ron Smith, never made it to the screen, despite appearing in Crumley and Hunter's first draft screenplay*

viewed as interchangeable, or even as strikingly similar. "Conan is an absolute outsider," Lippincott observes, "while Dredd is a loyal cog in the machine, like Murphy, who becomes RoboCop. He's not quite part of the establishment but he is an unquestioning agent of the establishment. In this sense the difference between the two characters reflects the difference in the time periods in which they were created. The image of the outsider hero doesn't resonate with people now as much as these guys do who are enmeshed in a corporate structure but still manage to hold onto, or to rediscover, their individuality. In this context the forces that make you start questioning things don't make you weaker, they make you stronger. This is an adult rite of passage story, a quest story. Like a knight of the round table who questions authority and spends some time in the wilderness fighting dragons and comes back a truer hero for having integrated his doubts."

An agreement in principle was easy for Pressman and Lippincott to reach; they were both enthusiastic about the Judge Dredd material. "But from then on," Pressman says, "the actual creation of the film took a long time. It was a question of finding the right

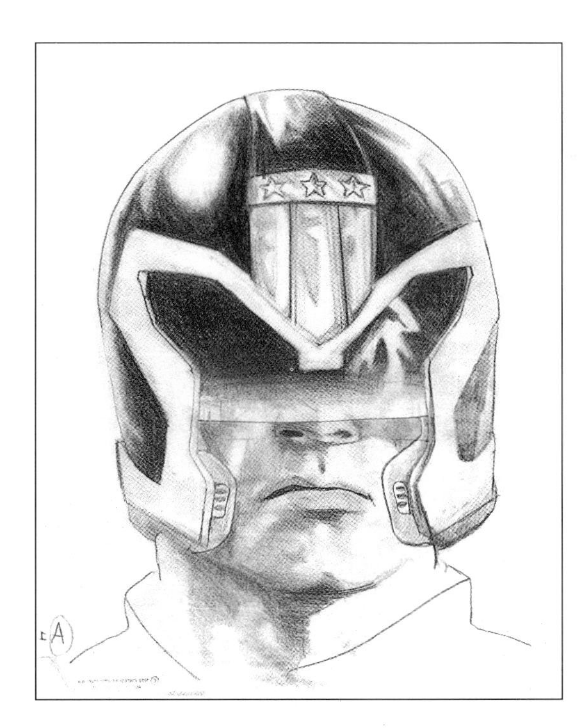

approach, because the approaches that *could* be taken were so diverse, from very comedic to very hard edged."

In 1987 the production was struck a severe blow by the opening and surprise success of a future-cop thriller that owed more than a little to the *Judge Dredd* comics. Pressman remembers "going to see a preview of *RoboCop* and coming out pretty depressed. It was a demoralizing experience because we realized how much had been taken from *Dredd*. It made our ability to move ahead somewhat more difficult. What we were selling didn't seem as fresh as it had before. From then on it was essential that we say to every writer and director that we talked to that it can't be too much like *RoboCop*."

Nicoletti, too, recalls the screening: "I know [*RoboCop* producer] Jon Davison, but I didn't get invited to the screening. That piqued my interest and Charley and I actually snuck into the screening. And we were like, 'Oh my God, not only is it *Judge Dredd*, it's so damn *good*.' So we're downstairs in the lobby and everyone is mobbing Davison and his face was beet red. I mean, his face is always red, but this time it was blazing. He looked at me apologetically and he just shrugged and said, 'It's *Judge Dredd* isn't it?' and Charley's standing next to me, nodding.

"After *RoboCop* we had to cool our jets for a while. We were no longer seriously pursuing *Dredd*."

But finally the process got underway. "With Pressman on board," Associate Producer Susan Nicoletti recalls, "there was a steady parade of writers. That's when it started getting crazy, because the writers sort of fell into two categories. They either

Dredd's helmet was always going to be controversial. In 2000 AD *he never took it off until he ceased to be a Judge,* below, *and went into the Cursed Earth*

Dredd belongs to a legal system exemplified by eagle sconces, clip-clop floors, gold, marble and granite. Nowhere is this more clearly illustrated than in the Hall of Justice, above

All the Judges are distinctively tattooed, below, *in another example of the all-encroaching nature of the Mega-City Law system*

knew the character of Dredd and were so in love with him that they did not want to do anything that wasn't part of the 'canon.' 'He would never say that, he would never do that, he would never wear that.' Some of these sticklers were British writers who had grown up with the Dredd character, some were American fans who got to know the character later in life. But they were all purists of one sort or another.

"The other category was writers who hadn't a clue who Judge Dredd was, and went off and did the research and came back and said, 'I hate this guy. This guy is a fascist.' And some of them would want the job anyway and would attempt to write a story about a character they hated. 'I'm going to stick him in the background and write a politically correct science fiction fantasy story that's a cautionary tale about excessive police power.'

"But then when [writer-director] Tim Hunter came along, he seemed to be the perfect mixture of the two approaches."

Ed Pressman had seen Tim Hunter's film *River's Edge* and admired it. "And then Tim came to our office in Burbank and said he would love to do it."

Pressman was sold, but Lippincott and Nicoletti were continuing to explore other options. They were excited about a little-seen thriller, *The Stepfather*, starring Terry O'Quinn and helmed by Bruce Springsteen's favorite director. "We were approaching a young director named Joseph Ruben," Nicoletti recalls. "This was well before he made *Sleeping With the Enemy*. But unbeknownst to us Ed was as good as promising it to Tim Hunter."

Nicoletti sighs. "Ed is one of the most exciting producers in Hollywood, but this is one of the things that can be frustrating about working with him. Charley's approach is much more deliberate. He wants to meet the people and weigh all the possibilities. Ed is impulsive. He would have already made the deal.

'Call the agent, sign the deal,' without even telling us what he was doing. Often when you think something's over and done with, it pops back up again. He'll have somebody come to a meeting and spout all this stuff, and everyone will say, 'Well, *this* guy's an idiot, get him out of here.' And then six months later Pressman is saying, 'Remember that idiot? I've hired him.' Peter Hewitt was in the picture for a while and then he was out of the picture and then two years later he was going to direct the picture. It was like a series of jack-in-the-boxes that kept popping up and down."

In the end, the potential for disaster (or at least for acute embarrassment) was averted. Hunter may actually have called his directorial rival and asked him to back off. But, for whatever reason, Ruben took himself out of the running. "He never was very enthusiastic about the character to begin with," Nicoletti believes. "I don't think he ever came right out and said, 'The guy's a fascist,' like some of the others, but that was the implication."

"Tim Hunter was one of the few American writers who was knowledgeable about Dredd, but wasn't so loyal to the character that he couldn't swing with some changes. He and his writing partner James Crumley (the acclaimed hard-boiled detective novelist of *The Last Good Kiss* and *The Mexican Tree Duck*) came up with an approach that we thought was interesting."

"Crumley was really fascinating to meet," Nicoletti recalls. "He's the authentic article, with a battered-looking face and a growly voice, the whiskey and cigarette voice. Charley and I met him at this old-Hollywood style restaurant, Musso & Franks, at the Raymond Chandler bar, and it was just perfect. He talks in these tough-guy metaphors, like all men are from Tijuana and all women are from Juárez. I mean, it sounds cool, but ... And Tim was going to direct at that time, that was the deal, and it looked good."

Crumley and Hunter's first draft screenplay, which was completed in 1988, is great fun to read. With a plot set in motion by an uprising among the mutants of the Cursed Earth to win recognition and social

As Cottie Chubb points out, there would be little point in hiring the likes of Stallone if Dredd never takes his helmet off. In the end, the movie's plot ensured that Dredd's face has to be revealed, below

At on point, Executive Producer Ed Pressman favored a plot centered on a confrontation between Judge Dredd and the lethal Judge Death, above

equality as human beings, it teems with grotesque supporting characters and down-and-dirty futuristic local color, and it incorporates several of the most vivid characters and storylines from the 2000 AD comic book stories, including the PSI-powered blonde amazon Judge Anderson and the scavenging Angel Gang from the Cursed Earth. At the center of it all is the cadaverous ultra-baddie Judge Death, a mirror-image "Dark Judge" who invades Mega-City One from another dimension.

Of course, it's one thing to read a script and something else entirely to consider committing your capital to realizing it on the big screen. For Pressman, at least, "The script that Tim and Crumley developed was very well written but was incredibly complex and drew from so many threads of the Dredd legend that it would have been impossible to actually make. It was too complex and expensive. The budget estimate was something like sixty million dollars, and this was several years ago. It just wasn't something we felt we could pursue."

Ultimately, Pressman and Lippincott went back to rolling the boulder up the hill. In fact, when Cottie Chubb joined Pressman as a production executive in mid July 1988 he looked over the firm's roster of dormant projects and recognized Dredd as a property that still had potential, and began pushing for it. But Chubb faced many of the same translation problems that had been dogging the character up to that time.

"The first thing," continues Chubb, who now works for the production company Alphaville, "was simply whether or not or to what extent we *wanted* to put the comic book character himself, intact, onto the screen. Whether you *wanted* to, because the character had a couple of major problems. He never took off his helmet, for one thing. He literally never showed his face. Which of course means that if you're going to be true to the comic in this respect you won't hire Arnold or Sly because, trust me, you're not going to pay the fee of a star like that and then never show his face. Even in RoboCop you saw his face, at least enough to assure people that there was a human being inside the suit. With Dredd it's never clear that there's a man inside.

"Now, there are Dredd aficionados who would say he would no longer be as much fun as a three dimensional character. You want to keep him as an exaggerated force of nature dealing with real problems in an over the top way. Shooting a person for littering, or whatever. It's only funny because of the exaggeration. But you can't ask the action audience in this country to go to a movie and laugh at itself for being insecure enough to want to see action movies with larger than life heroes.

"Luckily, Charley Lippincott was one of the strongest proponents of taking Dredd seriously and

giving him a more rounded character and a human personality you could identify with in conventional movie terms. But even when you say that, it's still a balancing act, because Joe Dredd certainly can't be turned into an everyman. He still has to be of mythic stature.

"And then you deal with, okay, 'Who is Dredd?' How do you make him human without turning him into a wimp? He is a guy who went to the Justice Academy. He had these ideals. He found himself. But he's in an untenable position and now he has to find out what it feels like to be hunted."

It was at this point that another comic book writer-artist, Howard Chaykin, was recruited by Lippincott and Nicoletti. In the mid-1980s, Chaykin was on a roll creatively. His *American Flagg*, a vaguely *Dredd*-like future-cop chronicle with a distinctive vein of sly satire, had recently become the first comic book series ever to obtain a Hugo Award nomination in direct competition with the year's output of short story science fiction. Flagg has emerged as a pivotal pop culture influence of the 1980s; neither Frank Miller's *Batman: The Dark Knight* nor the film *RoboCop* would have been the same without it. Chaykin should have been close to the ideal writer for a sharp comic book property like Dredd.

Scriptwriter William Wisher came up with the idea of basing the plot around Dredd's long-lost black-sheep brother Rico. Rico's first 2000 AD *appearance is in a brief comic book story,* left, *where he has been surgically adapted to hard labor on Titan. He was brought to life on-screen by actor Armand Assante,* below

Chief Judge Fargo in the Council Chamber, above, *played by Max von Sydow. Based on the* 2000 AD *character,* right, *Fargo's character emphasizes law and justice*

For people inclined to forget that ordinary personal problems, and ordinary problematic personalities, can throw a spanner even into the development process of a major film, the *Judge Dredd* vs Howard Chaykin story is instructive.

"Chaykin," Susan Nicoletti insists, "is one of the wittiest people on earth. He thinks on his feet like nobody's business and he's entertaining and funny. When he got up at an early meeting, he blew everybody away with a great pitch that had to do with Judge Dredd as the Lone Ranger. An astoundingly good pitch. And nobody took notes because there was the writer standing right in front of us. Everybody said, 'That's fantastic, go write it. Go do a treatment.' Well, to make a long story short, he came back with a treatment that had absolutely nothing to do with the pitch that he had given. The treatment had Judge Dredd out in the Cursed Earth having hallucinations about conversing with an animated statue of Blind Justice. It was just awful. There followed a long period of working with Howard and his partner (who shall remain nameless), who at twenty years old was having the first love affair of his life and could barely focus on anything else. He didn't want to be there, he was dreamy and love struck.

"It seems silly, doesn't it, that a potential multi-million-dollar project could get stalled by something like that. But this kind of thing actually happens all the time in Hollywood; maybe it has something to do with trying to be very businesslike about what is basically quite an unruly creative process. But for producers it can be maddening. You're trying to operate in a very straightforward, professional way, and all these messy personal problems keep interfering. It was funny, in a way, but it was also a nightmare. It was brutal."

Several other writers and directors came and went on into the early 1990s. Running conflicts developed over which of the multitudinous possible plot threads offered by the comic book stories should be plucked out for development. Pressman strongly favored the supernatural menace of Judge Death, which Lippincott and Nicoletti resisted – partly because a creature who looked so lethal on the page would be

almost impossible to bring fully to life on the screen. Inevitably, he would have to be a special effect rather than a human being. Perhaps even more importantly, a confrontation with the implacable and inhuman Judge Death doesn't help to define Dredd himself as a character, a point that was considered crucial in the introductory instalment to what everyone hoped would lead to a lengthy series of sequels. Lippincott

says Judge Death is still a strong candidate for a Dredd sequel, not least because computerized special effects techniques have improved to the point that it might now be possible to combine the performance of a real actor with some cutting edge computer generated imagery; imagine a walking skeleton in leather bondage gear with the leering face of a great character actor. But at that time, 1991, Judge Death was out of the question.

A contractual squabble with another producer helped stall the development process further, from a crawl to a standstill. As Pressman recalls, the conflict began with the sudden availability of a surefire megastar:

"At that time we still had no acceptable script and no development capital to get things moving, so Larry Gordon offered to develop *Dredd* with us, and we agreed. But then around 1992 we attracted some more investment and consequently had more capital of our own for script development. So I went back to Larry and said, 'I'd really like to develop this myself.' He agreed and we signed a document that basically let us out of any obligations as long as we gave him a first look at it. There was not even any commitment on our part that we had to give it to him; we simply had to let him look at it.

"But during that time Arnold Schwarzenegger came to us, out of the blue, and told us he wanted to be Judge Dredd. Now all of a sudden Larry started taking the position that we couldn't make the picture without him. We lost a good nine months over this stupid tug of war, this little greed festival."

The Largo/limbo period ended suddenly when the company's modestly budgeted thriller *Unlawful Entry* opened and made eleven million dollars in three days. According to Nicoletti. "Largo decided right then and there to stick to medium budget movies that could make a lot of money, and they backed away from *Judge Dredd*."

To Judge Griffin, on the other hand, law and order is everything. In 2000 AD *Griffin was also a Chief Judge, after Fargo dies,* left

Executive Producer Andy Vajna with veteran film producer Buzz Feitshans on the set of Judge Dredd, *above*

For Susan Nicoletti it was Cottie Chubb "who got the project back on track. He brought screenwriter William Wisher into the process, and Bill approached the job very unemotionally. He researched Dredd. He did whatever he had to do. He didn't come in and say, 'I hate this guy and I want to trash him' or 'I love this guy so much that I don't want to change a thing.' He was really the consummate professional Hollywood screenwriter, and I mean that as a high compliment."

"Well, yeah," Cottie Chubb agrees. "Billy's a great screenwriter, and I'm really glad that it worked out because I *knew* that he could do this. He got to the essence of it and he wrote a draft that would work, that people would go, oh, okay, now *there's* a movie."

It is not surprising that it was Bill who found the right approach, for he was the one who created a successful villain for *Terminator 2* with his old friend, James Cameron. They knew Arnold Schwarzenegger had created a villain that had revealed all his facets in *Terminator* and they had to find a new villain to top the first film.

Bill really liked the concept of Judge Dredd. "The notion that in the future things are so grim that the police have become judge, jury and executioner all at the same time. It is a great way to do a very exciting action-filled black comedy of where we might be going in the future if we aren't more careful."

It was Wisher's decision, after some extensive research into the character, to begin the Dredd screen saga with the bare hint of an "origin story" embodied in a single brief comic book story about Dredd's long-lost black sheep brother, Rico. There is nothing in the Dredd legend comparable to the episode in which the seeds of Batman were planted in Bruce Wayne's soul when he saw his parents murdered. There is no biographical prologue and there are no flashbacks in Judge Dredd. Instead, the secret of Dredd's origin is built into the solution to the mystery he spends most of the movie trying to solve; in investigating this case, he investigates himself.

It was this narrative choice, according to Pressman, that "catalyzed the entire project. I think the idea of doing the Rico story was originally suggested by Michael DeLuca [*From the Mouth of Madness*] and he did an outline that was sort of inspired by *Angels With Dirty Faces*. So the idea of taking a tried-and-true structure and working from that was a solid notion. But when Bill delivered his version it was all there; it was coherent and clear and told a story and was not overly absorbed with the artifacts. Once we had that script it was like night and day. Suddenly there were lots of possibilities."

Most of the key structural elements of *Judge Dredd* were introduced in William Wisher's first draft. Dredd is presented not as a thug or a brownshirt but simply as an overly rigid idealist, thoroughly indoctrinated by a demanding training process that began when he was all of five years old. The letter of the Law is the only value system he's ever been aware of. Meanwhile, the society of Mega City itself is at a turning point. Its merciless but even-handed justice system is being nudged toward full police-state status by an internal faction of reactionary Judges. A pair of contrasting father figures pull Joseph Dredd, and the entire city, in opposite directions: Judge Fargo, one of the original architects of the Judge system, whose emphasis is on law and justice above all; and Judge Griffin, for whom *law and order* is everything.

The way Wisher's clever plot has been worked out, the fate of the society hinges on the question of which of these mentors, and value systems, Dredd will finally support. And Dredd's choice is influenced in crucial ways by his discovery of his own origins. As written it's a very elegant and satisfying storyline, in which all the major themes dovetail smoothly.

"Moviegoers may not be conscious of that kind of structuring when they're watching a movie," William Wisher admits, ensconced in a spotless home office furnished with solid and unfussy old chairs and tables of oiled oak. "But people are affected by those things just the same. It's a large part of what makes a movie gratifying to watch. It's the symmetry that sends you out of the theater with a sense that the balance and proper order of things have been reestablished.

"As a writer I think it's partly just a matter of being a neatnik. You hate to see loose ends or extraneous elements in a story. You want everything you put in to fit and have a function. That's an ideal, of course, that you can never quite achieve. All you can do is keep trying."

After all those years of false starts and stops, Wisher's script was received with jubilation by most of the people who had been working for years to get *Dredd* made. A production memo written by Susan Nicoletti in November 1992 cheered the belated emergence of "a real movie." Only a few days later, the very same producers would begin work on new memos nit-picking Wisher's draft from almost every imaginable angle, and eventually a succession of new writers would trudge through the revolving door of "development." But for now, it seemed, the major

The shape of things to come, below. *This drawing by reader Danny Burgess appeared in* 2000 AD *in 1986*

In this spoof comic story, above, *Stallone appeared as one of seven dwarves battling with Dredd. Six years on, it is Stallone wearing the helmet*

problems were all in the past.

Wisher's was the script that solved the problem identified by Lippincott early on, of turning a rigid law enforcer into a hero. Wisher made of Dredd a protagonist who becomes a hero when he recognizes and overcomes his tendency toward absolute belief in the Law in himself.

"That aspect of the script was terrific," Chubb agrees. "I can say it was fun helping Bill work that stuff out, but that he deserves the bulk of the credit. The political elements are organic to the story; they aren't just tacked on. Which is always a danger, because nobody wants to be pushed and prodded by a movie. But when the writing is as good as Bill's was and is, it's priceless."

"When I read the script that Bill Wisher did, the one Ed Pressman brought to us, I thought this could be a really exciting adventure for a moviegoer," Executive Producer Andrew G. Vajna declared. "I like science fiction a lot, especially futuristic action, because you're creating a whole world. You really can go wild with the imagination. The challenge here was to also create, within an imaginary world, an exciting roller-coaster ride for the audience that is unmatched by other movies. So as much as I liked the script we had, I thought we had to come up with more new things and new ideas and new sequences that you'd never seen before."

Vajna is an entrepreneurial filmmaker who attracts big stars to his projects. Over the years he has been involved as either producer or executive producer on a long list of event films. During his early association with former partner Mario Kassar in their company, Carolco, they made the *Rambo* trilogy, *Jacob's Ladder*, and *Total Recall*. In 1990, Vajna formed Cinergi productions which has produced *Medicine Man*, *Tombstone*, and, most recently, *Die Hard With a Vengeance*.

Vajna is known for a quick, decisive approach in

personally financing the projects he likes. Once his initial questions were answered on *Judge Dredd*, Vajna moved swiftly to draw up a partnership deal, and to get it officially into preproduction almost immediately. "With us it's very simple," he says. "We have a simple organization. The buck stops here, the decision gets made here. It isn't being made behind some desk somewhere."

Vajna shares Lippincott's ironic sense that the major studios aren't always the most appropriate production entities for these big movies. "The studios are constantly being burnt with these films," Vajna says. "Even if they're successful, a studio has a very difficult time administrating them. These are the kind of films where a producer needs to stand toe to toe with the star, with the director, with everybody on a daily basis to make sure that those budgets stay within control. That's very difficult for studios to do because there are too many layers of bureaucracy."

It was at about this point, as Vajna recalls, that it quickly became clear who the star of the picture was going to be. "There was very little discussion about Arnold Schwarzenegger, or Bruce Willis, or Harrison Ford, or anybody else," he says. "Sly was the first person we thought of and the one and only person we showed the script to. He fell in love with it and we decided to look no further."

At this point, surely, Sylvester Stallone needs no introduction. Boot-strapping himself to stardom almost overnight with a picture he wrote for himself, *Rocky*, in 1976, he became a star, in part, because he seemed to represent ordinary, lumpen-prole urban American humanity elevated to iconic/heroic status. Over the years, in competition with the grandly cartoonish Arnold Schwarzenegger, his image (even his physical image) has undergone a steady evolution toward the full-blown superheroic. At this point it would be difficult to imagine Stallone playing anything like an ordinary human being, or anything

Off set, Stallone lights his cigar with a flame-thrower, below

but an iconic *über*-hero.

He is, beyond a shadow of a doubt, one of two or three stars in Hollywood who can gold-plate an action movie at the box office. However pivotal *any* version of any screenplay may be, no one who understands Hollywood would object to the statement that the performers in this elite group of superstars (and their super-agents and super-lawyers) exercise virtual life-and-death power over many movie projects. Dredd in the comics may have been modeled upon Clint Eastwood's *Dirty Harry*, and he may have looked to some observers even more like the lanky and lethal young James Coburn of *The Magnificent Seven* and *In Like Flint*. But in terms of current cinematic iconography his profile was sure to be a bit more mythic.

"Joel Silver told me that you can never forget who your star is, because the audience will never forget. You have to work with the natural resources the star brings with him," remarked producer Beau Marks. "The thing that Stallone does so well, is that he gets the shit kicked out of him, then comes back. That's his myth, almost, ever since *Rocky*. So the presence of Stallone confirmed our sense that Dredd needed to get knocked down to his lowest point, because Sly is such a great fighter when he's coming back. It was a good plot device in the movie, but it was also very sympathetic to who Stallone is."

Having agreed upon who was to play *Dredd* himself, the producers had to find the right director. "About three months after reading the script for *Judge Dredd*," Andy Vajna recalls, "I saw a very exciting, dynamic crime movie from England called *The Young Americans* which was directed by a young British director named Danny Cannon. We met with Danny and found that he had grown up with Judge Dredd as a fan of the comic book, and was very passionate about the material. He really had some terrific ideas about how to bring it to the screen. And then he met with Stallone and they got along great and from there on it was his movie."

"Screenplays would come up, and I would read

them, and I would go to the producers and say, 'Why do you think I should do this after watching my movie?'" Danny declares. "I was just desperately looking for a connection that I would have personally to Hollywood. I mean I was getting offered Westerns and things. I was ready to go back to England and make another low-budget film unless somebody wanted me for something that I could connect with. That was my promise to myself. But one of the meetings I had was with Andy Vajna on *Die Hard With a Vengeance*. I hadn't even been able to finish the script, but I said, 'You have *Judge Dredd* and just hear me out.' And what I did was just sum up the characters and the environment which had inspired me as a kid. I said what was different about *Judge Dredd*.

"The first thing I said was, 'Don't make a science fiction cop movie with a cop-story plot. Emotionally this film could be vast. You create a society which is just an amplification of what our society could become.' I was going on about how luscious this film could be. I was saying, 'Please don't make *Lethal Weapon* in space.' The cop hero now is just a guy in the front seat of a roller-coaster and we're all behind him and in lieu of a character, he's a movie star."

To say that the twenty-seven-year-old director Danny Cannon has a daunting amount of energy would be putting it mildly. He's practically a one-man melt down. Cannon was a self-taught teenage filmmaker in England who won the support of director Ridley Scott and a berth at London's National Film School on the strength of some remarkably accomplished, cinema verité style films that he shot in and around his own drab suburban neighborhood. His first feature, the street-level London gangster thriller *The Young Americans*, was probably taken more seriously at film festivals than it was at the British box office, where it was sniffed at by snobs who found it too flashy, too gritty, altogether too redolent of Hollywood. Which, in part, is why he decided to go there, to get an agent and try his luck.

The hiring of Cannon and the casting of Stallone did create some unexpected, non-financial anxiety. The actor had appeared in a 1993 SF action film called *Demolition Man*, whose young Italian director, Marco Brambilla, had been an eager candidate for the top spot on *Dredd*. At the time, a reconnaissance mission to the movies to check out *Demolition Man* and report back to the production bunker, had stirred up some anxiety. "The similarities are vexing," Susan Nicoletti had reported in an August 1993 memo. A couple of the more eerily familiar elements, like the existence of a literal underground of revolutionaries lurking in the service tunnels under the city, were dropped at that point. But with the arrival of Stallone himself, the pressure increased to mitigate the somber anti-utopian tone of Wisher's draft.

"When Cinergi came into it," Pressman says, "Andy

Director Danny Cannon with Stallone watching a playback on the Mega-City set, above

Director of Photography Adrian Biddle on set at Shepperton, opposite

Beau Marks with Andy Vajna at Shepperton, above

Vajna was really not familiar with Dredd, so a lot of the things that we had been taking for granted, he wanted us to account for. He wanted motivations, he wanted explanations. He wanted to know the rules better."

"Wisher is the one who had to sort out five hundred comic books to come up with a story," Vajna recalls. "What I didn't want was a very dark and downbeat movie, because I knew it had to appeal to kids. So I wanted to get a much brighter, much happier, much lighter feel to it."

"*Judge Dredd* is a comic book in the same way that Batman is a comic book," Cannon declares. "It's a part of our folklore. It's corny in a legitimate way. *Ben Hur* and *Spartacus* – would you call those movies corny? They are, but you don't think of them that way because there's an emotional passion about those movies. So what I said to Andy Vajna was, 'Let's make *Ben Hur* again. *Judge Dredd* can be *Ben Hur*. There's a way that we can justify being corny.' And when I read the screenplay that Bill Wisher had done for them, I thought it stood a chance, because he had a little respect for the character and the approach to Dredd himself was spot on."

As it turned out, somewhat to Cannon's surprise, the Cinergi crowd, which included production executive Tova Laiter, liked the sound of Cannon's pitch. Laiter says: "He came in and compared it to telling an epic Roman story. That the Council of Judges was like the Roman Senate. The way he described it you saw all the people with togas sweeping along the marble floors. We really liked that because we said, 'My God, what if you put a character in conflict against that epic background.' We thought it was a really wonderful idea."

For Cannon, a cop is just not a movie hero on a

grand society-encompassing scale, like a Spartacus or a Ben Hur, history-making men who embodied and shaped the fate of their society – in a way that a beleaguered public servant like a cop in a crime thriller never could, even against a "majestic" urban backdrop.

"I wanted to make a film where an audience could become interested in and lost in the story, because the story is bigger than this one guy. What I was saying was, 'Make it of international importance. Let's have an international cast. Let's make everybody in the film timeless. Let's not have any contemporary people in it, anything that gives it away as being a contemporary vision of the future. Let's not point the finger at how clever we're being. Let's actually create something that's quite low-tech and that people can get lost in.' All of sudden you're framing and legitimizing Dredd's actions, creating a context for them. He's working for the state. He belongs to a system and that system is exemplified by eagle sconces, clip-clop floors, gold, marble, granite. You create a group of people, the Judges, who stepped in to bring order to chaos and who have created some nice wealth for themselves at the same time. All of a sudden we've created a social reality that people can believe in, and we can be as corny as we like, then, because we're being so earnest about it."

The only elements Cannon didn't relish in the Wisher script, he says, were the overtly science-fictiony bits. "What I didn't like were all the mutants and aliens. I wanted it to be more human. I wanted to be able to shoot everything straight, without winking. I wanted to be able to say, 'This is a society that isn't far off from our own. I just went about then, working with Bill Wisher at first, and then with Walon Green [*The Wild Bunch*], a brilliant writer who always makes a certain amount of sense. But he wasn't on the picture long because he was writing a dark movie and at a certain point that became taboo.

Tova Laiter, an executive who worked on *Dredd* for Cinergi, is a great supporter of the "new energy" that another of Vajna's close collaborators in the business, screenwriter Steven E. De Souza, ultimately brought to the script for Dredd.

"The Wisher script was very dense," she says. "It didn't flow. There were lots of descriptions, and people were talking too much. It wasn't springy, you know what I mean? It wasn't light on its feet. Steve De Souza did a marvelous job from our point of view. He took the denseness out of the script, and he made it flow."

Vajna supported Laiter's verdict on the Wisher script and De Souza's rewrite. "Bill was and is a very good writer," he says. "But we brought De Souza in to give the whole thing a lighter touch, to clean up some of the story difficulties. He was able to step back and say, 'Let's just go for the ride.' He did a great job of just whipping us right through it so that we never stop to think about anything. Between the two of them, we got a really terrific script."

Steven E. De Souza has an enviable reputation in Hollywood for being involved as a writer on high-speed action movies laced with throwaway laughs, like *48 Hours*, *Die Hard*, *Die Hard II* and *Commando*, that large audiences find irresistible. De Souza was a natural choice to inject a little extra juice into *Judge Dredd*; he could give the heavy metal impact of the current action flick a glint of high spirits.

But Danny disagreed, "I think the thing where Steve De Souza lost his temper the most was with the character Ilsa. Rico needed a sidekick, and with

"What I didn't like were all the mutants and aliens. I wanted it to be more human. I wanted to be able to shoot everything straight, without winking. I wanted to be able to say, 'This is a society that isn't far off from our own'."

Danny Cannon, Director

Danny Cannon and William Wisher brought in the ABC robot, above, *from* 2000 AD *as a suitably emotionless sidekick for the characterless Rico*

Bill I had added a character from another *2000 AD* series, the ABC robot. I wanted Rico to have a mechanical friend because that's how void of character he is. But Steve wanted to create a character called Ilsa, I think as an homage to *Ilsa, She-Wolf of the SS*, who would be a female counterpart for Rico and they could be sexy together and then the girls can have a fight at the end. A cat fight. Which I found just incredibly crass. But of course once Steve had thought of that it was clear that it was going to happen, because Andy Vajna loves Steve De Souza.

"Ilsa at this point was a biker chick, and when Rico goes to see her she's kicking some guy in the balls, and she has tattoos, and things. And I was saying, 'If we are gonna introduce this woman, can she please belong to the world of *this* movie and not to some comic book we're gonna get bored with in fifteen minutes. We're not *Batman*. We haven't got the Penguin running around. We're making this stuff up and the audience has to believe in it."

Cannon had already pulled Rico himself out of the realm of the monstrously mutated; his deformations were now entirely emotional and psychological. Rico became a charismatic but sociopathic human being played by the world-class sinister smoothy Armand Assante.

"My Rico was a sophisticated, intelligent man, who could have been Dredd, but didn't turn out to be. Rico, you know, has the best line in the film: 'You gave up life to embrace the law; I gave up the law and embraced life.' In effect he's saying, 'I'm not a slave. They're using us,' and he makes a lot of sense. At the outset he really does see some aspects of the situation more clearly than Dredd. He makes a lot of sense. I tried to tell Steve that the best and the most deeply frightening villains are the guys that *almost* convince you. They're that close to being brilliant. But if you create a female companion for a character like that, she has to be more or less on his level, which the original Ilsa certainly wasn't.

"To fit her into the story better I made Ilsa a part

Danny Cannon wasn't happy with Bill Wisher's mutants and aliens, a basic ingredient of 2000 AD; *left is poor Otto Sump, the ugliest man in Mega-City One as drawn by Ron Smith*

of the cloning system, a member of the techie class in the city, a sophisticated woman who could help the plot along. She's the one authentic neo-Nazi in the plot, if you like. She gets off on the glamour factor of the jackboots and the leather. She belongs to the new order, a higher stratum, whereas [Dredd's partner] Hershey is a ground trooper and a no-nonsense, highly professional sort of person. At least that way you have a clash of personalities between the two women that might make people feel a little something when they start kicking the crap out of each other."

As it turned out, De Souza's concerns ran deeper than the traditional technical, tinkering functions of a script doctor, even with the mandate for "fun" hanging over his head.

"When the script came to me," De Souza explains, "I felt Dredd was a fascist and that the whole state was a fascist state. There were no civilians in the movie at all, apart from the anarchistic scum the cops were fighting. I wrote a scene in which some cops are complaining about the news media making the police look bad, but they don't take the reporters out and shoot them.

In the end Mega-City was populated by wild-looking humans. Here Cannon and Stallone pose with some of the film's extras

"This kind of thinking wasn't actually beside the point of my assignment at all. I think one of the things that most helped to lighten the movie was making the society it depicts less oppressive overall. Until that was done, no matter how funny you made the characters or how clever or amusing the dialogue, you could never really make the movie lighter. It would be innately oppressive.

"For me the key was to put a trial in the movie. To have a legitimate judicial process, not some kind of star chamber, and see that there's a defense attorney, a prosecuting attorney, rules of evidence. There's a key point where the Chief Judge sides with the defense in declaring some evidence inadmissible. So we can see there are still some checks and balances left."

Order for the sake of order, without a fairly high-minded and even-handed devotion to justice, would warp the story into a moral vacuum.

"There's a temptation in the material," De Souza argues, "that it's important not to give in to. I think anybody who reads the newspapers can see the frustration that people have with the court system. So it's important to show that Dredd is not a fascist, but that he's on the verge of becoming one and ultimately pulls back from it. He rejects Griffin and comes down on the side represented by Fargo. He helps the society to take a step toward real justice, as well, which is very much tied in with the idea of democracy."

De Souza's experience as a screenwriter on fast-paced commercial action films taught him that it's always a good idea to husband the resources of a story, to play out the string gradually, to save something for the home stretch.

"When I got to the flying motorcycle on page three, I thought, 'This is a great idea, but why show all our aces so soon?' You're playing poker with the audience when you make a movie. So you want them to be interested up until the very end. You'll see if you look into it that a lot of genre pieces run out of ideas halfway through. The crime has been committed, the hero has identified the villain, and that took twenty minutes, and then you have an hour and fifteen minutes of the audience sitting there waiting for car chases, explosions and fist fights. And then they wonder why the audience didn't like it? So I was determined that in this movie we would have surprises right up to the very end."

Obviously it would be highly uncool if a modern movie tough-guy seemed too knowingly political; that would be, in Cottie Chubb's phrase, "too on the nose." American film characters have always been more comfortable advocating commonsense "values" rather than overt political philosophies. Remember how much effort it took to persuade Humphrey Bogart even to pick sides in World War II in *Casablanca*! Judge Dredd's actions, too, needed to produce their political effects almost as an afterthought. He wouldn't be an acceptable, mainstream American hero if his motives weren't mostly personal and instinctive.

"Dredd at first is oblivious to the trends of the society as a whole," De Souza agrees. "He's too much a part of the system to step back from it. He has to be betrayed and framed and forced into the position of an outsider before he can see the current setup for what it is."

"The only thing that makes these movies better is their overview," Cannon asserts. "Their atmosphere is what you might go back and see the movie a second time for, not the plot. And I think this film has that in spades. There are layers in this film, because we cared to put them in. Yeah, it's a comic book, and yeah, it's got some elements you've seen in every other action-adventure film. But the truth is, when they looked at the storyboards I had a fight that they couldn't say no to. I had a robot in this that they couldn't say no to. The crash of a prison shuttle full of convicts, which they couldn't say no to. The Angel Gang fight, Mean Machine; they could not say no to them. I had motorcycles where the wheels went up and this thing took off.

"The point for me was it had to be a crossover picture. As well as being a cop and doing all these cool things, and getting the girl and the bad guy, Dredd has emotional problems, he has a history, and the city's in big danger because of it. All of a sudden the story becomes bigger and people get interested. I think everyone's gonna be happy. The kids and the grownups both!

"I mean, the kids are going to just explode to see this movie because, I mean, it's gadgets galore. If they were gonna pay me to do that, I'll give it to them."

Rico's female counterpart Ilsa Hayden, played by Joan Chen, is the one authentic neo-Nazi in the plot, opposite

Danny Cannon with Diane Lane rehearsing the fight between Hershey and Ilsa in the Janus lab, below

With the deal finally struck, filming could start at Shepperton Studios in England. Sylvester Stallone as Judge Dredd poses on his Lawmaster with actors and crew on the steps of the Hall of Justice

MAKING IT REAL

LEVEL 3

With the script edging towards completion, and a director on line, the first step in the long production process was to hire an art department to visualize some of the concepts that lay at the heart of *Judge Dredd*.

Director Danny Cannon remembers having great difficulties before there were any illustrations to show people. "You get everybody aroused at meetings, but they still stare at you like, if you walk out of the room at this point we're lost," he remembers. "It took an enormous amount of energy to visualize this for people and get them to trust in you. So the first thing we did was to create an art department because we thought if they could see it ... and sure enough, it helped. You just create an alternative future and the world is your oyster."

Nigel Phelps, an Englishman from Northampton who had worked on *Batman*, was taken on as Production Designer. He was joined in Los Angeles by three other British illustrators: Simon Murton and Matthew Codd, who now live in the US, and Kevin Walker, a comics artist for *2000 AD*, who Danny was very keen to use.

The four of them sat in an office churning out design after design. Nigel's ideas would often come out as thumbnail sketches, which the other three would develop into fully fledged drawings. As soon as anything was drawn, it was pinned up on the wall of the office. It soon became a crowded wall, but it was one that enabled everyone to see what was being done, what was working and what wasn't.

"The intent always was to have this enormous-looking and very believable society that we're setting the action in," says Nigel. "That was always the page-one thing. It's got to be totally believable, it's got to be larger than life, but at the same time you've got to be able to believe in it all the time. Otherwise the drama's lost.

"When you start off there's just a lot of thumbnail sketches and very rough ideas just to try to capture the essence of the film. And really you try to cover the board in a very sketchy form, and then work it up with all the other artists until you have much more detail, and you build up a picture that way."

"Working with Nigel was probably the greatest inspiration," enthuses Simon Murton. "That guy has a remarkable view and a remarkable way of putting it down on paper and really pushes you. Both Danny and Nigel really pushed us to come up with something."

The fifth member of the Art Department in these early days was a color photocopier which saved the human members a lot of work. Whenever a large illustration was needed for a presentation, the smaller version was just enlarged on the copier. It reduced many a week-long job into a job lasting a couple of

Production Designer Nigel Phelps, left

Kevin Walker's painting of the fantasy Mega-City One from fall 1993, below

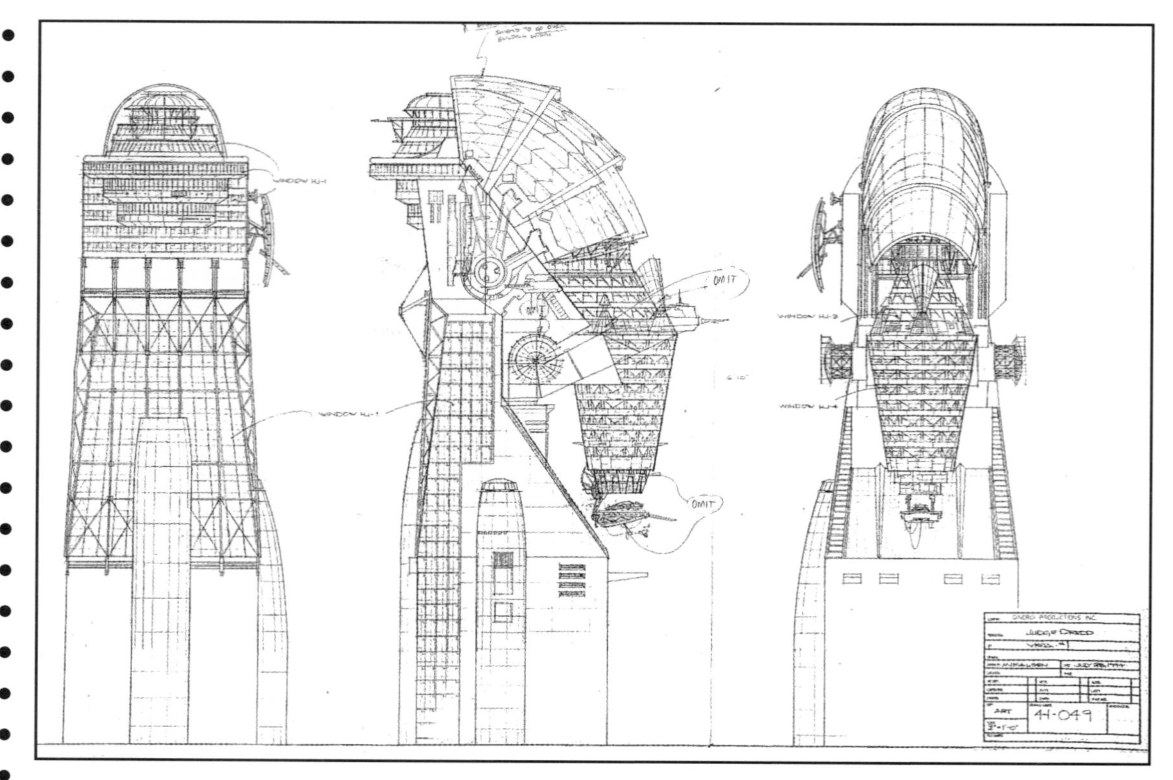

Mass.Illusion drawings of the acid-shielded upper portions of a Mega-City structure by Model Designer Kent Mikalfen, right

days. It was very important at the stage where ideas were still in flux and many of the illustrations would be superseded further down the production process.

The color copier was also able to change the hue and tone of pictures and the artists would experiment with colors by simply pressing a couple of buttons on the machine and letting it do its stuff. Those copies could then be worked on by other people without any concern that the picture underneath was being covered up.

"In the early conceptual stages we were trying to find and nail down the design language of the future," Simon continues. "One of the most challenging things was to design a future, one hundred and fifty years from now but make it look old, make it look used."

The comics were an obvious source of inspiration. They had, after all, been drawing the future for a couple of decades. But the work that ultimately came out of Nigel Phelps's department steered away from the styles established in *2000 AD*.

"It doesn't look anything like that," Nigel says. "Mega-City in the comics is totally different. It's much more ambiguous as to what's happening there. They have lots of domed buildings. Every artist draws them differently anyway, there's not a characteristic style ... When you do something like this you don't copy the comic book, you use it as a starting point. The most closely copied, if you like, is the Dredd uniform, but at the same time it's vastly different to the comic book, really."

The artists were told to let their ideas rip, to think up the best designs and leave the practical worries to later on in the production process. It meant being free to take inspiration from the comics without being tied down to them. In the beginning it was the artists' imaginations that spilled out onto the paper.

"Everyone in the department is a designer in their own right," Nigel continues. "I'm there to sow the seeds, so to speak, to get the first marks down, then steer people that are going in the right direction. If they're working in a certain way that I like, then I juggle them into particular areas where I think they're excelling. That's part of it. But with something like this it's not a one-man job. It's a big job and in trying to create a believable comic book future there are very few things that you can take from the already existing – whether it's architectural references or vehicles or food mixers or props or anything. You've really got to start from scratch on it. There's a lot of work there."

When production moved to England, Nigel took the preparatory work with him and brought in a new set of people to draw the future. Gradually the film began to take shape; some sequences were expanded, others dropped and the reality of what they were being asked to do began to filter through. The designs eventually had to match up to the capabilities of the budget and the needs of the filmmakers. Fabulous illustrations were drawn – like the bar scene – that never made it to the movie, but it was important to allow imaginations to run riot in the beginning. Only afterwards did the ideas need to be honed down to what was possible. It was better than starting with a list of restrictions that would have ultimately limited the vision of *Judge Dredd*.

Ten different places around the world were possibles when it came to deciding where to film *Judge Dredd*. Among the places that missed out were the USA, Mexico, Canada, Australia, Germany, Italy, Hungary and Czechoslovakia.

Mexico was an obvious choice because it had coped quite happily with films like *Total Recall*, but the fact that part of the studio was being ripped out for refurbishment ruled it out. Hungary was next in line.

"We've done a couple of very big movies in Hungary," says Executive Producer Andy Vajna. "Hungary could have been a real choice, but because of the technical requirements of this movie, Beau felt that probably it would be better to be in England where at least we understood the language and all the people spoke it."

"England became a favorite because I felt I could get everybody I needed out of London," says Line

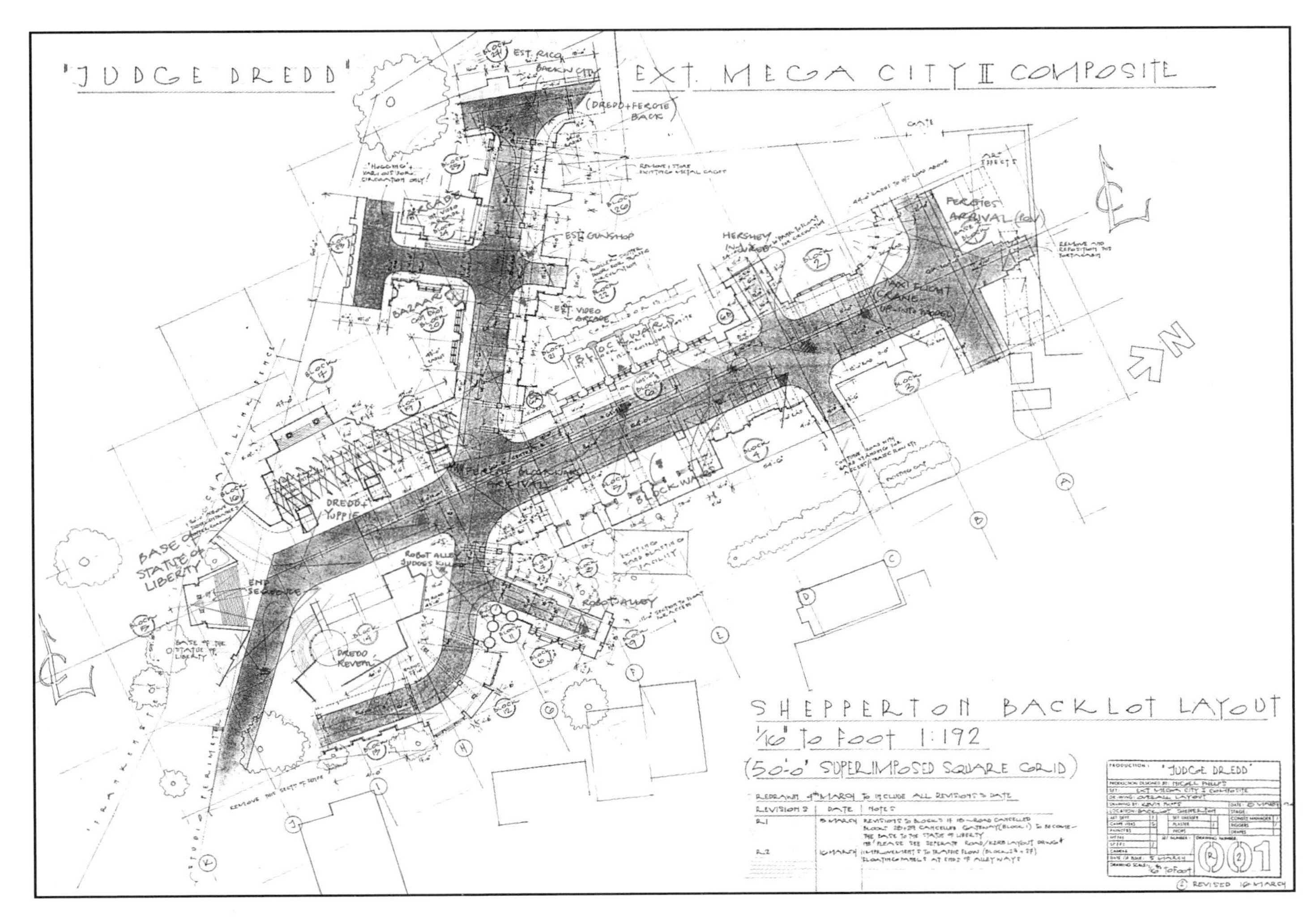

Shepperton back-lot layout for Mega-City One drawn by Kevin Phipps, below

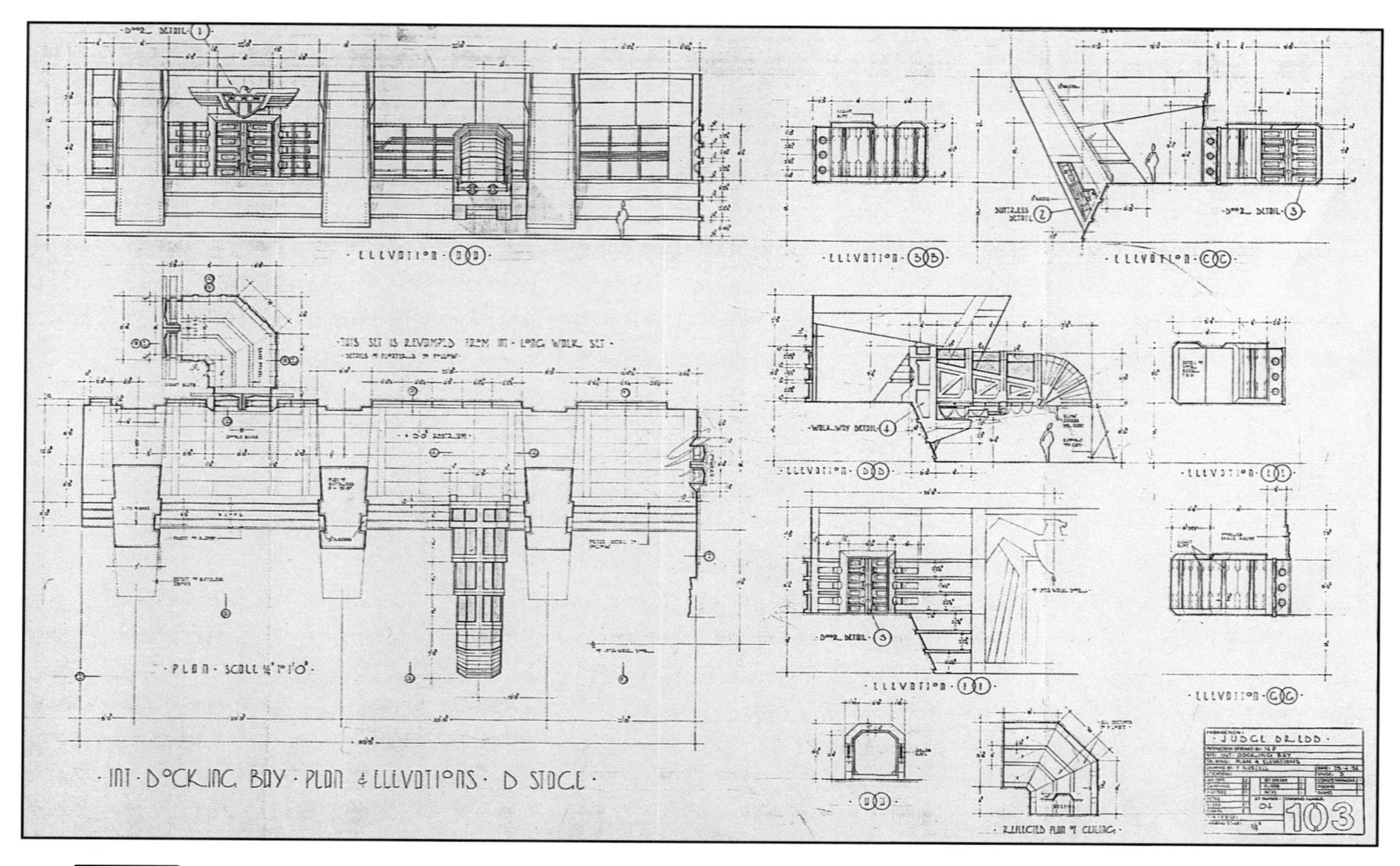

JACKING POINT

Peter Russell's plans for the final version of the prison shuttle docking bay, above

Notes from Martin Laing to the modelmaker working on the docking bay, right

DOCKING BAY MODEL.

1. EXTEND THE F/GROUND FLOOR BY 50%
2. EXTEND THE LOWER SIDE WALLS BY 50%
3. EXTEND FLOOR TROUGH INTO THE F/GROUND.
4. MAKE A SET OF BUTTRESSES TO PUT IN F/GROUND & FLOAT. (NOT SHOWN)
5. EXTEND THE CEILING & LIGHTS BY 50%

Producer Beau Marks. "I had an indigenous crew, so I didn't need to bring people in. I could save a great deal of money. I could save millions of dollars! And the quality of crew is phenomenal if you get their 'A' crews. The ability to build big they've demonstrated time and time again. The James Bond movies, *Batman*, even *Frankenstein* ... So you keep going through it; cost of crew, cost of locations, cost of all those things started to come down, and an English director. I felt that if I could support him with an English crew that he was used to, that would also be a plus."

So England it was. *Frankenstein* was just shipping out as *Judge Dredd* was shipping into Shepperton Studios, as the production team prepared for five months of filming.

The Aspen shuttle flies over the wasteland heading for the towering splendor of Mega-City One. The shuttle is returning the convicts who have served their sentences back to the community.

Director Danny Cannon wanted the shuttle to be

a bat shape swooping through the sky. In the preproduction stages in England he spent lots of time with the conceptual artists showing them what he wanted by drawing a bat shape over and over again. The original design for the shuttle followed that design, but the finished vehicle was quite different.

After the shuttle lands in the docking bay there was originally a scene where the prisoners try to escape with a big shoot-out. This was going to be filmed on 'H' stage at Shepperton Studios, which meant the shuttle had to be built life-size.

"Initially we had designed a shuttle just to look good," explains Conceptual Illustrator Julian Caldow. "When they realized that it was going to be done on 'H' stage, obviously the size was determined by the size of the stage and by the design of the docking bay that was put inside that. And gradually the shuttle got smaller and smaller and smaller. Once it

Operating the remote-controlled opening ascender rig shot of Mega-City One on a special track designed by Mass.Illusion, above and left

The official map of Mega-City One, right, *with the East River paved over with landfill*

was really huge, then the wings got shorter and it got stubbier. I was a bit upset that it wasn't as close to what I wanted to do."

Then the script was rewritten and the gunfight was written out. Essentially it became just Fergie walking out of the shuttle and entering Mega-City.

"You're not going to spend a lot of money building this massive set just for that," says Production Designer Nigel Phelps. "So we didn't build it, we made it as a model – the shot of the shuttle rising up through the wall and into the docking bay, that's a miniature. All we build physically then was a corridor, which is just one side, that you see Fergie walking off from. And then that money that we 'saved' if you like, we can put into something where there's more action going on."

"When I discovered it was done in miniature, that was really upsetting," adds Julian Caldow, "because they could have gone with the biggest shuttle design you could think of and it wouldn't have mattered. All that time shortening this and ..." he sighs. "Still, these things happen."

Making a film as involved and innovative as *Judge Dredd* is bound to produce minor casualties along the way. But it also allows minor miracles to happen. They are "happy accidents." It's what makes filmmaking one of the most surprising, exciting and frustrating businesses in the world.

MEGA CITY

The first striking image in *Judge Dredd* is Mega-City. After the gentle opening scenes, the audience is suddenly hit by the force of this towering combination of technology and power. All life is here, from the squalor of the "Heavenly Haven" apartments where Fergie is assigned to live, to the glory of the Halls of Justice. It is layer upon layer of living space, office space, factories, commerce, flying buses, road-going taxis and Judges.

It is a vision of how New York will be in the third millenium if the world of *Judge Dredd* is to be believed. In the *2000 AD* comic, the design was more spacious, with individual estates rather than towering buildings. Some of them were so vast they were self-contained blocks where people could work, eat and sleep without ever seeing daylight. But the film had different needs and requirements.

"It was very important to all of us that the city is a believable one," says Production Designer Nigel Phelps. "You believe in the characters and you believe in the environment that they are acting out in. We've stuck with the comic book premise in that things are larger than life and that they're theatrical, but we try and make them as believable as we can so we

strike a balance. It isn't how New York is going to turn out, it's hopefully something that's much more exciting and informative."

For many reasons, some of them aesthetic, some of them budgetary, and also because there was only a limited amount of space in the Shepperton back lot, Mega-City reached into the sky. It became something organized by socio-economic layers, built one on top of another. At street level it's a seedy, squalid, old and dirty place where the lowlife exist. As you go higher up in Mega-City, the buildings become newer and the inhabitants become richer, until you get to the very top where the air is clean and only the most powerful can afford to live.

"We've really tried hard to rationalize a believable society in this environment, with regard to the way that people live in it," says Nigel. "At ground level there's a lot of contemporary New York and as you move up the buildings they become more exciting, more robotic, more mechanical, until when you get to the tops of the buildings they have a very different character from the one they have at the bottom. They're chalk and cheese. The middle classes live up there and everyone flies about in aerial vehicles, whereas as you move down the buildings it's more and more roadways and public transport."

The script required three areas to be built. A residential neighborhood, a red-light area and a smarter Wall Street area. All these were constructed on the back lot of Shepperton in a fantastic array of shops, living quarters and functional buildings such

Building Mega-City One, above and left

Building and then dressing the set on the Shepperton back lot was a massive task – but the end result is highly convincing. From top to bottom, left to right, *these photos were taken by Kevin Phipps on: 21 March 1994; 8 April; 16 May; 7 June; 4 July; 27 July; 16 August and 7 October 1994*

NEW
BEAVER ST
ONE WAY

Construction was planned so that the same "buildings" could be quickly reworked to give a completely different appearance and appear to be a new location

as the bank and the Halls of Justice. Anyone who came to visit the set and needed to be impressed was taken on a tour of the city. It never failed. Even when there was no filming going on, all the neon signs were turned off and there wasn't an extra in sight; it looked incredible.

Building the set was a mammoth task, the biggest undertaking for the construction team on *Judge Dredd*. Once Nigel and his team had finished the initial designs, it was up to Art Director Kevin Phipps to oversee the project. He likens his role to that of the first violin in an orchestra conducted by Nigel Phelps. He started work on January 5, 1994, and kept an eye on things until shooting in the back lot finished in the middle of October. There were 154 building days with the construction team working on the set for twenty-five weeks, six days a week.

When Kevin started, Mega-City was only in sketch form and there were constant discussions about where to put everything. The Statue of Liberty was first going to be positioned at one one end of the street, then it was going to be at the other end, and then someone suggested it might be good if it was at the third end! There were, in total, seven major revisions at different times for different scripts. Eventually, as Kevin puts it, "We finally got to the point where we ran out of time and money.

"It's been a very challenging project doing what we've done in the time for the money," he continues. "It's been a very hard film in a way because it's been very tight in every single area to deliver on time and for the price. So however creative and wonderful your ideas are, you've always got to drag them back and achieve it within the budget."

Mega-City One started life as a gravel parking lot behind the sound stages at Shepperton Studios. There was literally nothing there until the builders came in. They laid down the roads, built in drains, and even constructed a series of tunnels to allow steam to be piped in and waft up atmospherically from vents in the road.

The requirements of the film meant it all had to be as solid as the real thing. "In the road construction we had to allow for the heavy vehicles and the construction cranes," says Kevin. "At one stage we were going to rent a SCUD missile launcher as one of the action vehicles and that was enormously heavy, so the road specification had to be good enough to take that kind of weight."

In the middle of building Mega-City, Construction Coordinator Michael Redding was heard to remark, "This isn't a film set, it's more like civil engineering." With real Land Rovers and Saracen armored cars thundering down the road, there was no room for cutting corners. The buildings themselves weren't real in the bricks-and-mortar sense, of course, but you couldn't tell by looking at them. Danny Cannon and Nigel Phelps's insistence that everything looked believable meant the construction team had to be very choosy with the materials they used, making the lower level of the street appear old and run down, while the newer upper levels are metallic and gleaming.

"Our main medium is tube," says Michael Redding. "Tubes and scaffolding are the background to all our finishes. Then we do it in plaster, which represents concrete. Into our molds we put all our decoration of the finish – caused by the environment, decay, aging – and that's why it looks just like the real concrete when it's up there. Then, of course, our painters come along and put all their runs and aging, green and orange rust decay. That's how we achieve our finishes. But also we've used a lot of metal and aluminum."

The next people to come into the picture were Set Decorator Peter Young and Prop Master Ty Teiger. Their task was to bring in all those little things that made the city look lived-in. All the knick-knacks that clutter people's lives and all the extra bits and

Luckily, nothing had to be built too high – computer effects would add the towering skyline

Dozens of shop signs were designed for use in the film, many involving crew names as a production in-joke

TY'S THAI KITCHEN {555} 2936

pieces that turn a building from being an empty space with four walls around it into a shop or an apartment. "A city like that will eat props," says Ty Teiger. "You can spend two weeks filling it up with trucks full of gear and you stand back and look at it and it's still empty."

Thirty lorry-loads of props, some 200 neon signs and 150 lights were swallowed up by Mega-City One. Ty had worked with Danny Cannon on *The Young Americans* before coming to *Judge Dredd,* which was his first big film as Prop Master. He talks enthusiastically about the eight weeks it took to dress the street. "You have to introduce all your big piping, your cabling, your barbed wire and stuff, just to fill it up, to make it look lived-in," he says. "Then you've got to age everything down like it's been there two thousand years, or whatever. It's an incredible process, it's brilliant ... If you could actually have a stop-frame animation of everything being done from day one to the end – now *that* would make a good film!"

Ty's name is up there in lights as *Ty's Thai Cuisine* for anyone who wants to study the movie closely enough to read the shop fronts. It's one of a string of production in-jokes that litter the street. *Mary Lou's Reptile House* was clearly inspired by Production Associate Mary Lou Devlin; Production Buyer Johnny Lanzer gets his moment of fame in *Lanzer Bacteriologist*; and Art Director for vehicles, David Allday, had such a useful name, it was turned into two shops, *Allday and Night Liquor Store* and *Allday Dining*. However, the best one as far as Kevin Phipps is concerned is the oriental diner: "We've got a chap with us called Jon Billington who's one of our assistants, and his name developed into *Bill Ying Tong's*," he says. "It's just a bit of fun, it keeps the buzz."

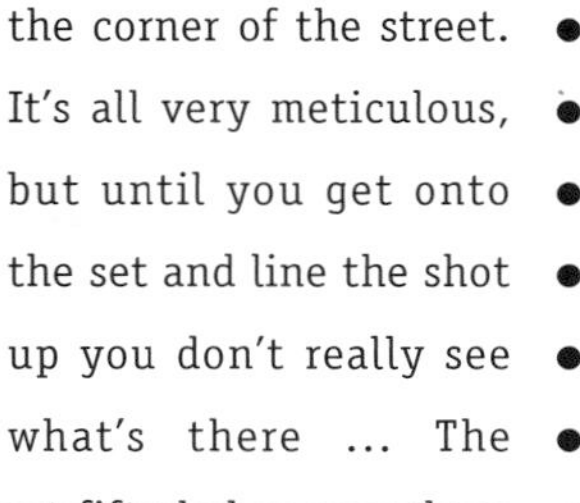

The final element that really brings Mega-City to life is the hoard of extras drafted in for the big scenes like the Block War and Rico's visit to the gun shop. "Danny wanted to make them look as if they had no money and they're just kept by the state," explains Emma Porteous, who designed all the costumes for the film. "They get fed by this horrible food robot that comes round and they just go to a stall and they get some garments given to them, so they [the clothes] have to be similar. Then they customize them themselves by either pulling out sleeves or whatever. So I went to a huge army surplus store and just bought hundreds of army surplus things and then we had them dyed different colors and pulled out sleeves and broke them down."

Once again, it was down to Ty Teiger to dig out some props to make all the extras look busy, which, despite months of planning, still turned out to be a bit of a spur of the moment thing. "[The extras] are either carrying bags or they're selling something on the corner of the street. It's all very meticulous, but until you get onto the set and line the shot up you don't really see what's there ... The Director will say 'Right, I want fifty hobos over there living in a shack.' So we actually muster it up and stick it together in about half an hour and then they shoot it!"

Most of the scenes in Mega-City were shot at night with all of the streets damped down so it wouldn't matter too much continuity-wise if it rained (which, despite the reputation of the British weather, it did only once). It was also helpful for the Director of Photography Adrian Biddle, "because you can get more control in where the light's coming from as opposed to days where you don't know if it's going to be sunny or overcast," he says.

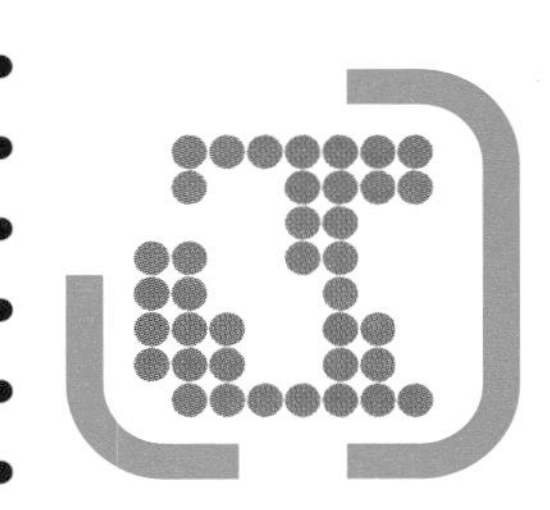

The set has been revamped to look different, below, *but that large diagonal pipe looks familiar*

Once the scenes were shot, the street was often re-dressed so it could masquerade as somewhere else for different scenes. "We had to do all these revamps very quickly over a period of twenty-four hours," says Kevin Phipps. "For one end of the street we had this huge window. So the taxi landing pad that you see right at the beginning of the film is magically transformed into a tenement block and a huge sign, a fifty foot sign, went up and said 'Elysian Heights' and the whole building was faced with this thirty-foot-square mirrored window. So all of a sudden you had no idea where you were. It assumed a completely different identity. And even members of the crew were turning round and thinking, 'Wait a minute, that wasn't there last time!' "

The revamping, along with the computer effects which added the flying vehicles, the extra buildings and height to the city, made Mega-City look far bigger on screen than it ever was in reality.

For a brief moment at the beginning of the film it seems that the future isn't such a bad place after all. As Fergie enters the city he does so with hope and optimism, his sentence at Aspen Prison has been served and he has been assigned a living space in the optimistically named Heavenly Haven Apartments.

He looks across at the gleaming city and at an image which the script describes as "a perfect utopian future of happy families circling through a green urban park." But of course it's just a video poster and it's one that is almost immediately replaced by a new video showing the drab prospect of the Law Enforcement Barracks. There is no utopia. This is the real future and one which is descending into block wars.

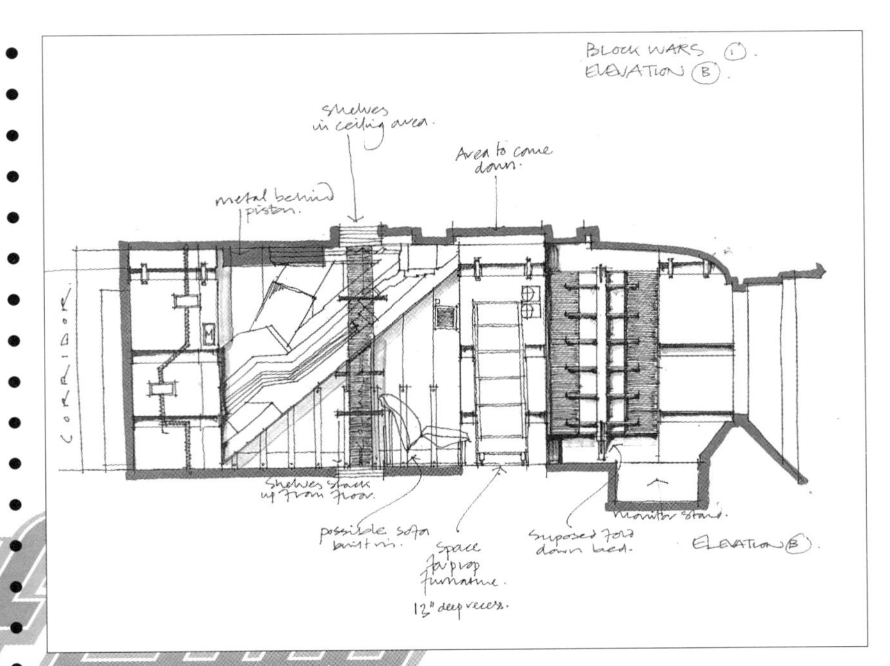

Detailed plans for the Block War by Martyn John, above, *and by Gary Tomkins,* below

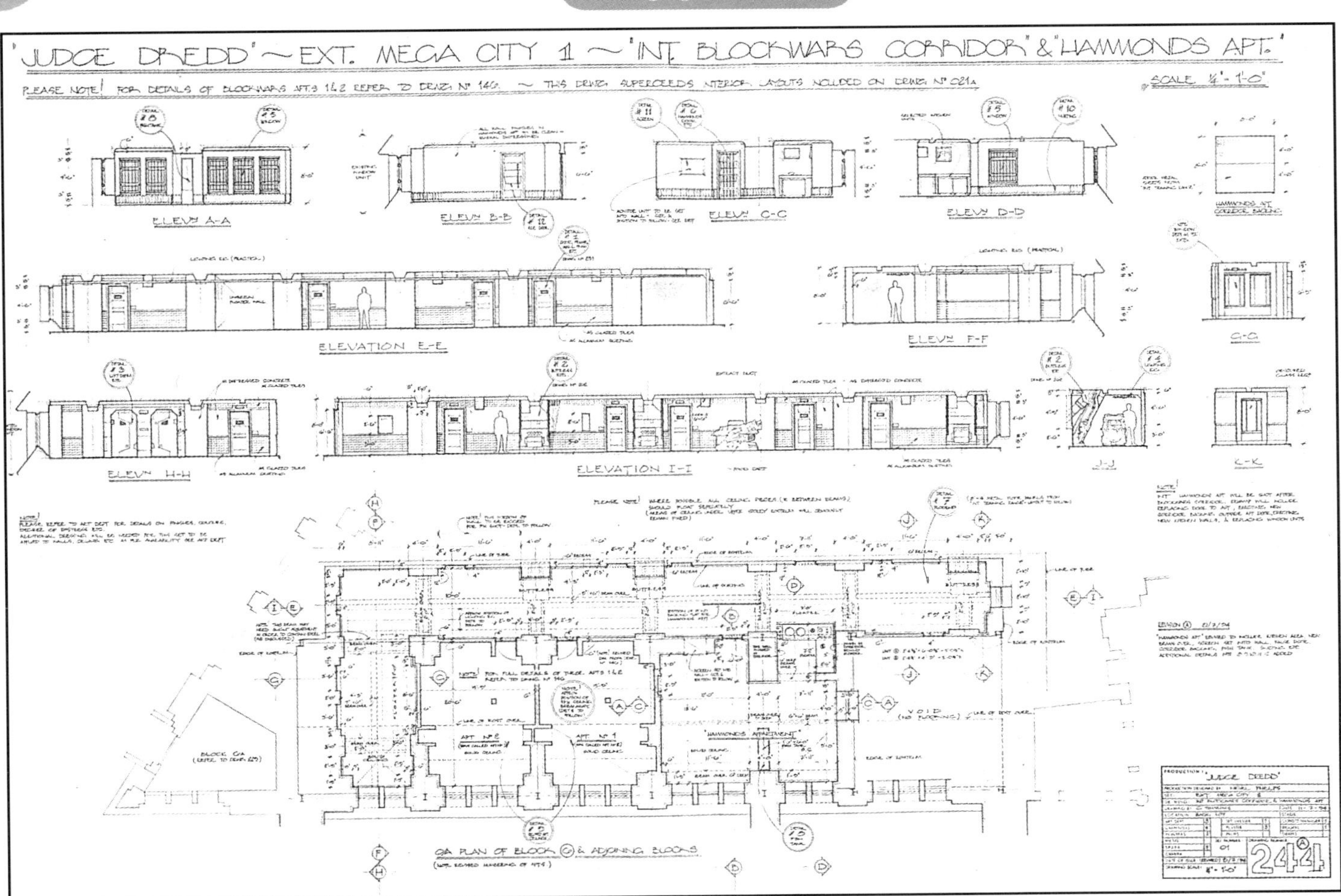

Orchestrating a major scene on the back lot set, above

This scene went through a lot of changes in development. In the comic, these fights were the result of groups of people striving for identity, to stamp their mark on a city that grouped them in a uniform run-down building. Groups of people would let out their frustration in an explosion of violence.

One early version had the Block War reflecting a theme from the comics, that of a civil defense group which is trying to protect the ordinary citizen (the character of Hammond who later became a reporter was originally the leader of this group). It brings up the whole question of how a group that upholds the legal system while at the same time lying outside it relates to the Judges. This version had a subplot in which Griffin was trying to take power away from the people by removing their weapons. However, this sort of political point-making was lost in the translation to screen, because it was never really what the film was about.

Instead, the Block War sequence shows a City on the edge, a city where the Law is breaking down, where people like Griffin are in charge and are spreading corruption from above. It is the corruption that Dredd, always the unquestioning upholder of the Law, will confront to some extent at the end of the film.

Kevin Walker tried to show some of this in his early illustrations of the scene. "This is where we find out how insane Mega-City's got," he says. "You can see down avenues off into the distance to show there's plenty of people who are quite oblivious to this death and destruction. They really don't care. They're going about their everyday lives while people are dying. Life is cheap in Mega-City."

To make the audience identify with the ordinary

citizen, a sequence was written in which a mother and child get pulled into the riot. But this was quickly dropped when it became very sentimental and seemed to be leading the film in the wrong direction. Instead, the Block War became a big action scene with an expanded riot at street level. It is left to things like the inside of the apartments to explain the situation in which the "rezzies" are living.

"You weave a storyline into all of those spaces just so that you can make it real," Nigel Phelps explains. "It's meant to be a very utilitarian place, it's welfare state, everyone's on handouts and credit, no one has any cash ... They're supposed to be two hundred years old and many families have lived in these apartments and there's the same sort of styling, the same sort of furniture, but everyone has ripped out units and put in some different ones.

"Every apartment has also got this jettison system built into it which you're all too aware of. You've got the door up one end, then on either side there are

A camera suspended from a gyroscopic monorail mount to shoot overhead footage of the Block War, left

Cleaning up the wreckage, below

The Mega-City streets were filled with suitably futuristic transport – underneath, the vehicles were mostly Land Rovers and Saracen troop transporters

these big mechanical units built into the walls. It's not ever gone into in the story, but the notion is that there is someone downstairs who can – if you're not paying rent, or are causing too much trouble – press a button and jettison your apartment. So they can get rid of bad debtors. It's just things like that you try to build in to make spaces more interesting. It works because it's so inhospitable. Because who wants to live with this fucking great machine rammed in your face all the time?"

The finishing touches that refined the living space came from Set Decorator Peter Young. The whole inside of the Block War apartments had to be decked out twice over, in what became the norm of last-

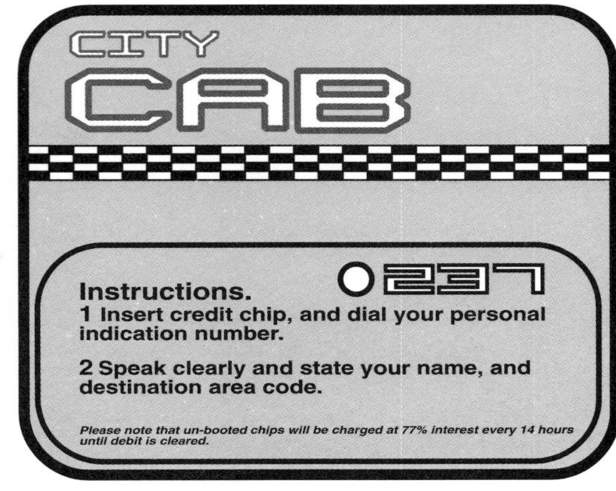

minute changes and late decisions that dogged the filming of *Judge Dredd*. "There was an awful lot of confusion," says Peter. "I discussed it fully with Nigel and Danny – I believed – and actually probably went in the wrong direction, i.e. I made the Block War apartment like a squatters' apartment and Danny actually didn't like it and changed it. I made it dead rats and barbed wire and more like a squat, which he didn't approve of. He wanted it to illustrate how people were actually living in one hundred and fifty years' time. He wanted it more decorated, with a bed, with a sink and a washing machine."

These scenes supposedly take place some three

The Judges arrive to take charge, above

Production shot of Dredd in the Heavenly Haven corridors

Judge Hershey under fire during the Block War, left, and protecting the rookie Judge Brisco after he is shot by squatters, below

hundred feet above street level. Naturally, building them at that height in the twentieth century is a little more than infeasible. The Block War sets were actually built at street level with the windows coming right down to the ground. They were then filmed side to side, with computer graphics filling in the rest of the street.

Once the Block War scenes were in the can, the whole set was revamped for use in a different scene. "We tore out great sections of the apartment and cunningly we built behind these apartment windows some derelict shop fronts. So instantly the building was no longer three hundred feet in the air, it was an arcade at street level," says Art Director for Mega-City, Kevin Phipps.

And thus it was set for another day, another scene ...

Two Judges on Lawmasters ride into town in the midst of the chaos, mayhem and bullets coming from the Block War above. On the leading bike is Hershey, followed by the rookie Judge Brisco, and ultimately Dredd himself arrives to restore law and order. It was

The Lawmaster's on-board computer terminal, right

Dredd rides through flames to enter the Block War, below

this image of Dredd and his bike (in actual fact, standing next to the flying bike) which was one of the main visuals that sold the film in the first place.

Nigel Phelps, who had drawn the initial design, had a strong idea of how he wanted it to look. He and Danny Cannon had their hearts set on a large, impressive machine with a huge back wheel. "We tried to ignore the conventional bike design," says Nigel, "and look for something that was going to meet the requirements of the Dredd character. It had to be something that looked very hard and very heavy."

David Allday was hired as Art Director for Action Vehicles partly because of his expertise in motorbikes. The worst thing about his job, he says, was the bikes. Although the design looked great on paper, it wasn't drawn by a motorcyclist. "When someone who doesn't understand motorcycles intimately decides to design one that's got, for instance, a back wheel that's about

fifteen inches across and expects it to go round corners, you've got technical problems that are going to challenge you," says Dave. "[Nigel] was determined, and Danny as well was determined, that this Dredd bike was going to be awesome. But the problem is when you're dealing with geometry and

The Lawmaster under construction, left and bottom

Production Designer Nigel Phelps tests a mockup of the Lawmaster, below

the physics of motorcycling, there are only certain things that you can do before the geometry and physics take over and the whole thing crashes to the ground."

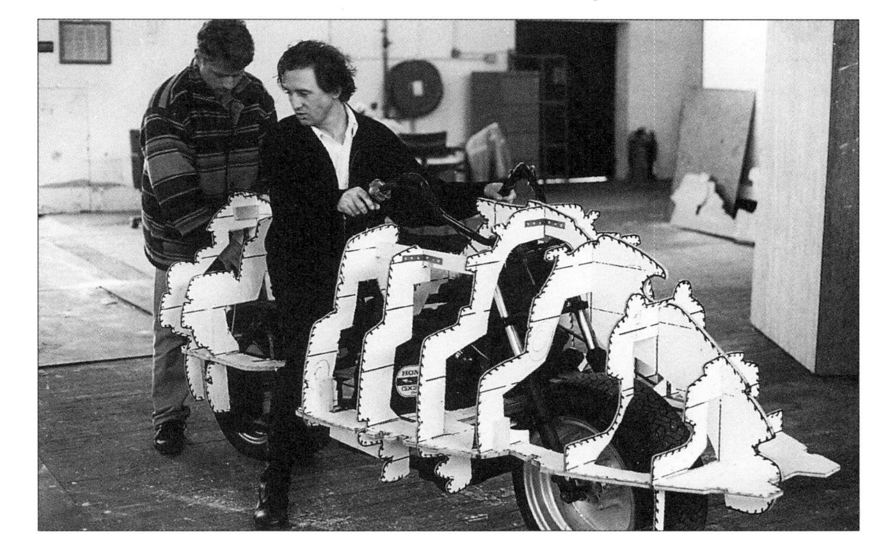

The Lawmaster design went through several stages before the final machine was built. First of all, a scale model was made by Chris Halls in the Art Department, again with a large back wheel that Dave Allday continued to insist wouldn't work. "I would come in and give my technical input and say, Look, if you want a motorbike to have a rear wheel that is fifteen inches wide, it isn't going to go round a corner.' And they said, 'Don't worry about it, don't worry about it, we're just going to get the look right.' So this went on for some time. In the end I was presented with this scale model which was approved by Danny and everybody and looked fantastic."

With the fat-wheel bike having passed the first stage, it was then built into a full-size polystyrene model about 4' 3" wide. "Eventually this first version in polystyrene was modeled up in a very rough state in about a week. We got everyone together and Danny sat on it and said, 'It's too big,' so that proved the point!"

By this time several months had slipped by and the need to get a bike built was becoming more pressing. A group of engineers were brought in to build a test chassis with a skeleton frame, two large wheels and an engine. This design was smaller than

the polystyrene model, but was still beefy enough to look different to a conventional bike. "When they finally brought the skeleton in with the wheels, the wheels are so wide the bike just stood up on its own!" says Dave. "I drove it up the road and decided the entire thing was a complete death trap and nobody would ever ride it. Even Beau Marks rode it and said, 'Make it work somehow, but it's not going to work like this.' "

By this stage there was no option but to compromise the design. A huge front wheel just can't turn a corner, no matter how many designers and engineers work on it. In the end it was decided to use a wide, but conventional front wheel and a slightly thinner back wheel.

However, the shooting date was now frighteningly close and the bike had to be built in a slightly unconventional way, otherwise it just wasn't going to be finished in time. The Art Department worked on sculpting the bodywork out of fiberglass, while a group of engineers were constructing the chassis several miles away. The amount of time, money and effort poured into the mini-project meant there was no turning back – it would *have* to work.

Dave Allday admits feeling a little nervous when it came to fitting the fiberglass body onto the chassis. "It was personally a very important moment," he says. "I knew if it didn't fit together there were probably going to be serious problems because my

They looked fantastic, but the Lawmasters ridden by lead actors, above, *were unkindly dubbed "mopeds"*

A special rig, right, *was designed to send a Lawmaster, with camera in tow, hurtling through a plate-glass window*

Judge Dredd's Lawmaster in full working order, left

Judge Hershey's Lawmaster is sabotaged and explodes with an earth-shattering kaboom, below

job was on the line. So it was an odd way to do it, but it worked ... The most important thing was it went down the road, it went round the corner and it looked fantastic."

There were eight Lawmaster bikes built. Five of them were powered by 650cc engines which were incredibly powerful and allowed shots of the wheels spinning and accelerating off into the distance to be filmed. They still weren't very easy to ride and only stunt artists were allowed to use them.

The other three bikes were unkindly dubbed "mopeds" and were ridden by the actors. They worked very simply. The rider opened the throttle and they started; the rider closed the throttle and they stopped. And that was *Judge Dredd*'s fleet of bikes. After all that, making them fly in the latter half of the film was easy!

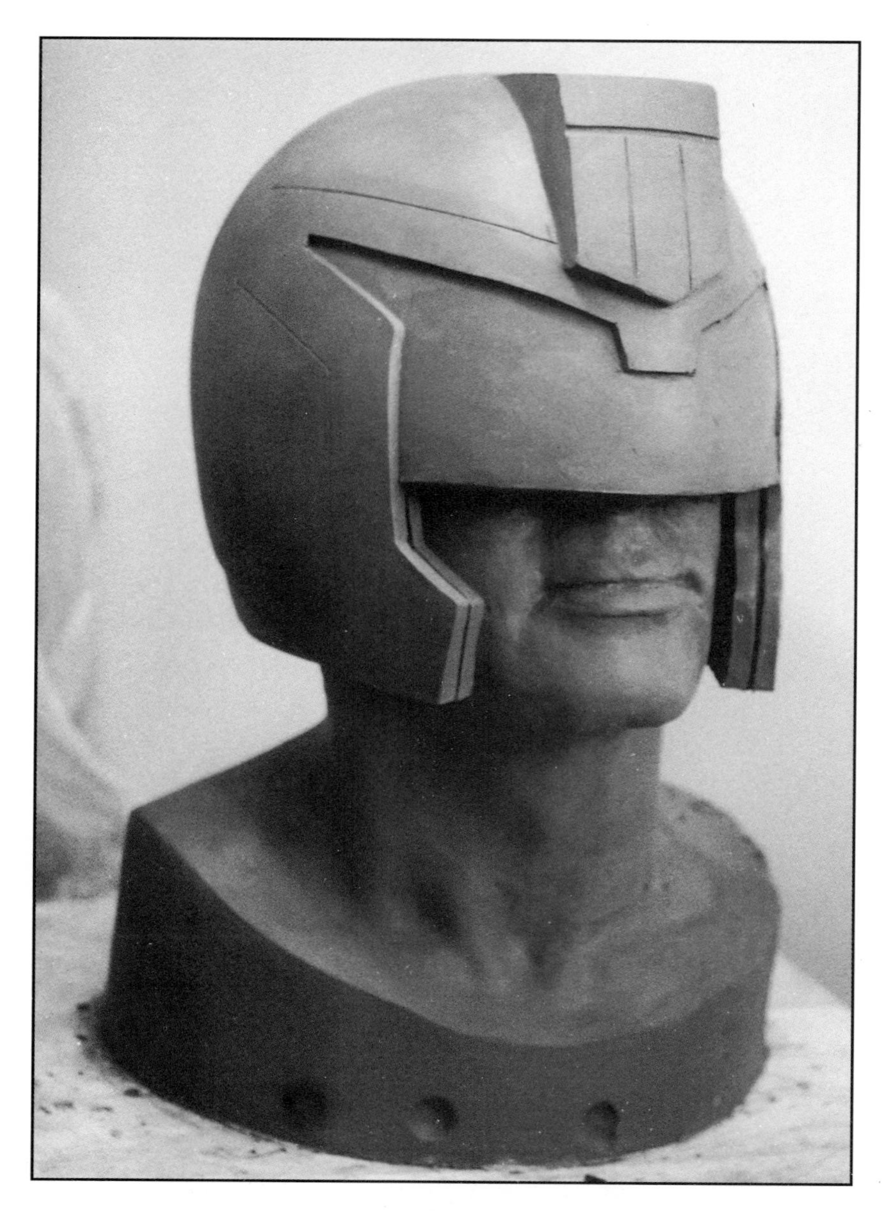

Above, *a clay sculpture of Dredd's helmet by* Chris Halls

The movie makes people wait for the moment when Judge Dredd appears on screen. Everything is set up so that when he finally arrives in the middle of the riot, he not only deals with the situation, he overshadows the ordinary Judges Hershey and Brisco. There can be no doubt that this is a man to be reckoned with.

One of Director Danny Cannon's ideas that didn't make it to the screen was to introduce Dredd in little bits and pieces. There would be shots of his boots, his gun, his hand and his helmet as he laid down the Law in Mega-City, building up to the moment when his face was revealed. It could have worked, but the idea was pushed aside as the scene began to develop in a different direction. Another idea, which was almost axed, was that Dredd would enter during the riot, stand in the middle of the street and decree: "Stop fighting! Drop your weapons!" Readers of *2000 AD* will recognise similarities between this scene and the Block War story.

But even before Dredd's entrance, came his costume. This was an important element to get right. Not only would it have a strong bearing on how the character was perceived, it was also the image that would play a major part in selling the movie.

When Costume Designer Emma Porteous first started on the production she was showered with offers of comics and other reference material. After so many years of waiting for *Judge Dredd* to come to the big screen, fans were anxious that he should actually look like the Judge Dredd they were used to. But Emma, who also worked on *Supergirl* and *Aliens*, knew from the outset it couldn't be an exact copy of the comic book.

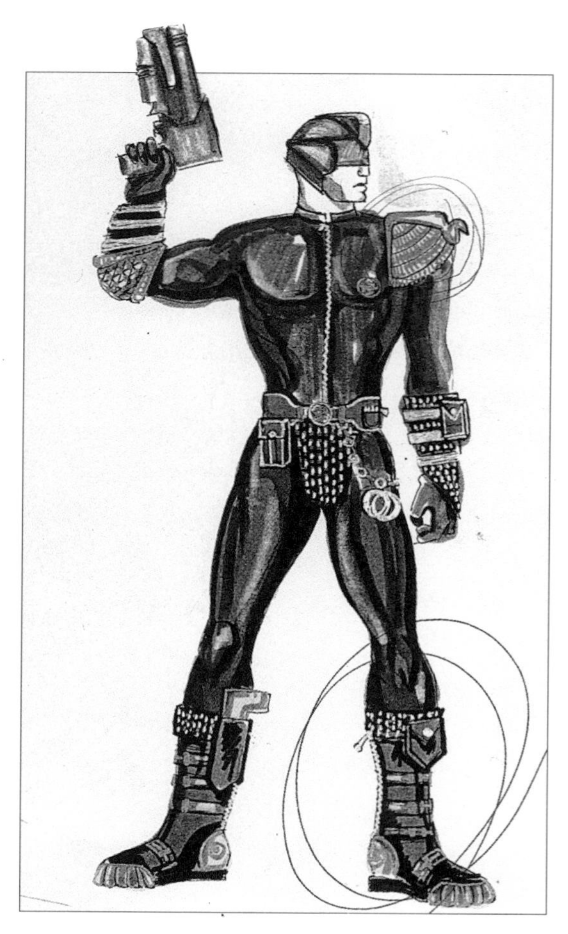

One of Italian designer Gianni Versace's suggestions for the Dredd look, right

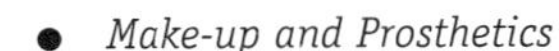

Make-up and Prosthetics Supervisor Nick Dudman's workshop, left and below; *the lifesize Dredd dummy was used to size the uniform correctly*

"I don't think you can do that," she says, "because you can do anything in a drawing, but you can't actually physically do things with an eagle balanced on one shoulder – which it is in the comic – and a football pad on the other with no visible means of support at all."

A physical representation of the original Judge Dredd costume actually exists. It was made by British publishers Fleetway for publicity purposes. "That's a literal translation of the comic, but it looks funny," comments Production Designer Nigel Phelps. "It doesn't look serious, it doesn't look scary, it doesn't look awesome. In the comic on 2D pages it looks fantastic, but when you translate it literally into the real world, it stands out like a sore thumb."

The initial designs done during the Los Angeles preproduction stage looked quite different to the familiar version in *2000 AD*. The man who Nigel told to "go away and do a Dredd picture" was comics artist Kevin Walker.

"We discussed in black and white line form what we would like to see done in comparison with the uniform in the comic," says Kevin. "In the comic the uniform has a zip straight up the front and a very large chain, which is connected to Dredd's badge. We decided to lose that for the first illustration. Dredd was designed in the seventies, so there's a great deal of seventies design elements which have remained over the years and have never sort of been refined

Every strap and buckle on Dredd's costume was endlessly discussed and revised

by the comic artists who've been doing him over the years. So we decided to lose the zipper and the chain and just do it as a straightforward badge on the tunic.

"In the comic his gauntlets and boots are a sort of drab olive green," Kevin continues. "We decided to lose that one completely because we didn't want any sort of natural colors. Nigel decided early on he didn't want any natural colors like greens, because everything is dead. There would be no reason for Dredd to be wearing green because he works in the city all the time. There's no camouflage reason or anything like that. It's just one of those curious comic things. It's like Superman gained his original red, blue and yellow colors because they were the easiest ones to print at the time, and it was for similar reasons that Dredd acquired his green gloves.

"The belt in the comic strip is just a series of pouches. It looks very much like Batman's utility belt. They're all the same in the comic, so we decided they definitely had to be different shapes and sizes and we wanted handcuffs and his nightstick hanging off his belt as well, just to get that sort of police feel in there. And instead of being black – as it was in the comic – we tried doing it as a very dark blue to keep the police connotations coming across there.

"In the comic the holster where he keeps his gun is actually on the side of his boot, and we figured out that if Dredd ever had to run he would lose his gun the first step he made. You just cannot run with this thing attached to your leg. It would be impossible."

The next stage was to take the designs to Sylvester Stallone himself. Nigel, Emma and Director Danny Cannon made the trip to Miami to meet him. They found he had some very definite ideas of how he wanted to look.

"I think when we first started the concept of the film, from Danny's point of view, it was a very serious heavy film and I think it got away quite a lot from the original comic," Emma explains. "The minute we met Stallone he wanted to look like the comic. And I have to agree, he was absolutely right. He insisted that we got as near to the comic as we could. And this is in fact what we did, and embellished it. There's

a lot of gold. He wanted everything really shiny, and lots of chains which we have in the comic and gold plates up the front of his boots, so he was a really impressive figure.

"In fact, his doing that changed the whole tone of the film, so everything became more comic-like, cartoon-like. Everything had a bit more color in it, a bit more life. So all the Judges had all these bits on, he wanted yellow inside the collar and all that. And I think it did help enormously and added a great deal to it."

The standard material for making superhero costumes is Spandex. It looks great and gives plenty of movement for the actor underneath. It's also been used many times before.

"Everybody was a little scared that he'd look a bit like Superman, a bit like Batman, so we were trying to get away from that," says Emma. "But in fact we had to come back to Spandex in the end because that's what worked best. It really looked tough because he's got a fantastic physique, Stallone, and all the other things just didn't work as well."

The costume was structured onto a piece of armor to make it look tough and like it has a purpose. It was made largely from molded plastic and rubber to be very lightweight for action sequences. It also

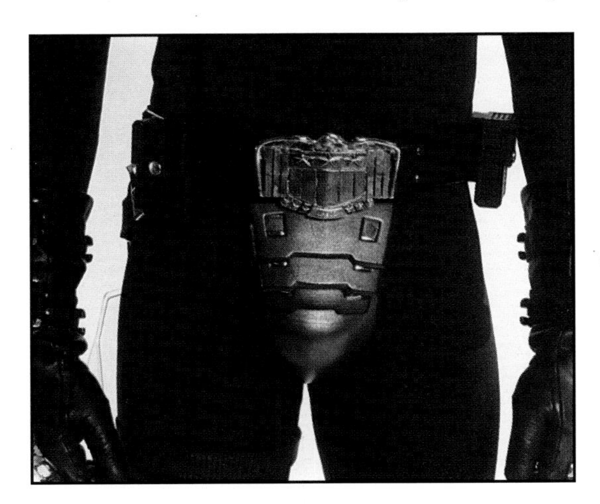

Sylvester Stallone as Judge Dredd, below

Even behind Dredd's menacing visor, above, *Stallone is instantly recognizable*

Version three of the Street Judges' helmet by Simon Merton, right

retains the eagle on the shoulder, which became the film's motif for the Law, and was something Sylvester Stallone pressed for at the meeting. The eagle, however, posed a few design problems.

"If you have something that is unwieldy, if you put your arm up – which you have to do all the time – you're going to knock your head off!" says Emma. "So we had to articulate all the feathers so when he moved his arm they all spread out so he could actually get his arm up and down. Getting the armor right took a long time because we had to do a lot of prototypes just to get the proportion right and then to actually get people to move in it."

The helmet is the most striking feature of the Dredd costume in the comic and Danny Cannon had a very definite idea about the visor for the film. He wanted it to come down just as far as Dredd's nose, so his mouth and chin were visible and recognizable as Sylvester Stallone. The brief was to make it aloof and menacing, and a lot of detailed tinkering was

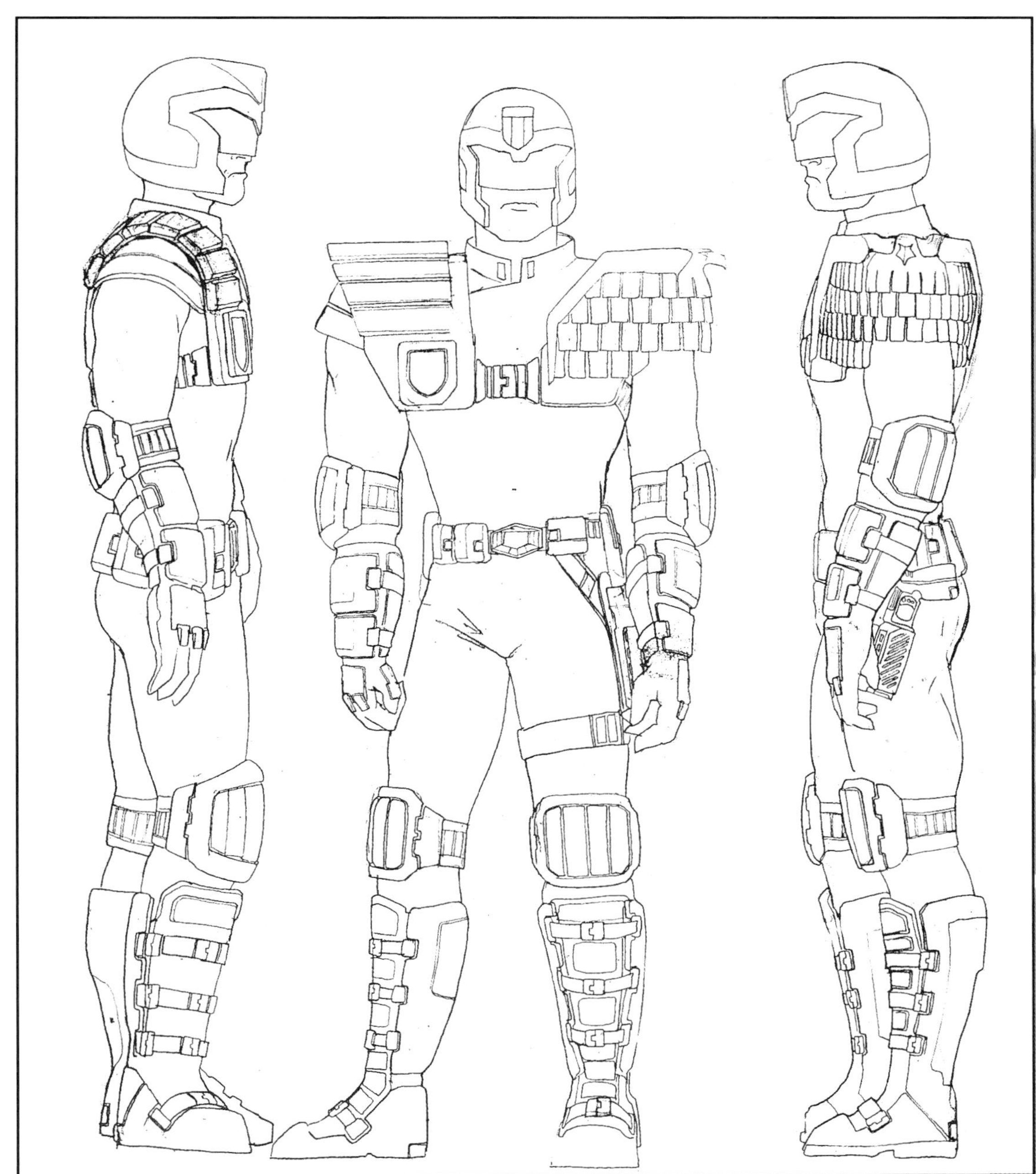

Final line drawings of three views of the Dredd costume by Julian Caldow, left

done to the design to get it right. Lots of photos, and even a bust of Stallone was made to help the design team. In the end the finished helmets were made out of lightweight fiberglass by a man called Martin Adams, who also made all the armor.

One aspect of the costume that no one watching the movie should have noticed is that inside one of the pouches on Dredd's belt there is a radio transmitter. It was used to relay a signal from a radio mike back to the sound recordist. Radio mikes were used a lot in *Judge Dredd*, especially when more than one camera was being used in a scene and a boom microphone would be seen in a wide shot. For that reason the costumes were specifically designed to allow a radio mike to be concealed in them.

The final element of the Judge Dredd look is, of course, Sylvester Stallone himself. It is said that he had pictures of Dredd hung up on all of his walls so he could get the characteristic Judge Dredd scowl right. So once he put the costume on, the 'look' was complete.

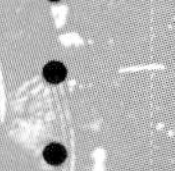

The terrifying Lawgiver, standard issue sidearm of Mega-City Judges, above

"Lawgiver! Awesome!" gasps Twist the Rezzie as Dredd pulls his gun on him.

The Lawgiver in *Judge Dredd* is the ultimate hero prop. So much about Dredd's world is symbolized in this object. It is the gun that allows a Judge to act as police, jury and executioner in the name of the Law. Its importance in the plot also means it is one of the highest-profile objects in the film.

The concept has changed very little from its comic origins. The Lawgiver was always able to fire different sort of bullets and operate through voice control. The one big addition was the DNA coding which allows only Judges to use the weapons and registers which Judge has fired it.

Director Danny Cannon had seen a drawing done in Los Angeles during preproduction and was keen for this to form the basis of the design. It was then passed to Julian Caldow in Britain who had been chosen for the job because of his extensive work with guns on other films. It was decided early on that weapons that fired beams of laser light in the tradition of *Star Wars* didn't fit in this hard future.

"This was one aspect of the film for which it was decided we should go for a real feel," says Julian. "The one in the comic is far more like a ray-gun, a fifties ray-gun. Apparently Stallone really liked that one, but they wanted a hard *Robocop*-type thing. And when you see this thing, it's huge in the hand and with the flames coming out of the front it really looks evil."

There are two main ways to get the impression of firing real bullets. The first is to use a gas-powered gun. Gas has the advantage that it's safer, but it was ultimately rejected because gas lines coming out of the back of the weapon makes it less versatile. The other option is to use a commercially available gun and put a futuristic casing over the top, which is what was used in *Judge Dredd*. In the case of the Lawgiver, the weapon chosen was a Beretta.

"We had in mind a Beretta pistol that fires like a machine gun," explains Julian. "But they no longer make those. So we had to alter the guns to try and

make them fire like a machine gun. And when the gun fires the whole clip is completely emptied in about three seconds – less. But you get a huge great flash coming out of the front which is about a foot long. It looks great!"

The casing, made of metal and fiberglass, was screwed to the actual gun. This made the Lawgiver larger than the contemporary weapon ,which was fine in terms of making it chunky and impressive, but not so brilliant when it comes down to the practicalities.

"That was the difficult thing on the Lawgiver, particularly, making the thing not too big," says Julian. "You can't cut into the real gun, all you're doing is adding. So that was a difficult juggling act to make it small enough to be believable.

"They were very thin around the handle. The designs of a handle of any pistol, or of any automatic – because the bullets are going up through it – the size of that is determined very much by the size of the bullet inside. So they have precision engineering just to get them comfortable in the hand so you can hold it and get as many bullets as possible in the magazine. Because you've got those two different equations fighting each other all the time, when you're adding even more dressing onto a real gun, it's got to be a tiny amount. In fact when you're holding the Lawgiver your fingers don't meet around the other side."

All the weapons were built by the Special Effects Department under the supervision of Joss Williams. He put his hand up during early production meetings on the Lawgiver and said, "Oh, I can make some of those for you" – and then suddenly found he had landed himself with a lot of work that doesn't traditionally belong to his department! He had volunteered to be in charge not only of the Lawgiver,

Dummy Lawgivers were made from rubber for the stunt artists, in case they had to land on them

Dredd fires the Lawgiver, below

Rico in the Janus lab after breaking out of Aspen Prison, above

but of the whole armory of guns as well. "The guns were a real pain in the backside for me to begin with," he admits.

The Lawgiver proved to be the biggest headache. As was the case with the motorbikes, the production team had already fallen in love with the design. Joss was therefore faced with the task of turning a piece of artwork into a functional prop. "It's a bit of a chicken and egg thing," he says. "The Lawgiver itself had been designed before the gun that was going to go inside it had been decided upon. It was the wrong way round and we had a major problem trying to fit the electronics in the firing guns as well as the practical gun. It was a bit of a squeeze to say the least!"

The delicate electronics that light up when a Judge uses the weapon caused the biggest problem for the Special Effects Department. "I was worried that the electronics we had to put in the firing guns would be affected by the mechanism of the actual gun firing," says Joss. "As the Beretta fires, the top part of the Beretta slides back and allows a new shell to come in. When you're firing that quickly that's a hell of a shock going on inside this poor little fiberglass case with these electronics that we put in there to work the lights. So I was stuck in a way. I had to go all the way down the line until I could find out the problems. Luckily – touch wood – it worked out okay."

Although it's possible to see lots of Lawgivers on the screen, few of them were working props. Another set of dummy guns, almost indistinguishable from the real thing, were produced without the Berettas and electronic flashing lights inside. These were used by extras and the main cast when they weren't being fired. And then a third set was made entirely out of molded rubber. These were worn by the stunt artists, who could then safely leap into the air without worrying about landing on the hard, unwieldy piece of equipment on their thigh; and for fight sequences, when it's far safer to hit someone over the head with a rubber gun than one made of heavy fiberglass and metal.

Joss Williams declares that the Lawgivers turned out to be one of the biggest successes on the film for him. "The guys that worked on them did a terrific job," he says. "I was very proud of them because they came out of my department and everybody that saw them thought they were terrific at the end of the day. But before we got there it was a pain in the ass."

We turn now from the concerns of the Judges and Mega-City to the man who poses a real threat – Rico.

In the original *2000 AD* Rico story, he was locked up in a facility built on Titan, Saturn's largest moon. It became Aspen Prison in the William Wisher screenplay because having people flying into outer space did nothing for the plot. Plus, keeping it on Earth helps develop the believability the film was striving for.

William Wisher put Aspen Prison on the Cursed Earth in the devastated wasteland of North America. There were many discussions about what type of a prison it would be. The original version on Titan required people to have their bodies adapted to survive the heavy doses of radiation that bombard the globe. Again, this just got in the way of the story. There was talk of it being a mining colony for carbon 4, a substance so dangerous that only convicted criminals were sent to dig for it. In the end, that was dropped and it became a prison for prison's sake.

For the Aspen interiors, the crew went to Bankside Power Station, an old rusted electricity-generating station on the banks of London's River Thames. It was closed down years ago and became a useful location for film crews when the asbestos was stripped out of it in the 1980s. However, it was far less ambitious than Nigel Phelps's original vision:

"I had initially hoped that we'd be making it out of miniatures where it just had to be this gargantuan environment. I was hoping to have the glass cells and elevated passageways and a real show-off piece. But as the script evolved, Aspen became very insignificant so no one was about to spend any money on something that was only that. In the scale of things it was a location that we had to try to find there to do those shots. And it looks terrific, but it has a different look to how we perceived it in the outset."

The earlier script had a riot taking place in the

The sinister Aspen guards, right, *looked like refugees from* Star Wars

Construction of Rico's cell, below

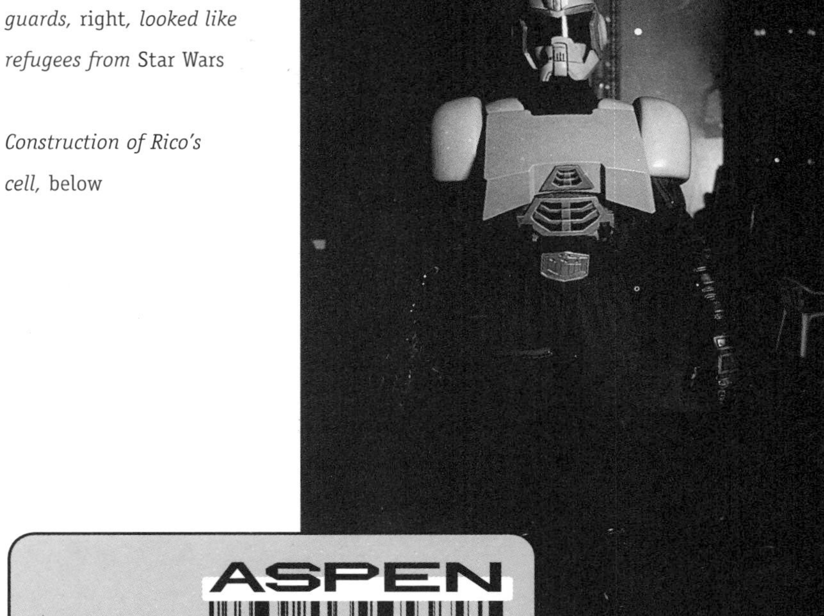

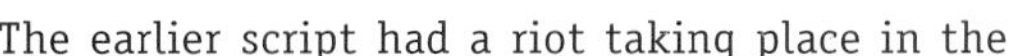

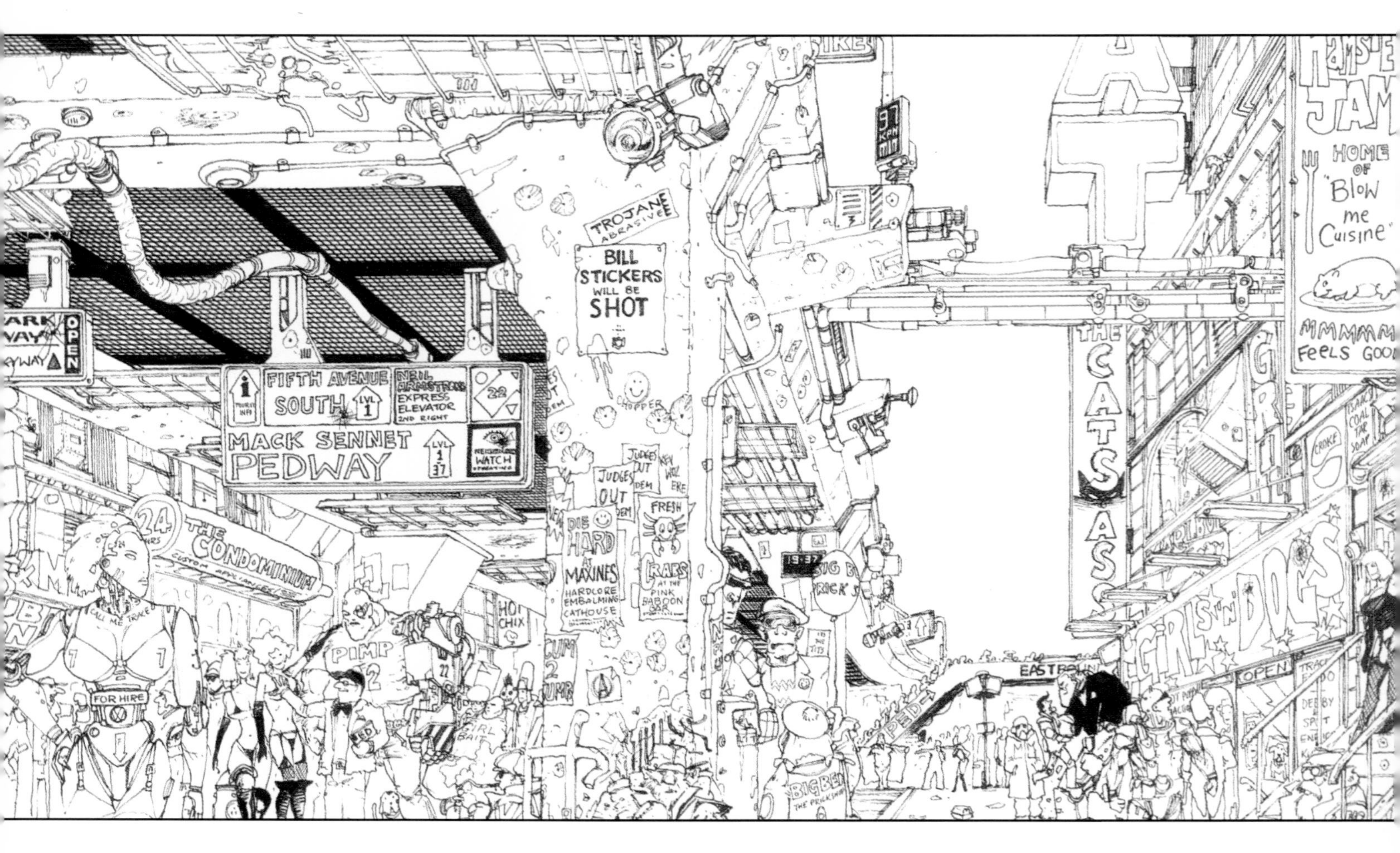

A version of the red-light district drawn by Kevin Walker – completely unfilmable, but a good starting point

prison. It had a scene in Warden Miller's office and Rico using Miller to get past security. One of the additions by Steven De Souza had Rico hidden in a building separate to the prison. Rico then escaped by stealing the vehicle that the warden had used to visit him. But when *Demolition Man* came out some of the scenes had a striking resemblance to those in the *Judge Dredd* script and the whole episode in Aspen Prison was scaled down.

The original design for Rico's cell, therefore, was far grander than the finished product. Matthew Codd did a wonderful illustration in the early preproduction days in Los Angeles of swirling gyroscope guns trained on a lonely prisoner highlighted by a shaft of light and trapped in a metallic sphere of firepower. But it wasn't to be.

"I thought it'd be really cool," explains Nigel. "We've got the most dangerous man on the planet here ... You've got all these cannons that are trained on him all the time and laser curtains. But obviously with that whole scene pared down, the concept has shrunk. But what we've ended up with is a much more simplified version of that.

"Instead of this very complicated series of mechanisms going around him now, he's still in a circular room, but it's vertical walls. He could be in an endless tunnel, still on an elevated platform, but instead of the gyroscope around him, there's now four towers with the cannons on him."

These autoguns were huge compared to the other guns in the film. They were about four feet long and, unlike the other weapons, were powered by gas instead of having real firearms inside. All the wires were simply hidden inside the turrets they were standing on.

It may not have been as amazing as first envisaged, but Nigel is still pleased with the results. "That's just the way a lot of sets evolve," he says. "You always jump off at the deep end and 'wouldn't it be great if we do this,' but it doesn't warrant it all the time."

When Rico goes looking for a gun in Mega-City, it's immediately obvious what type of area he's entered. He's in the red-light district, a throng of seedy activity that became a favorite for many of the film crew.

The first illustration of what the scene might look like was drawn by Kevin Walker. Even while he was putting pen to paper he knew it was an unrealistic concept. But it was a starting point from which the little bits and pieces of what was possible could be taken.

"[Danny Cannon] wanted it to be taken to a ridiculous degree," he says. "If this is a city of extremes, of the worst possible extremes or the best possible extremes, then the most extreme would be the red-light district. So he wanted everything to be in the face. There had to be advertising signs for every possible sex act you could imagine, things like that. Obviously none of this was ever going to be seen on the screen, but the feeling we were trying to get over is the seedy fluorescent lighting showing all that green color, and people out in the streets selling themselves. It's like an Arab market almost. Robot and cyborg pimps and things like that all out there. This illustration is a cartoon of a science fiction red-light district. I cannot see, personally, a real red-light district ever developing that way. Never, ever."

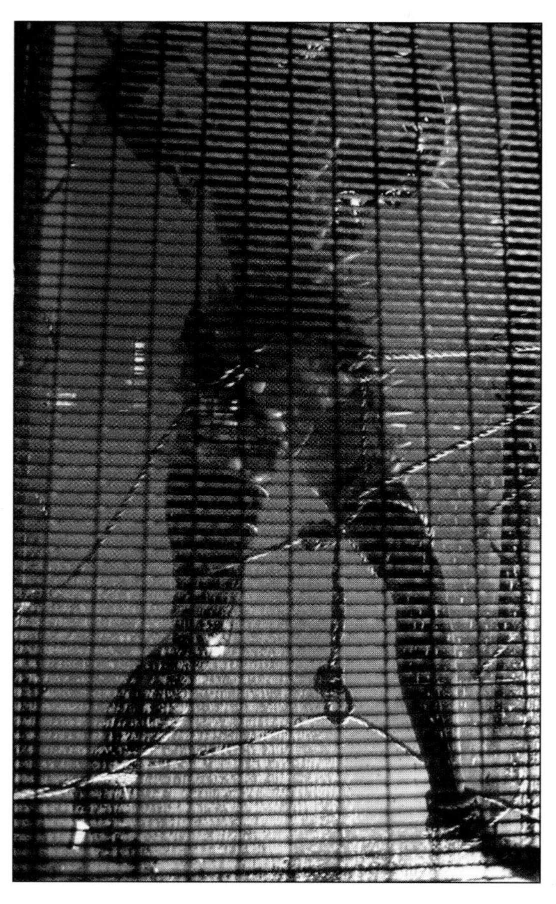

The scene as filmed begins with a shot focused on a fetish model in one of the shop windows before panning round to see Rico walking up the street. The rubber mannequin lady with a whip and a neon face was originally just one of the many set dressings on the back lot until the decision to feature her was made on the spur of the moment.

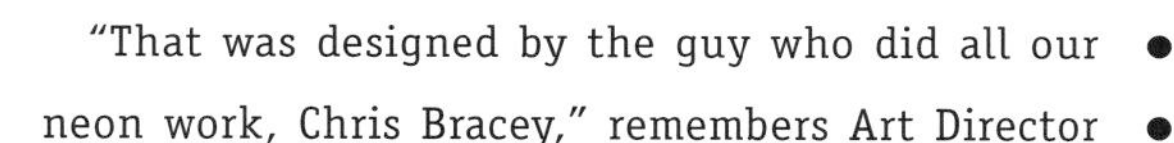

"That was designed by the guy who did all our neon work, Chris Bracey," remembers Art Director

The Costume Department could really let their imaginations run riot when it came to styling the inhabitants of the red-light district

Virtual Sex

360 Degrees of sex for 3600 credits

Kevin Phipps. "He said, 'How about doing this?' and it was fantastic, terrific and that became a key element at the beginning of that scene ... Something like that is not really considered and then it just kind of happens. You get these happy accidents all the time."

Apart from the set, the other element that really makes the scene come alive is the bizarre characters that inhabit this squalid area of the city. They were dressed by Costume Designer Emma Porteous. "We could really go to town," she says, "that was enormous fun. I had two young men – one, Craig Morrison, who dealt in rubber clothing. I went to see him and he brought me his collection which was quite mind-boggling, I have to tell you! Full of these extraordinary rubber neck bands and trousers and jackets. So he said he'd make the collection especially for me, for the film, so I just let him have a free hand and said, 'You can be as bizarre and as wonderful as you like.' And he came up trumps, they were the most wonderful long coats in rubber with huge spikes on them.

"Then I had another young man called Alexander who I met at a place called High-Tech and he's into leather. So we had a lot of strange leather-jacketed people. And then some of the kids came in their own clothes, which was wonderful. They came for auditions and I looked at stuff that they'd brought and we picked what we wanted."

The final touch was provided by a group of extras who were heavily into body piercing. These were real people who really have parts of their body pierced. "Through the ears, through the mouth, through the eyebrows, through other parts of the body one doesn't

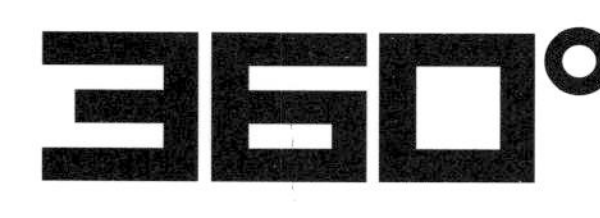

Store fronts and street scenes from the red-light district

mention in polite society! Extraordinary!" says Emma. "It's a sort of cult, they all do it. They have not just little studs, but enormous great screws and one young man had them all round his tongue. He apparently does an act in the evening where he hangs weights from it. Well, we didn't ask him to do that!"

Rico walks past the menagerie of bizarre characters into Geiger's gun shop. This was one place where Director Danny Cannon wanted to point up the violent aspect of American society taken to the extreme – hence the notice on the original drawing, "Children under the age of 12 must be accompanied by a RESPONSIBLE adult."

The outside of the building had to stick out from the throng of other shops without being out of place. This was achieved in a somewhat unconventional manner. Before Mega-City was built on the back lot, a model was constructed using little facsimiles of the buildings. Someone inadvertently put the gun shop on upside down and it looked so

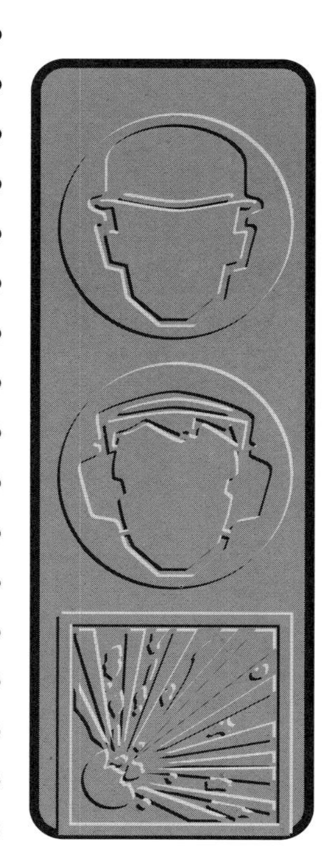

Building the entrance to Geiger's Bazaar, right and below

Geiger as played by Ian Dury, middle

much better that way they decided to keep it!

The idea of introducing the ABC robot, which Rico frees from the gun shop, came from Danny Cannon.

"Rico needed a sidekick," says the Director. "I wanted the ABC robot and put him in the film because I wanted Rico to have something mechanical that he used as a friend because that's how void of character this man is, and that's how much contempt he has for human beings."

The robot is based on Danny's favorite robot from *2000 AD*, Hammerstein of the ABC Warriors. Hammerstein, who gets his name from the war hammer he carries in one hand, is a relic from a far

more violent time. He is programmed to fight and destroy, and to enjoy doing it well. The original design looked very similar to the comic version with lots of body armor, which would make it easy for the robot to be played by a man in a suit.

Executive Producer Andy Vajna wanted the robot to be exactly that, a man in a suit, because he had never been satisfied by any purely mechanical robot in a film up to that point. But the general consensus was that here was a chance to do something different. So Conceptual Illustrator Chris Halls was set to work designing it and building an elaborate scale model. "I thought it would be nice to make it as if a lot of his armor had fallen off and you can see the skeleton underneath, what powers him," he says.

Several outside companies were asked to put in proposals to design and construct the ABC robot, but in the end the task was handed to Special Effects Supervisor Joss Williams, who wasn't too keen on the idea at first because he was already in charge of the weapons and the physical effects.

"One day I was called to Beau's office," Joss remembers. "Beau and Danny were there, and Beau

Construction of the ABC robot, left and below. *He started out as a lightweight*

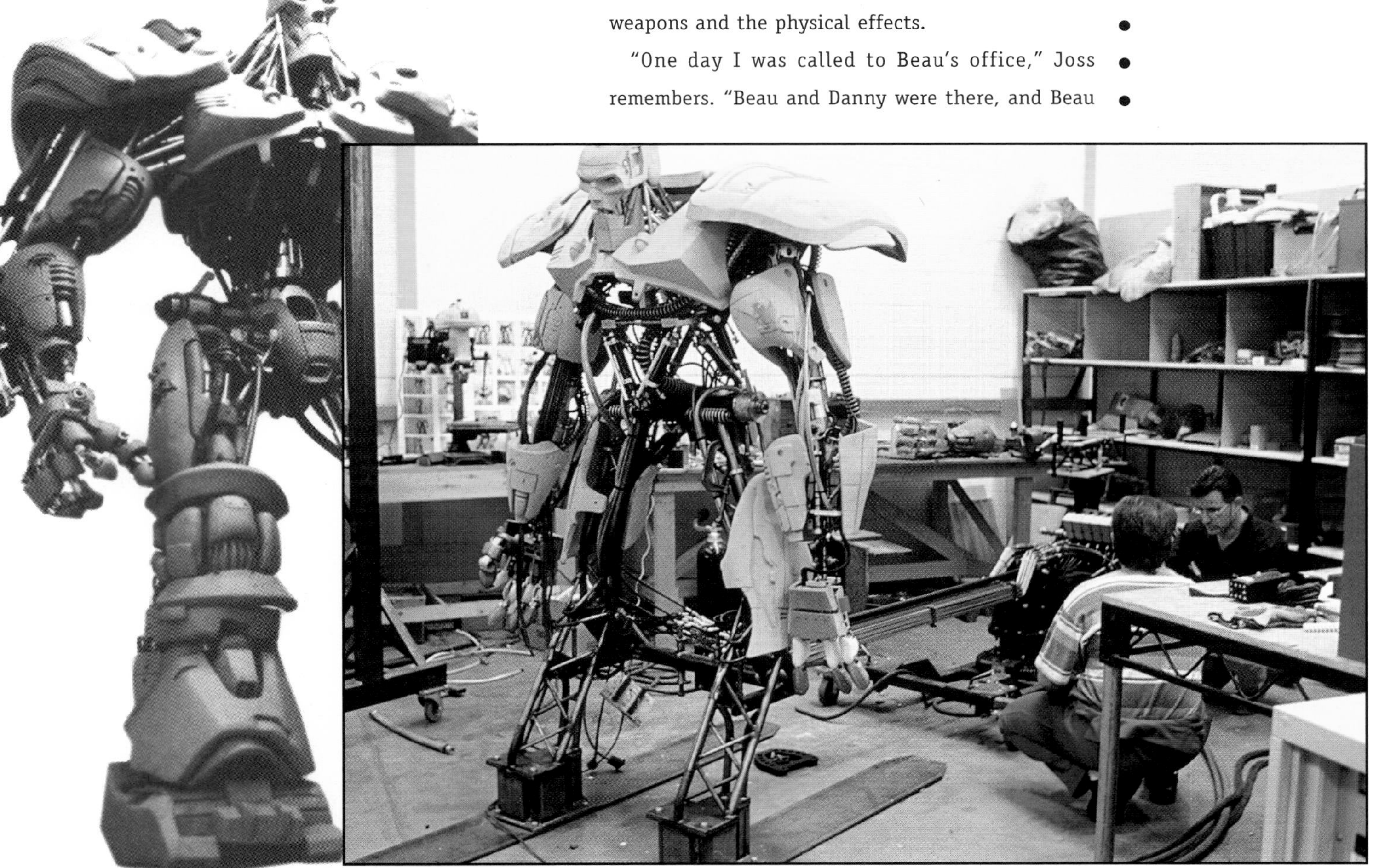

said, 'We want you to make the robot.' I said, 'Well, to be perfectly honest with you I've got enough on my plate as it is, thanks very much.' So they said 'Well, we want you to make it anyway!' So I said okay."

With Chris Halls' scale model completed, it was clear that in no way could the robot be a man in a suit. It was a great way to get away from the type of robots seen in science fiction classics like *The Day The Earth Stood Still* ("Gort") and *Star Wars* ("C3PO"), but provided a challenge for Joss's team. They spent four months building something entirely mechanical which, by the time it was finished, was a menacingly tall piece of machinery powered by hydraulics and controlled by five remote operators.

One man wore a harness across his chest and his arms which had sensors on it to detect the movement of his upper body, and was then replicated by the robot. Others controlled the ABC's head, eyes, legs and gun with a collection of levers. "The operators were my guys," says Joss. "They weren't puppeteers or performers or mime people who are used in these things. My guys knew what the thing could do. I

arranged for a movement performer to come in for a week and get my guys working together and understanding how this thing worked and how to get the best out of it. And once we'd done that, they were off and running."

Joss's team shot hours of test footage on video looking at the way it moved, the ways they could create expressions and, more specifically, the way it walked. In reality it wasn't able to walk anywhere, but it was made to seem as if it was walking by filming just the top half and moving the robot's thighs in the right way.

When the ABC robot first came onto the set, it

blew people away (and we're not talking about the gas-powered gun incorporated into its hand, here). There was a real buzz about the robot. Everybody loved it. "I think he's incredible," acknowledges Joss. "I'd like to see him used more, actually. I think in the whole of his involvement in the shooting we only held them up for about twenty minutes, which is saying something with a mechanical thing like that."

Dredd is back on the streets. This is the only time we see him dealing with petty crime, the normalities of everyday life for a Judge. A young upstart decides he wants to park in a space that is too small for his flash, gleaming car. The only way to do it is to bump the cars in front and behind him and he doesn't give a damn that he's crushing the other vehicles. It's his fourth violation and Dredd judges him by blowing up his car. Writer Steven De Souza sees this scene as

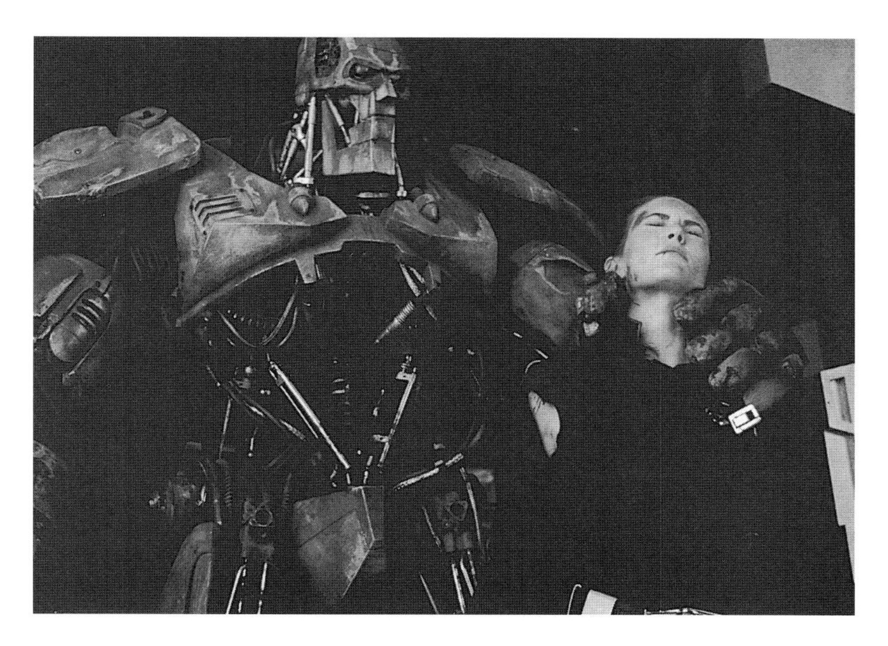

important in establishing the audience's sympathies with the Dredd character, especially after his harsh treatment of Fergie. The Law may be tough, but the little creep deserved it.

"I think right away the audience figures screw 'em," says Steve. "I think that's very satisfying. I was careful when he was extreme. He's destroying private property. I mean, you can make all these arguments on how that's totally fascist behavior, but in the context of our little story, I think the audience forgives Dredd for that transgression against property rights. I think it's important for Dredd in the beginning of the movie not to be a fascist but to be a prick. Because then he has somewhere to go."

The ABC robot attacks Hershey in the corridors of the Janus lab, above

Production shots of the ABC robot, opposite

A drawing of the flying taxi by Julian Caldow, below

Construction of the Future Yuppie car. The car was designed and built – only to be blown up – from wood and fiberglass

The car was built by David Allday and his team. It came to be known as the "Yuppie Car" because it's owned by a Fuppie, or Future Yuppie. It looked fantastic but had to go through a major respray shortly before filming.

"We decided it had to be a cliché color," says Dave. "The guy that's driving the car is a young upstart and it couldn't be anything else except Ferrari red. Now we looked at every single car color that actually exists and we chose the Ferrari color – quite right – but it was orange. When Danny finally saw it on the car about three days before we were going to shoot he said, 'That's not the color I want! I want red!' And we then changed it to Ferrari red. So we had to respray two cars in about a day and a half, which was crazy, but we did it."

After all that work, the car gets blown up! Explosions always look great on film, but Special Effects Supervisor Joss Williams thinks it wasn't as good as it could have been. "Everyone thought it was terrific on rushes, but for me it didn't work how I wanted it to work," he says. "There were certain things that I wish I'd done which I didn't do to enhance the effect even more. So I was disappointed with it, which in a way was a good thing because the next time something like that comes around we'll be wanting to improve. So improving on what you've done is the key to better effects. When you start becoming complacent about what you've done you start resting on your laurels."

As flames engulf what remains of the once-gleaming red car, its owner stumbles around helplessly in the street, trying to come to terms with his loss.

All the street-level scenes in Mega-City are augmented by the bustle of everyday life and a steady stream of road-going vehicles. The majority of these were made by Rover Group Limited in what is a movie industry first. Land Rover designers were brought in not only to help in the design process, but also to build the cars and make sure they actually work.

Car designs were drawn both in America and in Britain. After several months of beavering away, it became evident that the project would soak up quite a lot of dollars. The filmmakers was talking about having sixty vehicles, all of which would be of futuristic design. It was then that Producer Beau Marks approached Rover Group Limited and asked them to help out.

The proposal eventually made its way to the Product Design Director at Rover, Gordon Sked, who turned out to be very enthusiastic about the idea. "I said 'Why don't we go further than that?' " Gordon remembers. " 'Why don't we actually design something that would achieve the objective of the film, but also give the feeling of how you could develop the Land Rover mark that little bit further?' " At first he thought they would make just one car and let the film company have it on loan. "I was super-naive on that front," says Gordon, "I didn't realize they were after thirty of the things!"

A young Land Rover designer not long out of the Royal College of Art was put on the project. David Woodhouse was the latest in a long line of designers to draw sketches of what the vehicles should look like. But his expertise in road-going vehicles meant he solved the problems very quickly. He had also, coincidentally, gone to college with David Allday, the Art Director for Action Vehicles,

The car is rigged by the SFX team to explode, above

thought the whole thing was a practical joke! Negotiations took a frustratingly long time, and not only for the filmmakers.

After drawings were approved, a full-size model was built. "I have to say that it all got a bit eleventh hourish!" comments Gordon Sked. "Despite the fact that we didn't have the resources to be able to do it, and we certainly didn't have the budget to do it, there really was huge potential benefit in doing this thing. So I took the decision that we would pursue – at risk – a model on the basis that it might all fall apart, things might not happen and in the end the film company might not use it. But I felt it was worth the risk."

Building a working 22nd-century cab on a Land Rover chassis proved a new experience for Rover

and so the pair hit it off immediately.

"In one sense the pressure was off," says David Allday. "We had a design which was very exciting, but we didn't really know they could deliver. Obviously when you go outside the film industry, the delivery dates people talk about are completely different. People just don't understand how fast the film moves ... So, yes, it was very exciting, but it was a little worrying. Thankfully Land Rover were absolutely superb and delivered on time, but my God it was close!"

In fact, a story went around that when the final contract went to the financial boss at Rover it sat on his desk for two weeks because he

The model was built around an existing Land Rover chassis and cab using clay and plywood. With everything looking great (and the deal having finally been agreed), Rover went away and made the master vehicle with a molded outer body, gull-wing opening hydraulic doors and flashing lights. The rest of the fleet was made from the basic chassis covered with simple fiberglass bodies. The vast majority were

painted yellow and became futuristic yellow cabs, while a scattering were sprayed other colors and given different graphics to create a little variety.

To provide a final touch of authenticity, four armored vehicles were adapted for use on the film's back lot. After looking at several makes, the designers plumped for the Saracen, a six-wheeled British Army vehicle. Before the Rover deal was even considered, this was how all the vehicles in Mega-City were going to be made and David Allday spent a considerable amount of time going around Britain looking for the right ones for the job. "Because of the way the country unloads a lot of military hardware at the moment, you can actually procure this stuff extremely cheaply and in large numbers," he says. "The other useful thing about military vehicles is that they're extremely sturdily built, it's very easy to weld things to them and create a completely different look."

A hood and a bumper was added to cover up the front of the Saracens and they were given bigger wheels and mudguards to make them look even more imposing. An engineer was brought in to fix the bits that weren't working (some of the vehicles had been sitting abandoned in a field for six years!) and then the Art Department added the finishing touches. "I'd been looking at a lot of aerospace hardware, bits of engines and things like that we'd found in various places. I found these – I think they're called afterburners – from a jet plane and we stuck them on the side, four of them on each one and the whole thing looked awesome."

With that, the fleet of road-going vehicles were completed and ready to go on set with no problems – almost.

"We had a few moments with them," Dave admits, "but I would say that they were superbly engineered and the way they performed was perfect. When one considers the amount of things that can go wrong with this sort of thing in terms of what happened on set. We had a lot of last-minute panics, particularly with the Land Rovers filling up with exhaust and that sort of thing. There were a lot of little adaptations that had to be done at breakneck speed. But, basically, on set they performed beautifully."

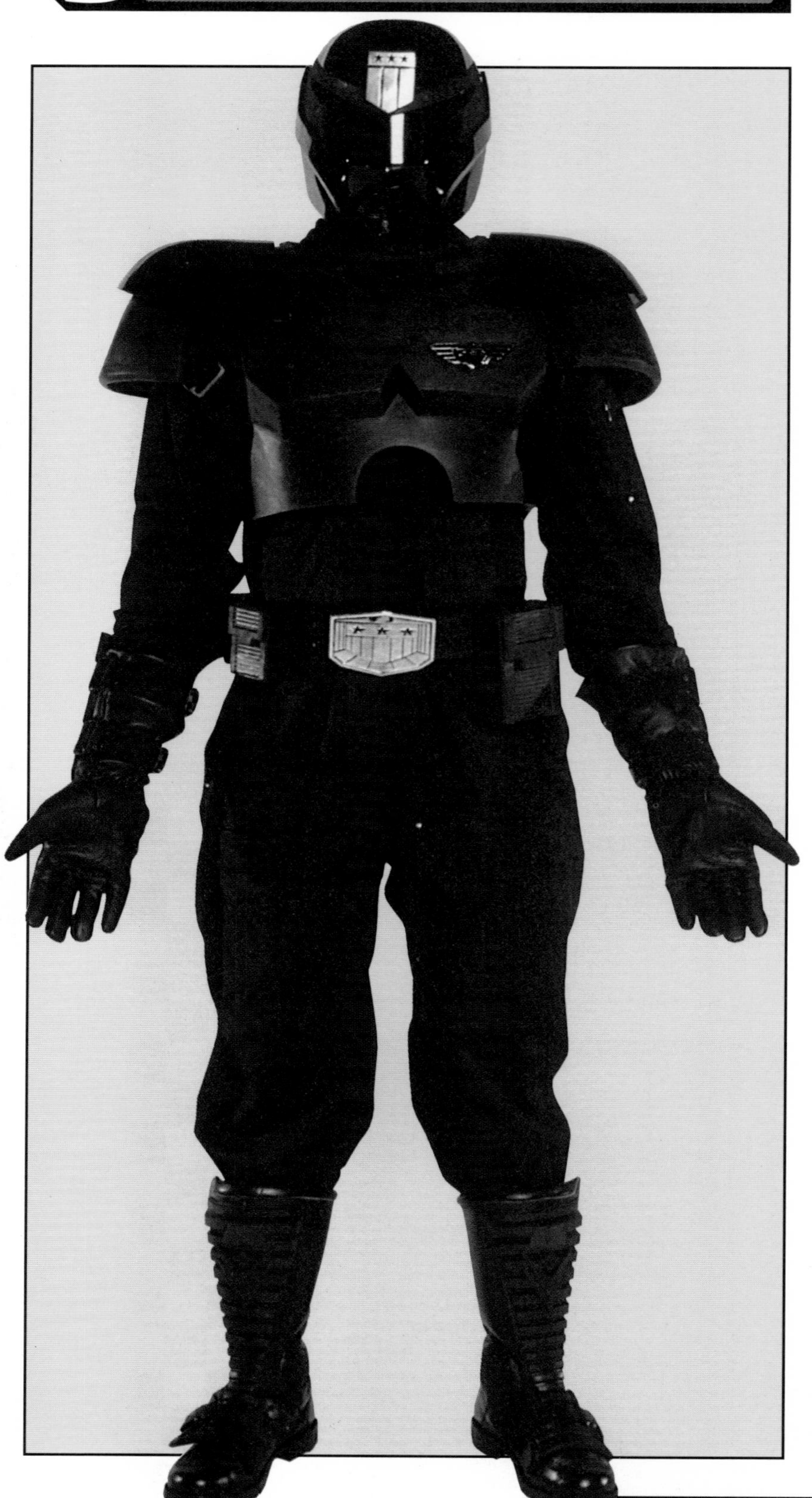

The reptilian Judge Hunter outfit, above

"Judge Hunters," says Dredd under his breath. These are the figures that have come for him, who in the comic are called the SJS – the Special Judicial Squad. Their function in both mediums is to watch over the Judges, the name change simply being there to make it easier for the audience to understand their purpose.

They are tall, menacing, totally clad in black and don't allow one trace of humanity to slip out from beneath their helmets. Their weapons are also black and create a wonderful effect in the film when they fire up a dark corridor – all that can be seen is the silhouette of the Judge Hunter, the gun's red lights and then a flash from the barrel.

The Judge Hunter guns, as well as the Aspen Prison wall guard guns, were built around AK-47 Kalashnikov rifles. Although future technology usually makes things smaller, the designers went in the opposite direction for *Judge Dredd*.

"We went for the chunky thing because it's so much more visual," says Julian Caldow, who worked on all the gun designs. "For instance, millions are spent all over the world by arms people making the muzzle flash that comes out of here [the end of the barrel] as small as possible so you can't be seen where you're firing from. Our priority on this film was to get the muzzle flash as big as possible, purely because it's such a beautiful visual thing to see, this huge great star-shaped muzzle flash coming out of the end of a gun. It would be less dramatic to see a guy holding a pencil-sized thing in his hand, rather than hiding behind something that looks like it can take out an entire building!"

The casing around the weapons had to make allowance for the internal workings. In the case of the AK-47s, they have a real stop movement that goes backwards and forwards incredibly fast, and the casing around this section was made out of metal to stand up to the force of the cocking action. Diagrams were made of the side of the gun designs to give the special effects team all the information they needed to make them. This turned out to be a little deceiving because it was a totally different story when the guns were subsequently drawn in three-quarters.

"We do a plan and elevation and they look fine," says Julian. "Then you put them on three-quarters and you realize that holding these things would be like holding a brick! They're vast, really wide. We built them all in polystyrene before we went ahead. It was my secret plan to get the guns as ludicrously big as possible, but not so big that they didn't look like someone could physically hold them. We discovered pretty soon that the guns were huge, quite stupidly big. The breadth was the problem. We were trying to whittle away the width as much as possible. You can have them as long as you like and as high as you like, but when they're really wide they're very difficult to hold."

The other weapon featured in the film is the "Judge pump" which Dredd uses later on. This was constructed around a Remington pump-action shotgun. However, for some scenes – as with the Lawgivers – rubber facsimiles were made. "There are certain scenes that Sly's got to do where he's got this thing slung over his back where it would be uncomfortable and too heavy to have a fiberglass casing with this real gun inside," Joss Williams explains. "So we made lightweight rubber ones for that so it would be easier for Sly."

These sort of weapons, the "hero props," were designed to stand apart from the guns wielded by the populace. "In the movie all the police stuff is shiny," Julian explains. "All the police weapons are gleaming lovely, have got lights all over them. And when you go to the Block War scene, for instance, all the guns look like they've been

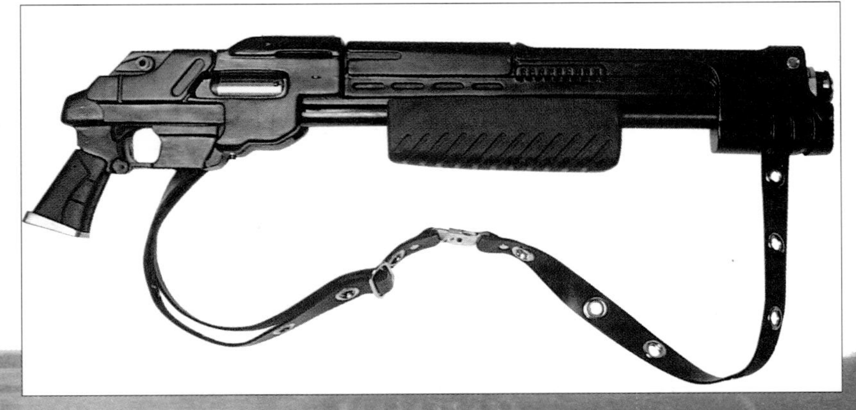

Compare and contrast: the Judge Pump, a modified Remington pump shotgun used by Judge Fargo, above, *and the sawn-off shotgun used by the squatter Link during the Block War,* opposite bottom

Aspen Prison guards pose on set with their impressive weapons, below

Construction and decoration of the entrance to the Hall of Justice, above *and* right

stored in a sewer! And that's realistic."

And the same can be said of the buildings themselves, from the grimy squat right up to the glorious Hall of Justice.

Dredd is sent for trial in the Hall of Justice, the dominant architectural building in Mega-City. In the comics it is a building with an eagle just strapped to the top it. But the designers had a much more ambitious idea for the film. They wanted to incorporate the eagle into the structure of the building itself.

"We wanted to have a certain sort of pop motif that would stick out from everything else that's going on," explains Production Designer Nigel Phelps. "Bearing in mind how chaotic the city would look, it seemed as if there would be something quite awesome about having an overall rationalized building that was a total design concept from beginning to end. It's the only building in Mega-City that is."

The idea was that the Hall of Justice, even if it wasn't bigger than any of the other buildings, would stand out. The eagle embodies the regimental feel of the Judge system, with a very definite style of solid geometric shapes and art deco. Nigel had been working on the idea with Simon Murton in LA when Kevin Walker – who was supposed to be working on something else at the time – had a brainwave.

"Rather than trying to describe it to Nigel," he says, "I went away and spent half an hour putting together a small painted drawing just to try and get the impression across as quickly as possible before it went out of my mind. It was the actual relationship of the head and the wings as parts of the building that Nigel had been looking for to get that very dominant and superior feel of the structure across.

"He'd already come across with the concept of the actual entrance, with pillars and huge rows of steps and things like that. So I incorporated that in with the shape of the head and the wings, using the tops of the wings as landing pads for the flying Justice Department vehicles and making it a massive block of a building with lights everywhere."

The eagle is most prominent on the front of the building, but it is a motif that is repeated throughout the film, from the badges on the Judges' uniforms, to the Hall of Justice and inside the Council Chamber.

"The American eagle has been contorted into a fascist eagle," says Nigel. "It's still the symbol for freedom and independence, but just like the system's gone wrong. Even though they're the good guys, they're doing everything right, it's all gone too far.

"It's the same with the styling of the Hall of Justice. It's quite classic in its format. It's a futuristic classicism. It's very totalitarian in its outlook, it's very symmetrical, it's very sharp and crisp and looks expensive – it's where all the taxpayers' money's gone. So there's a lot of

Eagle decorations occur throughout the Hall of Justice, above

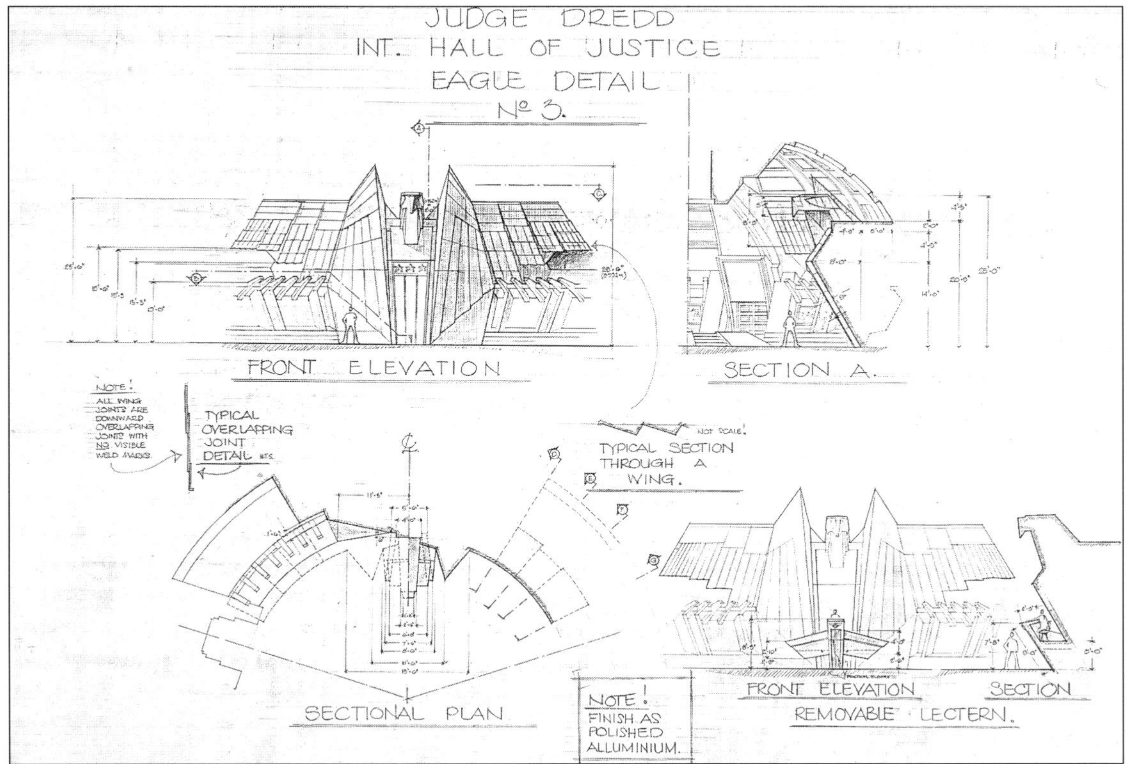

Elevations of the monumental eagle for the Hall of Justice by Martin Laing, left

Cadet Olmeyer, played by Balthazar Getty, right

Judge Esposito, played by Peter Marinker, far right top

Hershey defends Dredd during his trial, below

Judge Silver, played by Angus MacInnes, in the Council Chamber, far right below

Judge McGruder, played by Joanna Miles, prosecuting at Dredd's trial, right

Max von Sydow as Judge Fargo, below

Judge Dredd is stripped of his uniform and handcuffed by the Judge Hunters, left, *and imprisoned in the Hall of Justice,* below

polished granite and steel and bronze."

Judge Dredd's trial takes place within that hard and severe environment. It's the same set as was used for the Council Chamber earlier in the film. The round table, which harks back to the legend of King Arthur, was simply replaced by a bench and several rows of chairs.

The viewie that displays the picture of Dredd's "family" is essentially a very simple idea. It's a futuristic photograph that lights up as you open it, revealing an image as bright as a TV screen but as thin as an ordinary photo. However, creating this effect in the twentieth century wasn't easy.

A search was mounted for some kind of material that could reproduce that effect. Some special stuff was eventually imported from America and incorporated into the prop. But as filming progressed, it became clear that it wouldn't work. Although it lit up okay, it wasn't bright enough for filming.

Another prop which took a lot of to-ing and fro-ing was Judge Dredd's scanner, as Property Master Ty Teiger remembers: "You go through that whole exercise of things being rejected," he says. "You make a hundred of something and then on the day someone will go 'Oh, that's not quite right' and you have to scrap all that and start again. I'm probably not supposed to say that because it's a waste of money! It's the whole prototype principle. I mean, this scanner was actually rejected. We went through five different stages of actually making it less round. That took me about three months just to come up with something that was right. It's not as if you're actually going to see much of it on the film, but I'm not supposed to say that either!"

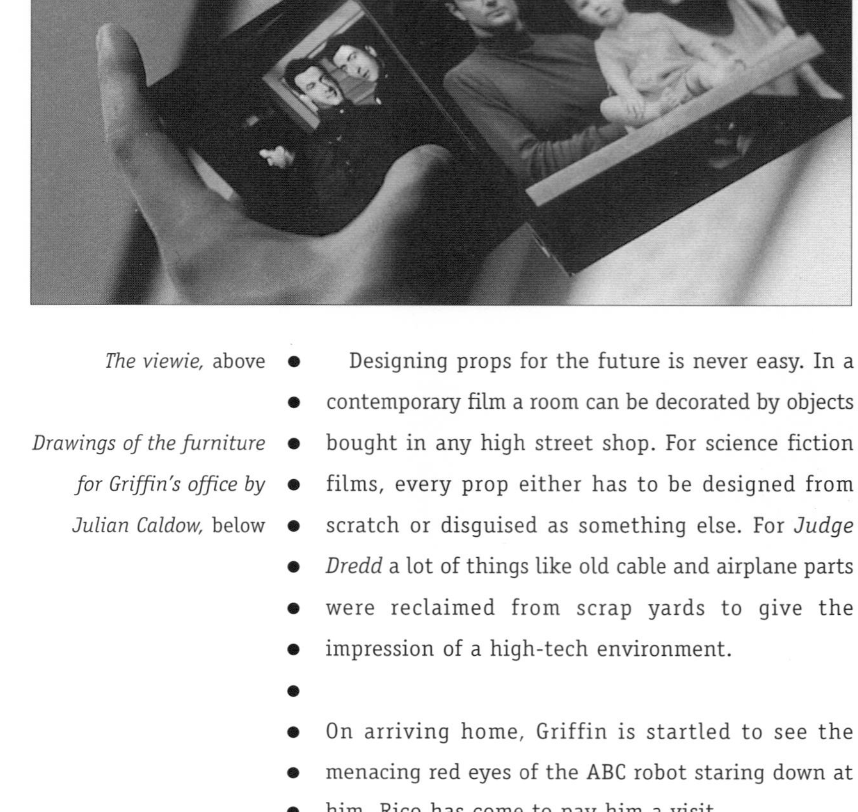

The viewie, above

Drawings of the furniture for Griffin's office by Julian Caldow, below

Designing props for the future is never easy. In a contemporary film a room can be decorated by objects bought in any high street shop. For science fiction films, every prop either has to be designed from scratch or disguised as something else. For *Judge Dredd* a lot of things like old cable and airplane parts were reclaimed from scrap yards to give the impression of a high-tech environment.

On arriving home, Griffin is startled to see the menacing red eyes of the ABC robot staring down at him. Rico has come to pay him a visit.

The idea behind the character was to make him honorable, even though what he is trying to do has destructive consequences. "You set up chaos in a city that is horrendously overpopulated," explains Producer Beau Marks. "You have the president [Griffin] who wants to become more repressive, and take the Council to a conservative bent, thinking that more conservative laws would be laws that would help society. And one of the difficult tasks that we had was that we always saw Griffin as Nixon, as a man who absolutely believed what he was doing was for the betterment of the country."

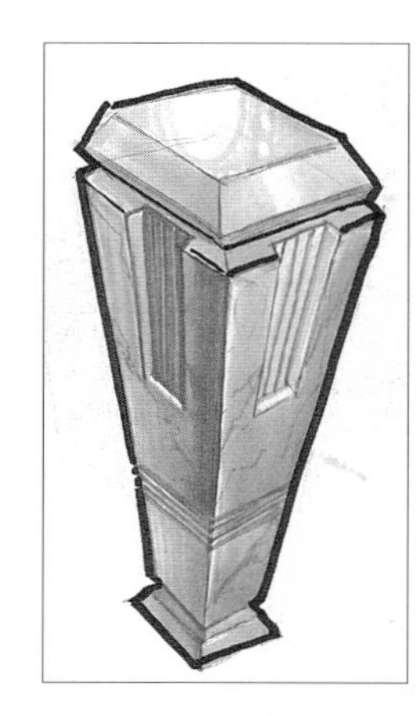

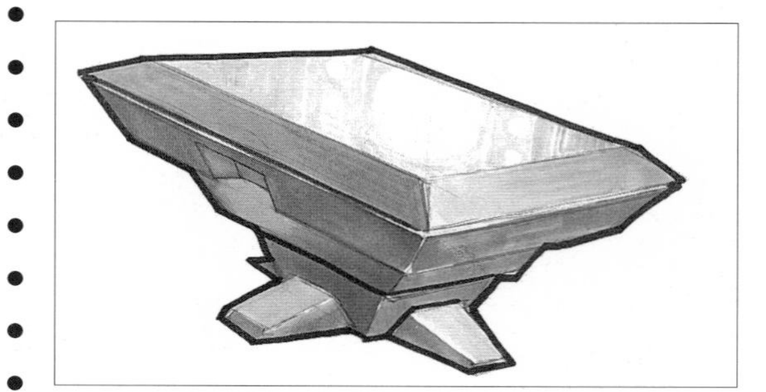

Griffin's apartment is the first living space we see of the upper-class community in Mega-City. There was originally a scene in Griffin's office as well, but finances put a squeeze on things and it was moved to the apartment. The apartment was supposed to have been a much larger affair to reflect Griffin's status. But again the budget wouldn't stretch, it was scaled down a bit and part of it was recommissioned from another set.

"When we finish shooting on a stage and the set gets struck, a lot of the sets have ended up out on the back lot augmenting a lot of the buildings and plugging up a lot of the holes," says Nigel Phelps. "Likewise in this instance, the walls that constitute Griffin's apartment all come from the Hall of Justice corridor. So we're not remaking things time and time again. We reuse this one set, painting it a different color and doing some stuff to it."

A lot of elements were put into Griffin's apartment to give it character, like the fireplace, the fluted columns and the big window. The type of furniture used in this scene and others came out of discussions between Danny Cannon, Nigel Phelps and Set Decorator Peter Young.

"If you talk about one hundred and fifty years in the future, what is an antique?" says Peter, stating one of the main dilemmas of his job. "We had to go to Milan Fair to look at what futuristic modern furniture was available."

Ideally, Danny Cannon wanted to use the work of furniture designer Philip Stark. "Well, Philip Stark is not cheap," says Peter. "What I'm saying is that a table or a chair, if it's Philip Stark, is five or six thousand pounds, and if you want three of them because it's going to blow up, it's not going to be practical as you get into it ... There's no wood, there's no vegetation in the future – or that's what they said, that's the restriction and what we were given as a guideline – so therefore you're left with metal, steel, glass.

"Because of the restrictions, and because Danny and Nigel didn't like anything that was anybody else's concept, [most of the furniture] was actually designed and made. Julian Caldow also drew a lot of it, and it was much easier. Danny preferred it to be drawn before his very eyes, and you actually saw it being made in-house in Shepperton Studios."

But where Griffin's apartment was concerned, Danny put in an objection. "He didn't like the color," Peter remembers. "He said it was too garish. Whether that was my fault, Nigel's fault or his fault or whatever, but he changed sofa colors four times."

The scene was originally down to be set at nighttime, but was later changed to dawn, which gave the apartment a different ambiance. "It's going to be a very cool scene," says Nigel. "As an environment, it's quite simple. Not a lot to it. But it would be nice if it was bigger."

The road to hell for Dredd is the Aspen shuttle, the squat little vehicle crammed with prisoners that he and his kind have put there. And now he is one of them, the most famous convict catcher of them all trapped in a confined space with a group of convicts who all know who he is.

The interior of the shuttle was inspired by that of a Roman slave galley. The prisoners sit in a subordinate position either side of an elevated gangway, so, as Production Designer Nigel Phelps puts it, "The guards can strut along the aisle and

Squat, cramped and bearing a deliberate resemblance to a Roman galley – the Aspen shuttle, below

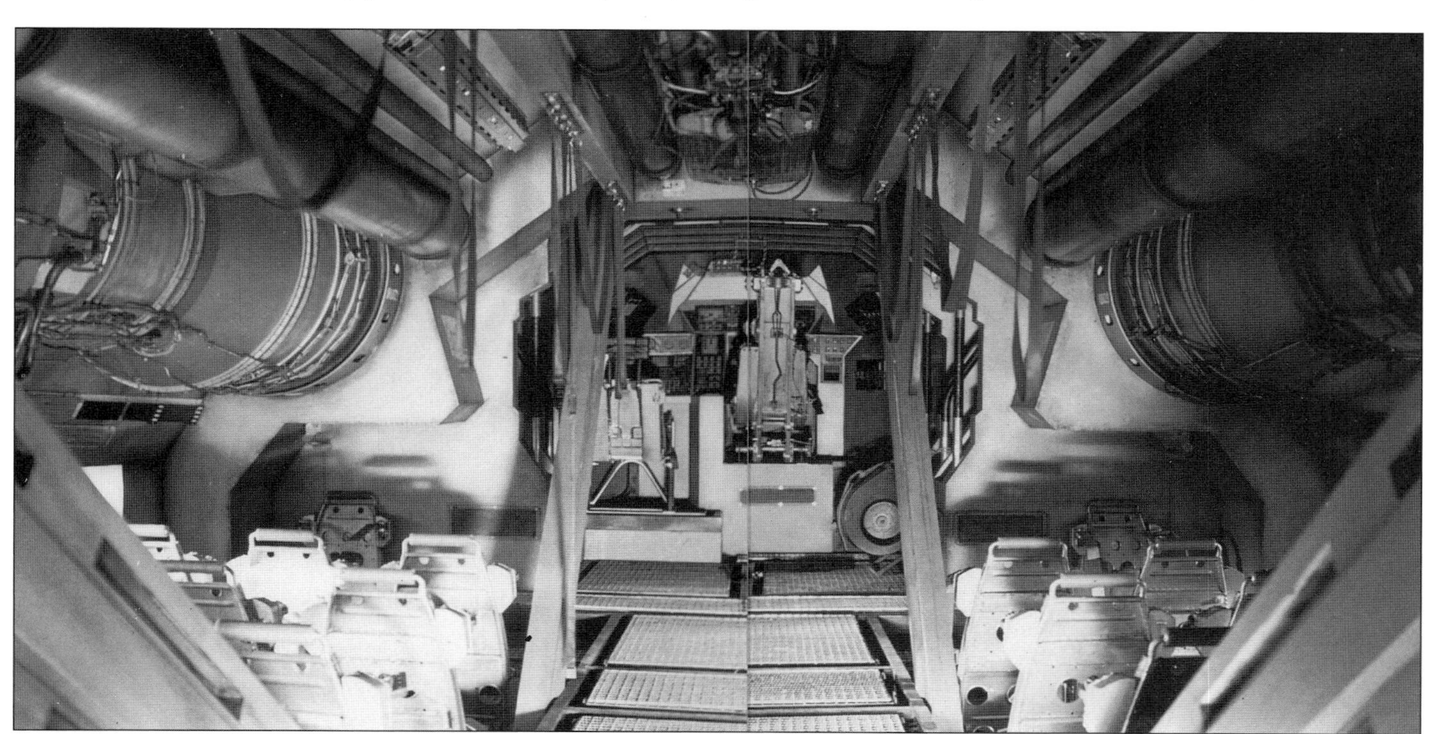

Dredd and Fergie aboard the Aspen shuttle, right and below

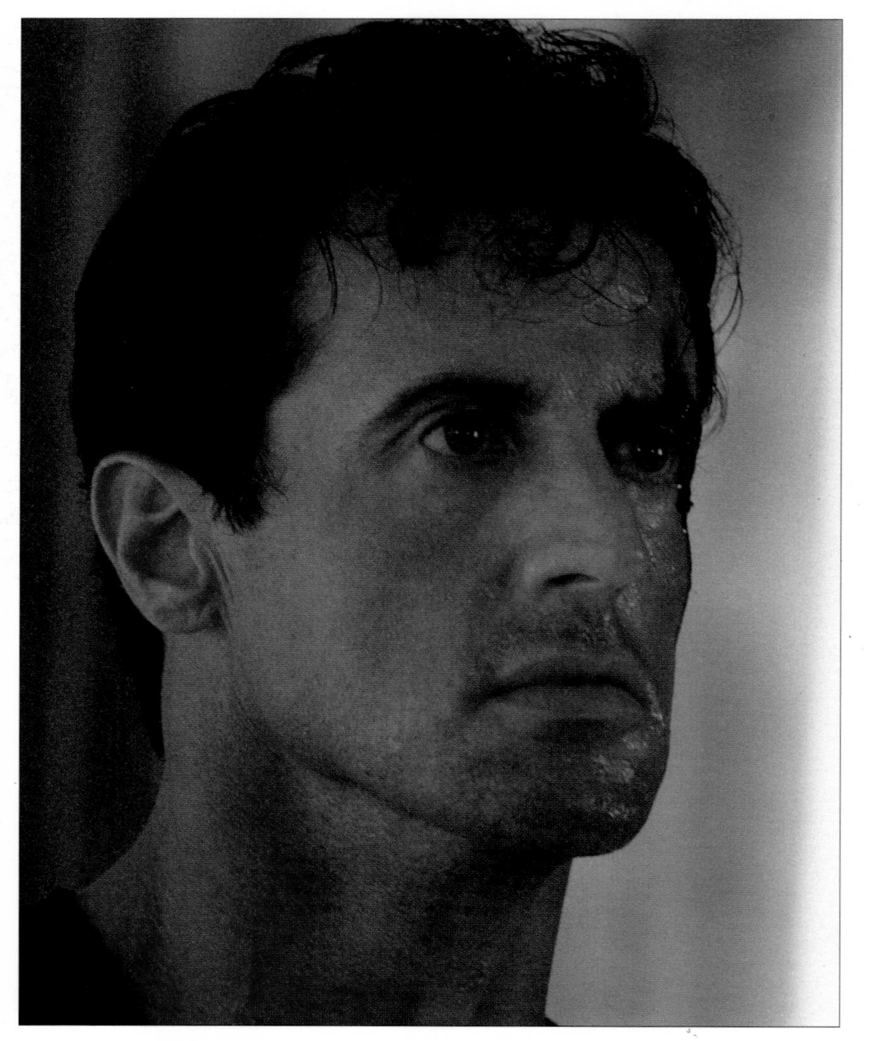

if they don't like the look of anybody they could kick you in the head!"

"We added interest into it by bringing the main engines down into the environment," Nigel continues. "You're aware that there's nothing pleasurable about this. Everything is hard about it. Nothing's cushioned and all the edges are sharp. And it's just a horrible, horrible way to travel."

But it gets worse.

The shuttle is blown up by a group of cannibals – the Angel Gang – intent on eating the people inside and salvaging everything possible from the wrecked craft.

The bomb itself was actually a product from the Second World War. It's a cluster-bomb fuse which was gutted, tarted up a bit and connected to an LCD display to make it look more like a futuristic bomb by the Props Department headed by Ty Teiger.

"I was lucky with this bomb because we did actually find it on the floor of a gun hire shop," says Ty. "I said, 'Jesus Christ, that's the one!', picked it up, brought it back to the studio and everybody said, 'Yeah, that's great, perfect.' It could have taken months of meticulous drawings."

The shuttle shakes violently when hit by the bomb.

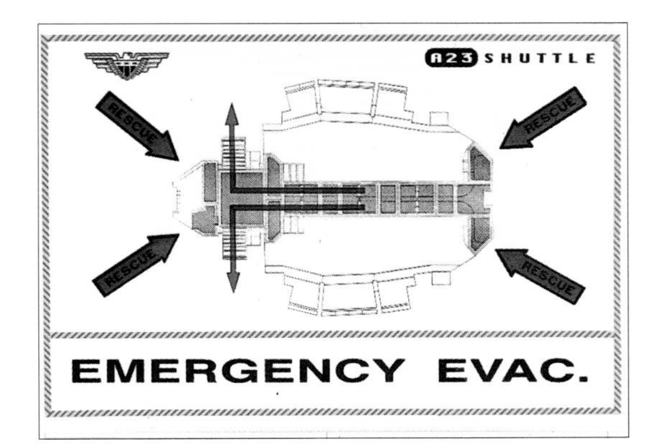

Emergency evacuation warning poster from the Aspen Prison shuttle

For this, the whole set was built on gimbals which rocked backwards and forwards as the shuttle plunged towards the Cursed Earth. The exterior shot for this was filmed in Iceland, and was discovered coincidentally when the crew were flying into the airport.

"I looked down and it looked like a crash site," remembers Nigel Phelps. "In fact it was. I think it was a Star Fighter, something like that, that the local fire brigade used for fire practice."

It was another piece of good fortune that the fuselage from the wrecked aircraft was about the same size as one of the shuttle engines. It was re-dressed and set alight and actually forms part of the burning shuttle seen on screen. The rest of it was matted in afterwards.

Model of the vaguely bat-like Aspen shuttle, above

The compact flight deck of the shuttle, left

Max von Sydow as Judge Fargo preparing to take the Long Walk into the Cursed Earth, above. *Painted by Dermot Power, over a photograph*

Iceland provided a suitably unreal landscape for the shuttle crash in the Cursed Earth, right

The Cursed Earth is a bleak unforgiving landscape that has become a penal colony where Mega-City dumps its undesirables. It's the wasted remains of North America, destroyed by the excesses of modern life and a series of catastrophes. At first the production team were thinking about places in North Africa, like Tunisia, where they could film in a desert-like environment.

And then they hit on the idea of Iceland. "Iceland is a black desert," proclaims Producer Beau Marks. "It's gorgeous, it's beautiful, it's perfect."

There are conflicting stories as to where the idea to send the location crews out to this little-used, isolated country came from. One story has Director Danny Cannon coming up with the suggestion, which in turn came from Icelandic pop singer Björk. The alternative version has Beau Marks and Production Designer Nigel Phelps simultaneously coming up with the idea. If one believes the latter version, Nigel was inspired by a travelogue on the country, while Beau had seen a newspaper advert.

"It was the fact that we were, by that time, so in sync with one another that it hit," says Beau. "The fact of the matter is that this process, to make a film this big with this much complication for as little money as we did, required all of us to always be bouncing off of one another, both creatively and in organizational ways."

In the end it doesn't really matter who thought of it first because there's no arguing that the location is ideal. "It's this volcanic island, basically," says

Nigel. "Just lava flows and a dead landscape. It's just awesome because it's got tremendous scale, but selective places. It's this black landscape. It could be on the moon, you don't know where you are. It worked perfectly."

The dark, dilapidated courthouse where the Angel Gang torture Dredd and Fergie was a set built in the studios to match the Iceland location. It wasn't pleasant.

"The scene that everyone hated was the ruined courthouse," remembers Camera Operator David Worley. "That was because it was smoky, we had fires on the set, the floor was covered in cinders. Everyone was filthy and black and couldn't breathe and a few tempers got a bit frayed."

This was not the only part which had to match the Iceland footage. In fact, the Angel Gang actors never got the chance to go to Iceland because all their stuff was filmed at Shepperton. The Iceland footage was recorded by a second unit crew in July 1994 before principal photography got underway, and was later composited with the other elements. There *was* a plan to go back to Iceland and do some more work in November, but this never came off – which is just as well because the country was snowbound at the time!

For a long time, no one was sure whether the Angel Gang would make it to the film or not. Script revision after script revision had them in; then had them out; had them back in again, or had only some of them in. Danny Cannon was the person who was really keen to see Mean Machine in the movie, and so in the end the whole family (with the exception of Fink and his pet rat, Ratty) made it to the screen.

They are a ragtag group, scavenging on the unforgiving Cursed Earth, and generally living a cannibalistic life. When Dredd first encountered them

The Angel Gang spot the shuttle approaching, left

Junior Angel (Ewen Bremner) aims at the Aspen Prison shuttle, below

in *2000 AD* (Prog 160), it was in Texas City, another Mega-City that incorporated a few of the characteristics of the American Wild West. They are probably the part of the film that sticks closest to the original comic strips.

"They're unbelievably evil, but wonderful fun to do," says Costume Designer Emma Porteous. "Danny wanted them to have a mad spaghetti western feel about them, so I was really able to go to town. They've all got these really big duster coats. Everything was unbelievably filthy. We bought a lot of undergarments which I found all over London, things just caught my eye. Then we had a band of people come in to break down the stuff, professional breaker-downers! They absolutely mangled everything, made it filthy dirty and broke it down and holed it. We found belts and wonderful bits of things to hang round their necks, and old teeth. I really enjoyed that bit."

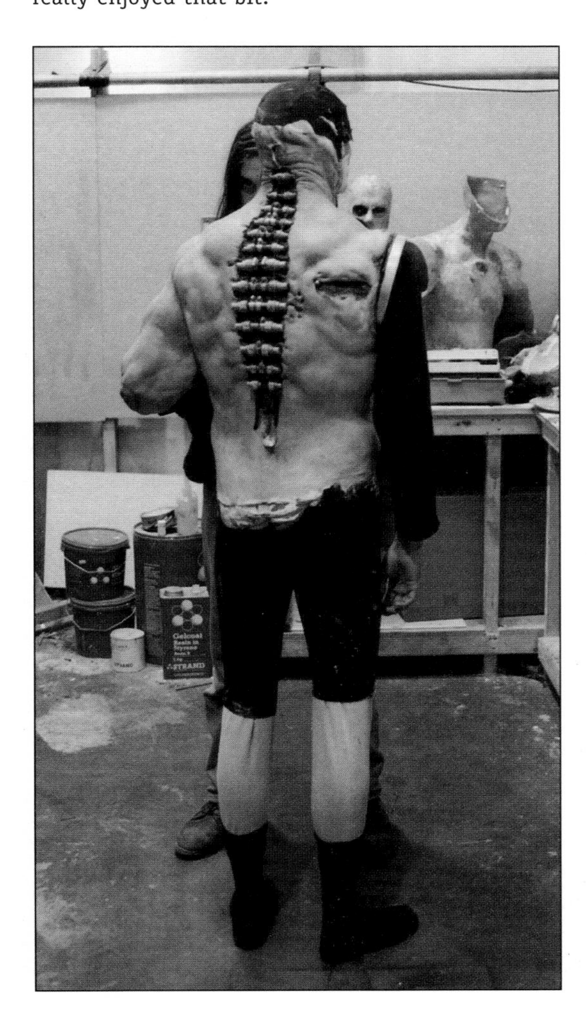

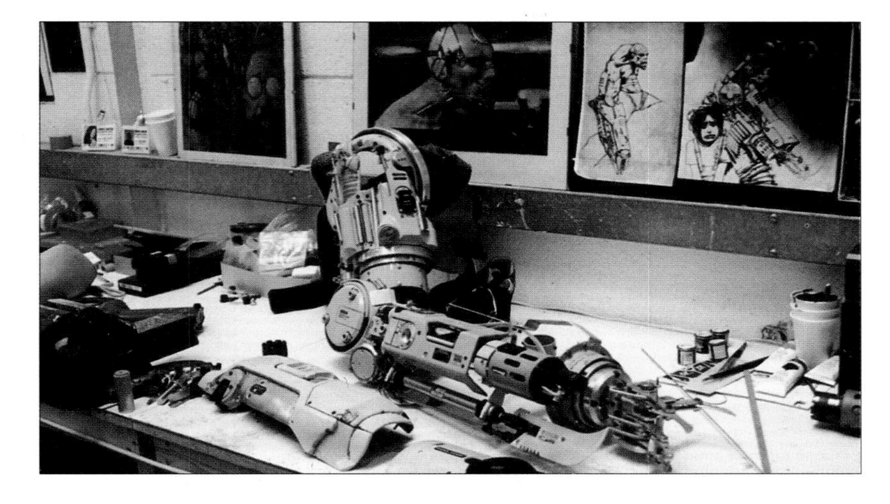

Center stage is Mean Machine, an elaborate cyborg designed by one of the UK Conceptual Artists, Chris Halls. He had drawn Mean Machine in the comics, which was where Production Designer Nigel Phelps first saw his work. The way that Chris had drawn the mechanical arm meant he would be the ideal sort of person for the project, not only in designing Mean Machine, but also incorporating some of that mechanical detail into the buildings.

It turned out that Chris had a history of working in film. He had done creature effects for six years and was in the middle of taking a two-year sabbatical to work on comics and improve his drawing when he was approached to work on *Judge Dredd*.

Chris's background meant adapting Mean Machine for the screen posed few problems. "I'd kind of drawn him in the comic based on how I would have made him if I was ever going to make him," he says. "All the time I was thinking how he was going to work in 3D, so it wasn't really much of a transition."

Some changes were made for the film – specifically making the robot arm smaller and more manageable – but Chris was careful not to stray too far from Mean Machine's origins: "The thing is that in the comic he's a half-wit, a psychopathic half-wit, and I didn't

Chris Halls's desk, top: *his artwork is pinned to the wall above the mechanical arm*

Clay model of the face prosthesis, above

Half man, half machine and all mean SOB: Mean Machine, opposite

A strong yet wiry actor was needed to fit inside the bulky mechanics and prosthetics required for Mean Machine, left – *Chris Adamson fitted the bill*

Chris Adamson takes a break in fitting the Mean Machine body, above. *He had to tuck his left arm up inside the costume; spot the zipper in his armpit*

Dredd confronts Mean Machine in the ruined courthouse, right *– an uncomfortable shoot for all involved*

want him to look too disturbing and frightening because you're supposed to laugh at him in a way. When he tries to head-butt you and you move out of the way and he crashes into a pillar it's supposed to be half-funny and half-frightening."

Chris was able to follow through the project from the design stage to the sculpting – which he did himself – to looking after the actor on set. The man cast in the role of Mean Machine was Chris Adamson, whose slender build was a distinct advantage. It allowed all the mechanics and prosthetics to be fitted on to him without making him look ridiculously huge.

"I didn't want him to look like he had stuff stuck on top of his body," Chris Halls explains. "I wanted him to look like his shoulder stops and then blends into a robot arm, so it looks like things have been stuck into him rather than onto him. Like the skullcap and the bits and pieces in his body, they're not overlapping skin, they're actually on the same level as the skin. So where the skull ends on his nose, skin starts, so it looks as if he's had his skin torn away and replaced with these new parts."

The costume basically encased the actor in rubber, aluminum and bits of plastic. The mechanical arm was attached by a harness under his costume, which supported most of the weight. Over the top of that went the rubber chest part, which was built up to make Mean Machine look more muscular and hide all the mechanics. The actor's head was then encased in a two-section prosthetic with a third section for the face. It was attached with glue, and finally the contact lenses were put in.

But like all prosthetic makeup, it brought with it its own characteristic challenges. "I think it was the heat more than anything," says Chris. "We had problems maintaining him on set because it's so hot that the sweat comes underneath the foam rubber and it starts coming away, so we have to keep maintaining the pieces round the eyes and his nose all day long. He can't eat either because the greasy food makes the pieces come off."

The arm was maneuvered simply by the actor's own arm, with the help of internal mechanics that allowed him to control the three fingers. There was also a knife that shoots out from a pneumatic piston at the end of the arm. Although it was possible to give the actor control of this part too, it was actually worked behind the camera with an airline running down the inside of the arm. It was just too risky to do it the other way in case the knife shot out accidentally and injured someone!

The arm was made, as Chris puts it, "on the cheap." Only one copy was produced, so there was a lot of praying and crossing of fingers hoping that it would stay in one piece. "I was very worried," Chris admits. "I didn't use glue on anything; every single thing on there is bolted together because it's too frightening the thought of it falling apart ... Luckily it survived the shoot, survived a lot of action."

One piece of engineering that never made it to the film was connected to Mean Machine's dial on his forehead. It was built with a motor which would turn on its own when Mean's mood changed. However, when it came to filming the scene, the other Angels moved it manually and only the flashing light was seen to work.

Mean Machine has turned out to be one of the successes of the film. During interviews with other members of the crew, the subject of how wonderful Chris's work was would often come up unprompted. Chris spent four months on the project and is delighted with the way it turned out. "It's the best job I've ever had," he says.

Mean Machine Special Make-up Effects Designer Chris Halls performs a little on-site maintenance on "the best job" he ever had, left

The highly detailed model of Hershey's apartment, above

Brian Bolland's artwork for Hershey from 2000 AD, right – *the severe haircut made it into the film*

The script describes Hershey's apartment as having "enough personal things to tell us she's both a danger-crazed athlete ... and a romantic." But the set ended up being constructed out of other pieces of the Academy. It was part of a resource-saving idea developed by Nigel Phelps when a scene in Olmeyer's apartment was moved to the training range.

"I came up with a solution there of making a block component system that you could turn sideways, shoot it one way and turn it lengthwise and have it the other way, and each way would look absolutely cool. So it's like a modular system that we could turn any way up and create a different space from it. So Hershey's apartment was one of those component systems. And so the Academy has a homogenized look to it because in fact they're the same pieces seen in a different configuration.

"And her apartment is quite a small space. We wanted to keep it tight. We've got sunken floors in there and all the furniture is built in to a large extent. And there are lots of raking searchlights all the time. It works very nicely."

One of the props, however, caused a few problems. Hershey's computer is featured quite prominently and, like the other computers in the film, had to look futuristic while still looking like a computer.

"In a perfect world Danny would have liked an electrical image floating in midair with no tube or depth behind it," explains Set Decorator Peter Young. "The thinnest screen that we could obtain was a liquid crystal display. We actually tested it in April to the Producer and the Lighting Cameraman's satisfaction, but unfortunately it would only work if you shot it straight on. If you came off one inch or six inches either way to the left or the right, the top or the bottom, the resolution was not clear enough for filming. And that proved an embarrassment for our department."

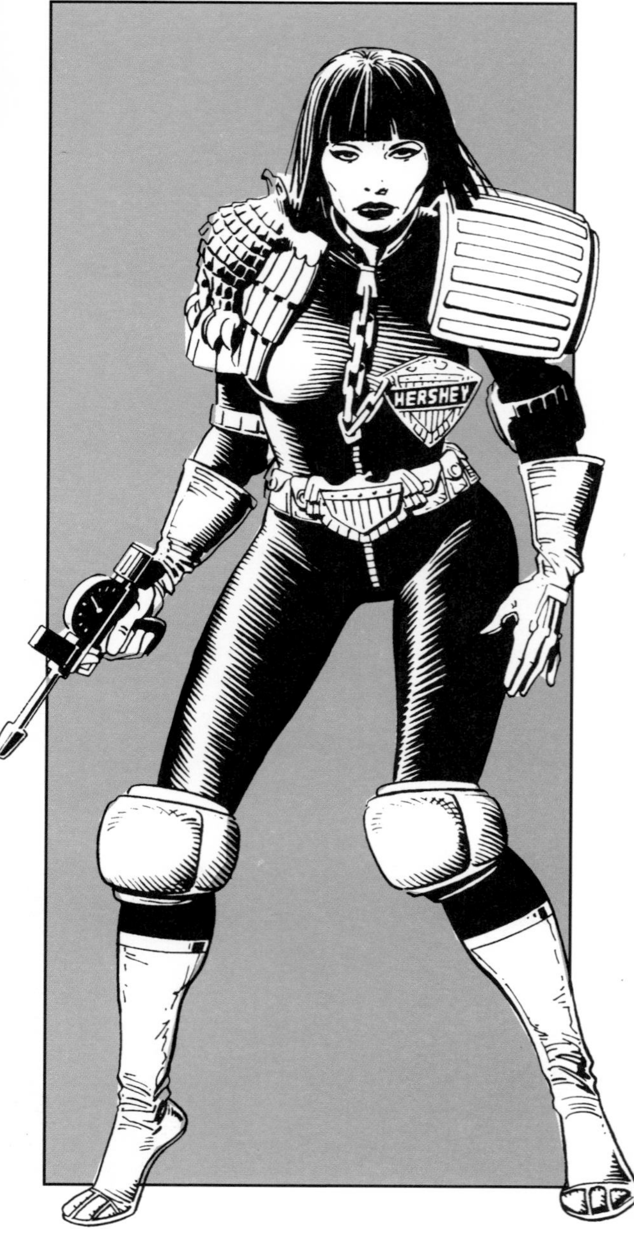

While Dredd is wondering how the hell he is going to escape from the Cursed Earth, pandemonium is breaking out in Mega-City. Judges are being killed left, right and center, as demonstrated by the way the bank explodes in a shower of sparks, debris and flying bodies.

This scene wasn't originally in the screenplay. It was added when Danny Cannon saw the finished building on the back lot and liked it so much, a sequence was written especially for it. As for all the explosions in the film, Special Effects Supervisor Joss Williams was in charge of making it look spectacular. Joss's secret and his motto for doing these type of scenes is "Test, test and test again."

"I insist on testing everything before we get into the shooting," he says. "That has two implications. Above all it enables me and my crew to see what's required, the minimum amount that we can get away with pyrotechnically to achieve the right effect. And also by testing up front on preproduction I can go on the set months after we've tested and be confident that we're going to get the shot in one, rather than in two or three – provided nobody else screws up! So far as the effects are concerned, I feel confident I can say to the director, 'This is what's going to happen, this is how far things are going to go, this is how big it's going to be.' They can never, in all fairness to them, visualize it because unless you do that stuff all day you can't."

Essentially the effects team placed explosive pyrotechnics at strategic places and packed them with lightweight debris which is blown outwards

Judges approach their Lawmasters outside the Mega-City bank, above left

Special Effects Supervisor Joss Williams has a motto to help ensure spectacular – and safe – explosions: "test, test and test again."

The bank explosion looks extremely dangerous, above, *but no one was hurt and the set wasn't damaged*

when the charges are set off. The building appears to get blown up without actually damaging the set. They videoed all the tests and then watched them frame by frame to see what happened to the explosions. Using that information, they were able to position the stunt artists and the cameras to make it seem more dangerous than it actually was.

"The effect is designed so that it looks as if the explosion has engulfed people, it's wiped them out, the flame or the debris has wiped them out, but in fact it's missed them," says Joss. "And that's what we did with the bank, that's what we did when we blew up Hershey's bike. All my charges were angled in the bank in such a manner that the stunt people were underneath the charge, it was going over the top of them. There was in fact no danger to them at all.

"Obviously there's always the inherent danger when you're involved with special effects. Regardless of how much testing you do, how much preparation you do, there is always that element, the unforeseen. We are making action movies, we are dealing with potentially dangerous materials and creating potentially dangerous situations. So you have to think of everything you can to illuminate as much as possible all the dangers. But there is always the unknown. And that is when experience comes in, in trying to predict what the unknown is going to be by – how can I put it? – if the unknown is going to happen, it's going to happen in such a way that it doesn't affect anything or anybody. That's the key, really. That's the secret. And being able to do that comes from testing, so we test everything to the hilt."

For Joss, what makes the explosions that much more exciting is the people who are caught in the middle of the action. It's the interaction between special effects and people that creates the effect. "I could quite easily have said to the Director and the Producer, 'That's going to be too dangerous to put people near it or in front of it,' which is my prerogative to say. But it's also my responsibility and my wish to give the best effects I can. So I don't want *not* to put people in there, I want to put people in there or it might just as well be a model shot."

Stunt Coordinator Marc Boyle was in charge of putting people in the middle of the explosion. The biggest problem for the stunt artists was they were in the Judge costumes which are not very stunt-friendly. "You get heat on that, it just burns," says Marc. "So they all wore fireproof underwear, but the suits still got burnt and there's not a lot you can do about it, you just try and protect yourself as much

as you can. We use a material called Zel-gel which you soak your face in, your neck, to stop burns. It will keep some of the heat out. And you rehearse it without the explosion so everyone knows they're in the right place at the right time. And then you do it.

"For the boys it was very hard if they were doing something in the Judges' suits," he continues. "You couldn't put as much padding as we normally do. You try and wear knee, elbow and maybe hip pads if you're hitting the ground because they're the points that hit first. We tried to place stuff on the ground if we could. But it did make it very difficult."

Unlike many films, most of what the moviegoer hears when she or he watches the sequence is the actual sound produced by Joss's pyrotechnics. Director Danny Cannon has a hatred of post-sync sound and was determined from the beginning to get the real thing in the can. Sound Mixer Chris Munro was in charge of making the on-site recordings which he did using digital technology. "I shoot a lot of that stuff in stereo," he explains. "The reason being that's what gives the film the real stereo effect ... On this particular film a lot of the bangs are loud and they're very real." That raw tape was then passed on to the sound mixer to use as a base on which to add the extra touches to take it into the third millenium.

Exploding the bank was a major success for the technicians. Quite a few journalists had been invited down to the set that day and watched from a distance as broken glass flew across the street and stunt Judges were blown off their feet. The explosion was so fierce it was possible to feel the impact, even at a safe distance. Several cameras placed in strategic positions got the shots from different angles, and afterwards the crew gathered around the monitors to see the video playback.

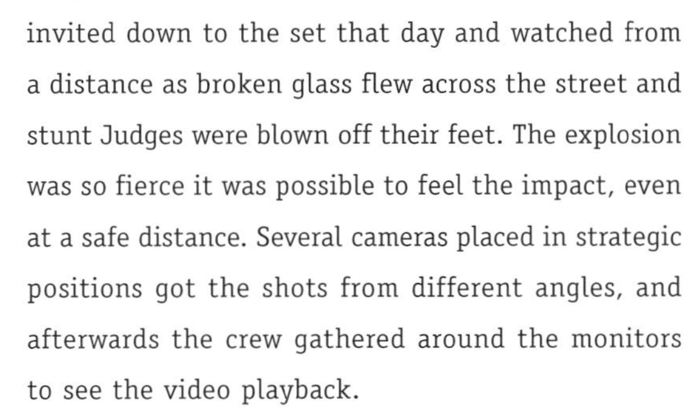

When Dredd and Fergie escape the Cursed Earth, their only way back to Mega-City is down the incinerator chute. They run down the chute with the fireball

The gloomy incinerator chute, below, *started life as two-and-a-half steel freight containers*

Fergie runs from the fireball in the incinerator chute, above

Production shot of the incinerator sequence, right

chasing them and at the last moment Dredd fires into the floor and creates an escape route through which they both dive as the fireball rolls on above them.

The set for this scene was one case where necessity was the mother of invention. There was no budget to build a set from scratch and the designers couldn't use any timber because of the risk of it catching fire. And so they lined the 100 foot-long corridor with two and a half steel freight containers.

This shot was going to be composited together using separate film of the fireball and the actors, until Special Effects Supervisor Joss Williams stepped in and said, "We can do that full size, for real. We've done all that stuff, that's what we do."

The idea of having a raging fireball and Sylvester Stallone in the same room quite naturally left the producers a little apprehensive. After several of Joss's famous tests everyone was convinced it could not only be done safely, but that it would look great. "It's not a problem as long as you shoot it the right way and set it up the right way," says Joss. "I tested it until I was satisfied how big a fireball I could put in there, how far I could put the artists away from it, how safe they would be and what the best camera lens would be to achieve the effect, to make it look as if they're right by the fireball when in fact they've got their safety distance from it all the time."

The fire was produced using propane gas projectors which fire bursts of flame down the set. The artists were too far away to be in any danger, but, just in case, their costumes were made fire-retardant. The ancient trick of using a long lens on the camera to

create a foreshortening effect made it appear as if they were in mortal danger.

Originally, this wasn't how Dredd was going to return to Mega-City. An earlier draft of the script had him impersonating a guard and trying to get through the gate in the perimeter wall. But he is recognized and there is a fight. This scene, along with the fight in the docking bay that was also axed, was intended to show the strength of the defenses along the wall. Instead, the idea of Mega-City being a hemmed-in place designed to keep outsiders out was skated over.

It was replaced by the journey through the incinerator chute, but in the Steven De Souza version the scene was far more significant. It had Dredd mounting a split-second rescue of Fergie, rather than firing through the grille to create an escape route. The version that appears in the film leaves Dredd's change of attitude towards Fergie to be confirmed several scenes later when he apologizes to him for wrongful arrest.

One of the most breathtaking sequences in the movie is when Dredd jumps on the Lawmaster and takes to the air. It presents a whole new view of Mega-City as he flies in between the buildings and through the video poster, pursued by Judge Hunters. These impressive shots were compiled by the visual effects team at Mass.Illusion, but there was also a lot of important work being done on the ground.

The flying bikes, although they were conceived of first, owed much of their design to the road-going Lawmasters. "We decided with the flying bikes we really had to stay with the same bodywork because we knew that with the schedule we'd never have the time or the finances to cope with building another version that was dramatically different," explains David Allday, Art Director for Action Vehicles.

"So the basic bodywork and fiberglass construction was the same. But the way they were rigged was completely different because obviously they didn't travel along the ground, they didn't have a motor in

Fergie and Dredd prepare for a wild ride on the flying Lawmaster, below. *The green screen enables a Mega-City background to be added afterwards*

them. They were made to look like they were flying by a combination of computerized gimbals inside, shot against green screen, and then a hydraulic rig was made for them to fly through the wall of the Academy as well, which was constructed by the Special Effects Department ... The amount of engineering that went into the flying bikes was phenomenal. I think the crew that worked on that side of it were extraordinary."

There were three alternative versions of the bikes made to tip and sway in different ways. The rigs were mounted several feet in the air to give them enough room to do that. The green screen was there to enable the visual effects team to drop in the background of Mega-City behind. The whole process required exact lighting, exact programming of computers and a hell of a lot of patience. One crew

Clay sculpture of the flying Lawmaster by Chris Halls, above

This early production sketch of Dredd with the flying Lawmaster by Kevin Walker, right, *was instrumental in selling the whole idea of the film*

Three different flying bikes were built, made to tip and sway in different ways, left

Fergie's outfit for the climactic bike chase, below

member commented that he popped into the studio for a quick visit one day, and when he returned three hours later they still hadn't got around to shooting one frame of action!

A lot of the scenes included dialogue, and as soon as they had been filmed, the actors trooped off to the office of Sound Supervisor Chris Munro. There, they disappeared into a tiny recording booth about the size of a wardrobe and re-recorded everything.

"We weren't able to get actual original sound on this green screen because we've got these great wind machines, we've got all the effects and things and there's just no way of quieting them," Chris explains. "So we video everything. They actually run a video just for me of all the stuff we've done with dialogue. And I have a booth here and we have the actors here, we run the video back and we do on-the-spot post-syncing. Rather than, as would be normal, Sylvester Stallone or Rob Schneider going off and making a period film and then being expected to come back and do his post-sync for *Judge Dredd* where he's completely forgotten how he's played it or he's just out of the mood of playing it. So what we've done is get them straight in here and done it almost immediately after shooting."

The flying bikes sequence was the final thing to be filmed in England. After that the key people flew across the Atlantic for the lengthy postproduction process, while the cast and English crew went on to other projects. Meanwhile, as far as the story was concerned, the climax was yet to come ...

Rico reveals the clones in the Janus lab, above and right

The climax of *Judge Dredd* takes place in the Janus lab. Here lies the result of all Rico's plans, where he injects his own DNA to clone himself and create the ultimate psychotic army. It is here where Dredd and Rico face each other as two brothers with equal strength and equal ability. The setting for this confrontation had to be impressive.

It had to be very bright and clinical, while giving the impression that it had been sitting there for twenty years waiting for someone to throw the switch and reactivate it. It was constructed in aluminum and lit from underneath the floor to give it a look distinct from any of the other sets.

The way it turned out, the set has a close resemblance to Julian Caldow's original drawing. "I was very pleased with that," he says, "because there was a time when they were very worried about the cost of the design of the Janus lab. They asked me to come up with more designs and I came up with [an idea] which would have been nine times more expensive."

In fact, the Janus lab went through quite a lot of

changes as the filmmakers tried to take account of the budget without compromising their grand ideas too much. "You shoot for the moon," explains Julian. "You'll always fall short, but at least you tried."

Allowing the designers' imaginations to have free reign eventually paid off when they found a way of living up to the exciting ideas that can be seen in the drawings. Rather than building the Janus lab entirely from scratch, they reused the ceiling from the Hall of Justice. "It's a revamped set," says Production Designer Nigel Phelps. "That was as much a time thing as anything else. There simply wasn't the time once we'd finished filming on the Hall of Justice to totally strike that set – because it was a big build – and build a brand new Janus lab. The ceiling, I felt, was the one thing that we could suitably disguise and that wouldn't be a problem because there's a lot of circular sets in this film and that was part of the styling and motifs that were repetitive.

"That goes part of the way to homogenize the look anyway," he continues. "There's a lot of different styles going. You want to see something – forms – repeating themselves ... You start off designing everything and whittle it down into 'Well, the reality is ... ! We haven't got time, we haven't got the money to do all that.' You've got to think on your feet a lot. But as long as we've got everything schemed down to begin with, then it's relatively easy to pare them down to make it affordable."

The set was filled with more than seventy clones. A lot of them were dummies, some were made of expanded polyurethane foam and kept in the background, while the models in the foreground were made from a central core of fiberglass and polyurethane with an outer see-through silicone layer, allowing them to have two levels of color. There were also stuntmen in suits and extras in full all-over body prosthetics.

The clones themselves were designed by Make-up and Prosthetics Supervisor Nick Dudman, who was the man who led the team which ended up making them.

Dredd attacks a clone, left

Make-up and Prosthetics Supervisor Nick Dudman's workshop, below, *where the clones were constructed*

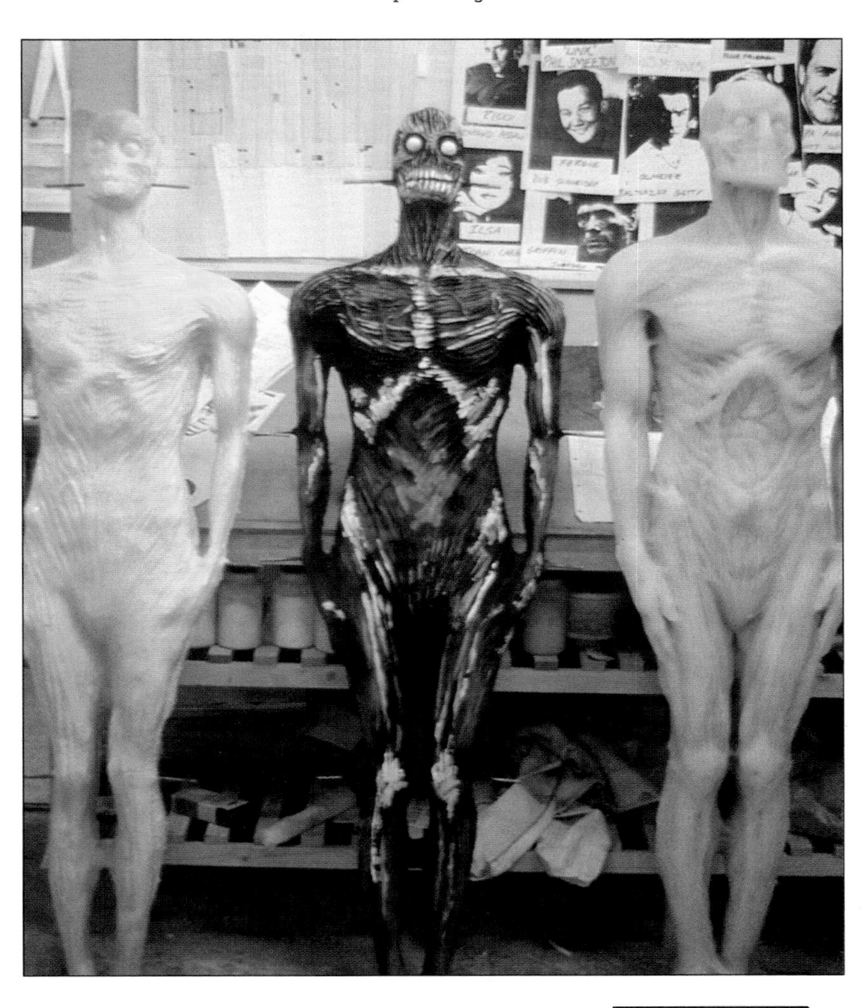

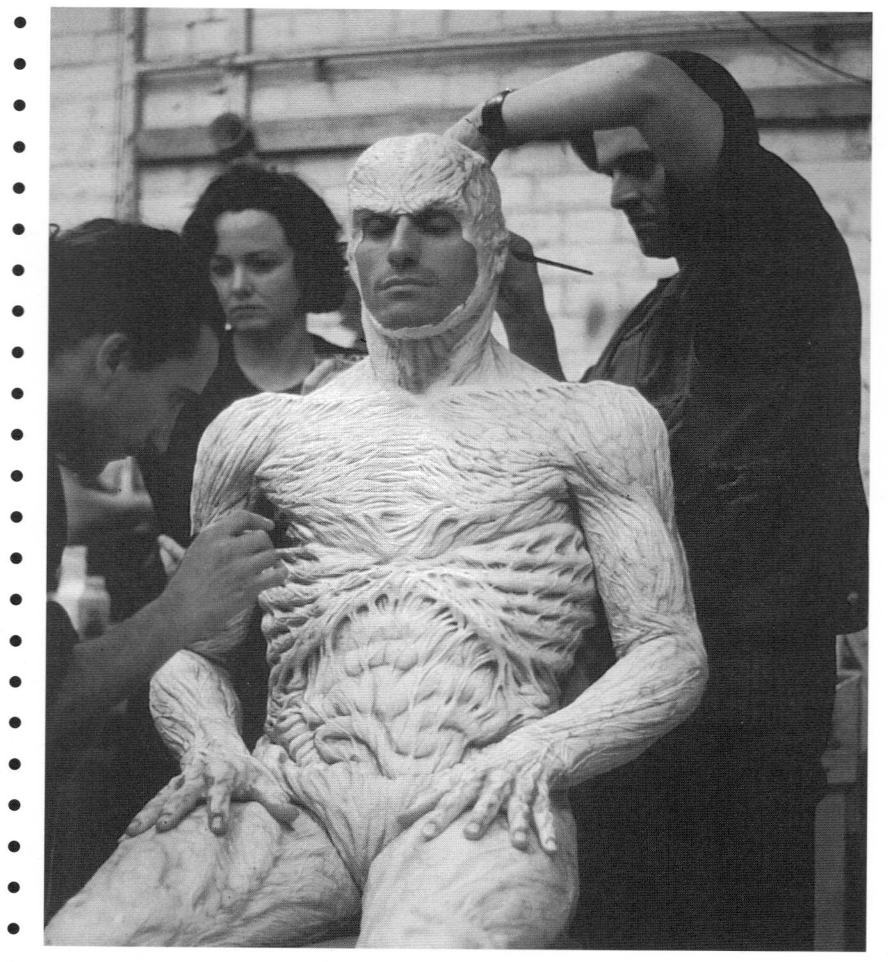

The clone prosthetic make-up took five hours to put on and two hours to take off – which meant only fours hours' sleep for Nick Dudman and his team

His experience includes working on *Batman* where he turned Jack Nicholson into The Joker. Therefore he knew the comics world and was careful not to do anything that would offend Judge Dredd fans.

"I just sat down and did a series of airbrush paintings," says Nick. "For an initial concept I don't do a lot of research for something like this. I might go through some of my medical books, but then I just sit back, close my eyes and listen to some music and start sketching. After about eight or nine things ending up in the bin you start to come up with something ... I wanted an anemic translucent sort of feel to them, so they didn't look like animals, they weren't bloody or *Hellraisery*."

When Nick had a portfolio of designs, he met with Director Danny Cannon and they decided which ones to go for. "He just looked through, picked one out and said, 'Yes, I like that.' And since then he's been in, he's seen various things at various stages and he's had input – 'more veins here, more color here' – that sort of thing. But by and large they pretty much follow the concept that I originally had."

Prosthetic makeup has been around in the movie business for a long time. It turned hordes of actors into apes in the 1968 science fiction film *Planet Of The Apes* and is still turning people into aliens, like the Klingons in the various *Star Trek* films. Technology has improved the finished result over the years, but the technique remains basically the same. A cast is taken of the relevant bits of the person who is going to wear the prosthetic. This is then used to create a mold in which the mask is made. It's fitted onto an actor with glue. In the case of the clones in *Judge Dredd*, the actors' body hair had to be shaved off before gluing every inch of skin and sticking the prosthetic on top in sections.

The make-up had to be maintained and repaired constantly between every take, below

It all sounds fairly horrible. "It takes a long time, but it does give you wonderful body movement, it does look like skin," says Nick. "But I wouldn't pretend that it's a joyride for anyone."

For the Makeup Department it was two weeks of concentrated work. Nick Dudman, speaking just before the scene was going to be filmed, anticipated long hours and very little sleep. "Prosthetic makeups will take five hours plus, and we'll be starting them five hours before unit call at eight o'clock every day. They'll take two hours to get off, the last part of which involves putting them in a bath of solution to get the stuff off. We'll probably get away around midnight. So we'll be doing the week on four hours' sleep a night. On top of that a lot of the stuff we do has to *work* on film, it isn't something you can just chuck a powder puff on and walk away. Every second the camera's turning, you're watching and checking. And in between each shot you're repairing and maintaining. Every one of my crew will be on set, they'll be busy all the time. It will be physically exhausting."

On top of that the actors have to be looked after. Working under studio lights when your body is encased in rubber means you are likely to get very hot, to sweat and become dehydrated. Nick's team had to have glucose drinks, oxygen and fans on hand to keep the actors cool and prevent anyone from passing out.

And yet all that work becomes a background for the main action as Dredd and Rico meet up for the first time to confront each other face to face.

The stunt artists arrived for the rehearsals of this scene with a fight sequence all worked out. But by the time the actors had got hold of it, it had completely changed. With scores of action thrillers under their belts, Sylvester Stallone and Armand Assante were keen to put in the best moves and make

Rico fails to convince Dredd, below, *who is shocked by what he sees in the Janus lab*

Rico and Dredd battle it out in the Janus lab, above

the fight as spectacular as possible. Director Danny Cannon, on the other hand, was trying to restrain the action, knowing that the subsequent duel on the Statue of Liberty had to be bigger and more exciting.

"That happens all the time," says Stunt Coordinator Marc Boyle. "I look at the script and try and talk to the Director – but often, he's thinking about other things – and you go away and put something together with the stunt guy and say, 'Fine, we'll try this, this and this.' So you've got a form with which to work from, you've got some ideas. Because directors work in different ways. Often they'll come on a set and say, 'Fine, show me what you've got,' so the best thing is if you've got something and you can run through it and they go, 'Well I don't like that bit, but I like this bit,' so then you can move it around. And often I do them in sections, so you take out different sections if you want, and you can move them around. And you've got to be able to think on your feet. If they don't like that bit, fine, we'll take this out. To walk on a set with nothing, and a director and a lot of actors, you find too many people say, 'Well, if he did this ...' and it becomes a committee and difficult to do. So it's always good to have a plan. Whether it's right or wrong is immaterial, at least you've got something to show them, then you can either change it or stick to it.

"With someone like Sly who can throw a punch and everything, it's great," Marc adds. "Some things you may have set up, some things you may not like, but if he feels comfortable doing it and it works, that's fine. And he came up with some nice ideas because he's very experienced. It's great working with him and Armand. Armand was very dedicated. He's a method actor and he'd get very into it."

The Janus lab set on which that fight sequence takes place was all gleaming metal which looks great, but becomes problematic for stunt work. The skintight costumes meant there was no room for protective padding.

Rico's sidekick Ilsa confronts Judge Hershey in the Janus lab, left

Camera ascender rig for the Statue of Liberty, below left, *includes a radical dolly track to zoom in on the fighters in the broken cranium*

The full-size "picture head" of the Statue of Liberty, below. *The model in the foreground constructed by the Art Department has the cut-out section clearly marked*

"That was difficult," Marc acknowledges, "because any falls or anything we had to either cut [the shot] just above the floor so we could put a little mat in, or we'd come in tight on the double hitting the floor. But then for the double it was really quite hard. Very hard because of all these metal sets. A stuntman's nightmare!"

The stuntmen got their revenge in a way because the set was destroyed at the end of the scene by a series of explosions.

Dredd and Rico's final battle takes place inside the head of the Statue of Liberty. In the comics this icon of American values has been superseded by the Statue of Law, an effigy of a Judge that towers above the crumbling and neglected lady and her beacon of light. In *Judge Dredd* she is just as much abandoned, but instead she is dwarfed by the buildings, the realities of commerce and power.

The head of the Statue of Liberty in which Dredd and Rico fight was sculpted out of polystyrene and was twenty percent bigger than the real thing. The lightweight material was used so the riggers could put it on a high platform (about ten feet) from which

Dredd dangles perilously over Mega-City. The scene was filmed on one of the sound stages at Shepperton against a green screen with the splendor of Mega-City filled in later using computer technology.

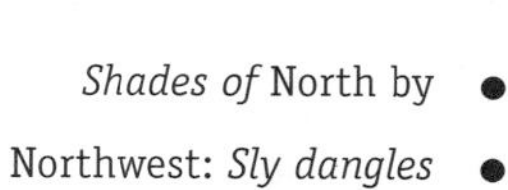

Shades of North by Northwest: *Sly dangles from the Statue of Liberty,* above

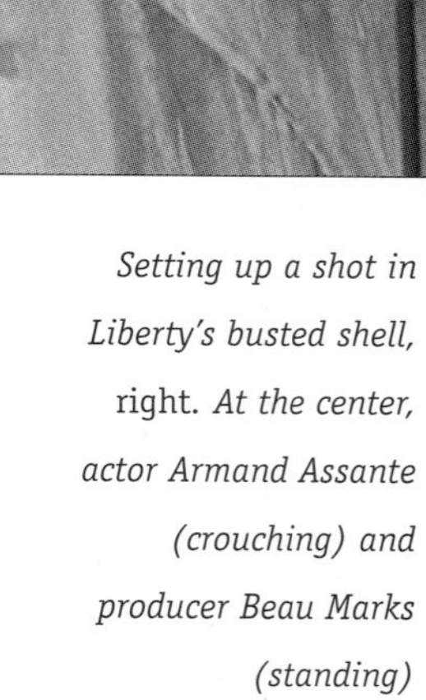

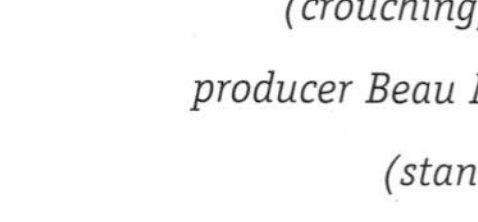

Setting up a shot in Liberty's busted shell, right. *At the center, actor Armand Assante (crouching) and producer Beau Marks (standing)*

The breathtaking shot where Dredd is hanging off the edge was actually performed by his stunt double, Ignacio Carreno, who's an accomplished gymnast. "Often you do that on cables and wires," says Stunt Coordinator Marc Boyle, "but he's such a good athlete that we do a shot where he's right on the edge. They've had a fight and he's fallen and Armand kicks him, and he flips up. In fact, he's holding onto this bar. If he flipped up he'd land facing the wrong way. So as he is kicked in the air he changes hands and he flips himself round, which is some stunt to do. Not a lot of people can do that."

As with all good action films where a sequel is a possibility, the hero lives to fight another day. Rico plummets to the ground and Dredd is left without his brother, but victorious. He even gets a kiss from Hershey (a moment Sylvester Stallone wanted to have in the film, while others were still arguing about as it was being edited).

It appears to be a happy end. And yet for another group of people it was just the beginning – the beginning of a long postproduction process that took all the raw elements of the film and constructed an extravaganza of action.

Hershey and Dredd after he is reinstated as a Judge, below

POSTPRODUCTION: AN OVERVIEW

The Statue of Liberty in the model Mega-City One, opposite

Quarter-inch scale building tops on the gantry stage, below

It is said postproduction can turn a bad movie into a good movie, or a good movie into a bad movie.

No matter how good the filmed material is, the way that it is brought together is vital to a movie's success. Editing is not just joining pieces of film together, it's about value judgments, about choosing the shots, trimming the excesses and adjusting the rhythm so every action sequence and every reflective moment works to the optimum. The excitement and the mood is heightened by the music which is specially written; countless sound effects are seamlessly added to give impact to crashes and believable noises to opening doors; and in the case of *Judge Dredd* a massive special effects project added up to 180 shots to the movie.

The late decision to add the three-minute flying bike sequence to the film kept the postproduction team on their toes right up until the end. It was a major change that helped to create the "roller-coaster ride" Executive Producer Andy Vajna was after, although it added extra work to an already packed agenda.

"Everything with regard to the production schedule changed in order to make those shots as real and exciting as possible," says Andy. "Whenever we get

Roy Berkowitz, a member of the Mass.Illusion editing team, above

Like the city (Los Angeles) in Blade Runner, *Mega-City's appearance is largely due to the skill of the special effects team. Right, the gantry stage camera moves through the Mega-City canyon set*

to a situation like that we do the best we can, take a deep breath and realign the schedule to make sure that we can get the shots that we need."

While the visual effects wizards at Mass.Illusion in Massachusetts were busy producing the chase sequence, the editing was underway in Los Angeles. A total of three editors were brought in to meet the tight schedule which stipulated a release date six months after the end of principal filming in England. They were all given a different portion of the film to work on.

"You have a certain amount of finite time in which to get the work done, so four hands are better than two. Consequently we added editors as we needed them when we felt we were falling a little behind, and we sort of dismissed them when we caught up ... It was all supervised at that particular point by Paul Hirsch, who looked over everybody's shoulders to make sure that we got the right feel and the right beat in the movie, so that we wouldn't have pacing problems between reels, it would flow the same."

One of the people with a large stake in the film's success was actor Sylvester Stallone who spent a considerable time sitting in on the editing process.

"When you get a fresh set of eyes looking at the movie, they notice things that we are so used to looking at that we no longer notice, and I think he gave us some great ideas and some great hints about how to improve it further," says Andy Vajna. "Sly himself is a filmmaker who's produced Academy Award-winning material, so his involvement as far

as I'm concerned was really appreciated and sought after. Because, first of all, he knows best for himself what really works and I think his creative influence was a great asset throughout the movie, throughout the process, whether it was changing or improving lines or selecting cast or ideas in general about the action."

Calling the shots at the top of the tree, of course, was Danny Cannon. The director's cut was finished at the beginning of March 1995 at which time everyone looked at the film and decided more work needed to be done. This is nothing unusual. There have been many highly publicized disagreements between producers and directors over changes made to a director's cut. This wasn't the case with *Judge Dredd*, according to Andy Vajna, who was pleased with Danny's version. It was just a case of stepping back and reevaluating the material.

"I think when you get a director's cut usually you

Another view of the model Mega-City, above. *This is a "beauty pass" on the gantry stage*

Once filming was completed, left, *Sylvester Stallone took an active interest in the editing process* get the movie full of the shots that the directors are in love with, and then you see the movie, you figure out 'Is that shot really necessary, is it part of the story-telling or just a pretty shot?' We went through the movie and made sure that everything that was in this movie had a real definite purpose and it moved the story along, and I think that's really where we ended up."

The finished article emerged from the edit suite at the end of March, still with most of the visual effects shots to be added (the general impression and the pace of the piece was maintained by including the rough versions of these shots).

Lab Technician and Editorial Assistant Roy Berkowitz of the Mass.Illusion team, below, *manipulates one of the green-screen flying bike sequences filmed at Shepperton*

This was then taken to the composer to add the music. Originally Jerry Goldsmith was penciled in to write the score, but as the postproduction schedule got later and later he had to drop out to work on another movie he had agreed to do. Alan Silvestri was brought in as a replacement. His name may not be as familiar as Goldsmith's, but according to the *Dredd* production team who picked him, he's just as good.

"We have to play totally opposite to what is on the film," says Andy. "The film is based on a comic character, and I think the key is to have fun with this character, so the music should really play into that fun ... This is an action movie, but it's a roller-coaster ride so it needs to have a *Star Wars* score, which is basically also an imaginative kind of score, but it's got grandeur and it's large and harmonic and hummable."

Special effects have always played a major role in science fiction cinema, using the power of the imagination and technology to bring the as yet impossible to the screen. Every decade has brought its landmarks of the genre, beginning as early as 1926 when *Metropolis* created a vast gothic city of the future. In the thirties it was H.G. Wells' *Things To Come* and after a break for the Second World War,

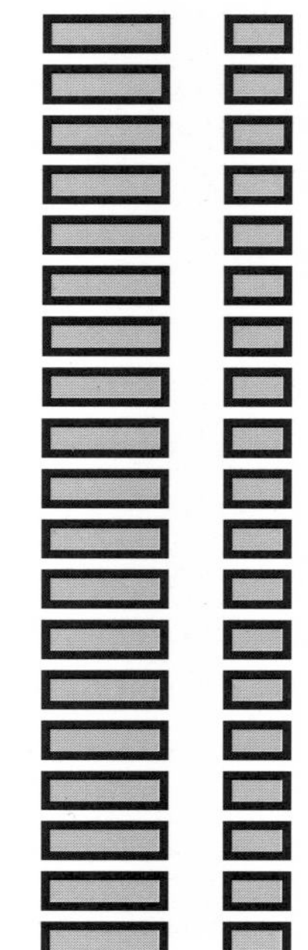

Joel Hynek, Visual Effects Supervisor, right

Visual Effects Producer Diane Pearlman, left

The model shuttle docking bay, below

the stunning *Forbidden Planet* arrived in 1956. What was supposed to be a cheap-effects film (because the monster is invisible!) turned out to be the most expensive, but impressive FX film of its time. It was never really surpassed until 1968 when *2001: A Space Odyssey* developed new techniques in making convincing spaceships. In the 1970s it was *Star Wars* that amazed audiences with startling space battles, and in the eighties *Blade Runner* produced a city of the future in all its run down, polluted, crowded and technology-ridden glory.

But as SF cinema moved into the nineties, it gave birth to the subgenre of the "effects film." Computers had already come into their own and were expanding the barriers daily with technology becoming more sophisticated and technicians more adept at using

Director of Photography Dave Stewart on the gantry stage, right

Detail of the top of the "Ernie Kovacs" building, below

it. Now it seems a new landmark film emerges every year. *Batman, Terminator II, Jurassic Park* and a host of others have arrived on each other's heels, each claiming to be bigger and better with state-of-the-art effects that put their predecessors to shame. The latest to follow this new trend is *Judge Dredd*.

Visual Effects Producer Diane Pearlman observes: "A project like this has enabled us to push the limits in order to get the shots ... You're trying to make a director's vision happen. The only limit tends to be time and money. But with enough of the right brains in the right place, you can really figure out something that's really new or some way of doing it. I think that we have a real hotbed of talent here in terms of solving those technical problems. Out of it comes something that's never been done before."

It's not that *Judge Dredd* is trying to be one-up on *Jurassic Park* or any other major special effects film,

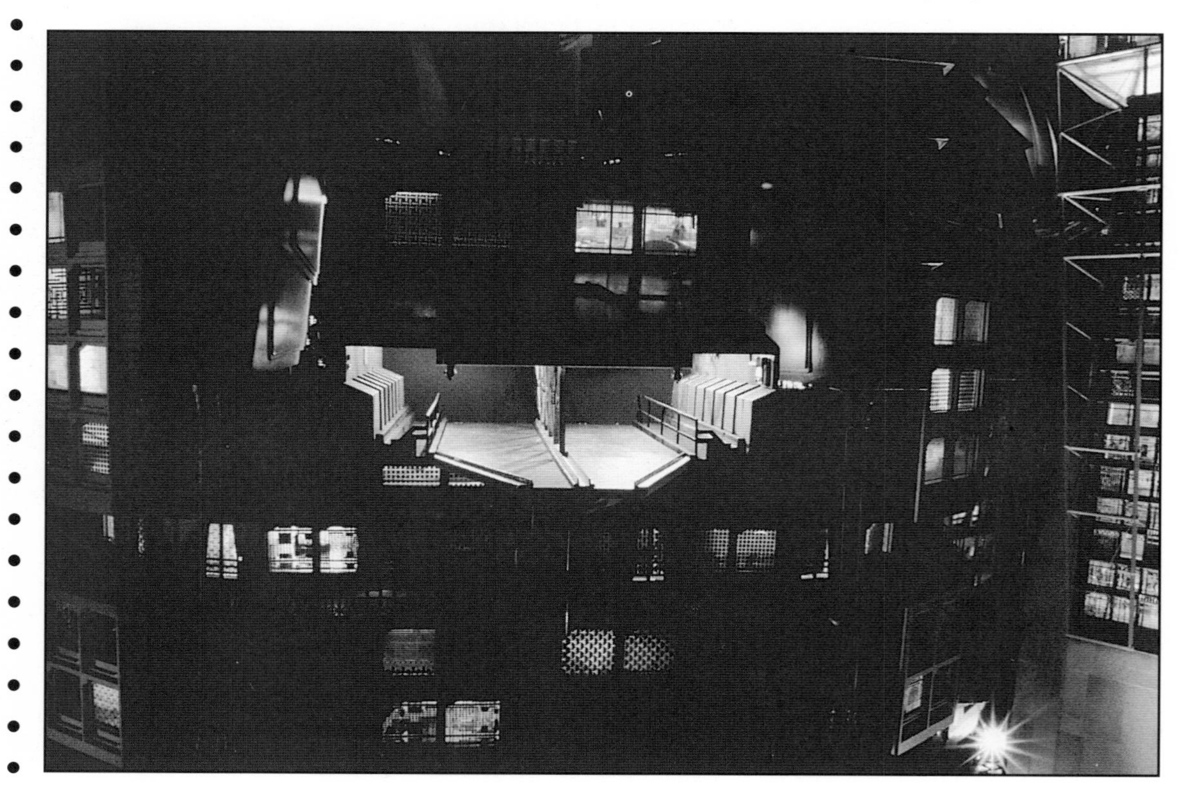

it's that technology is making it possible to do more spectacular things. More than ever, filmmakers are able to wonder 'What if ...?' and actually make it happen on screen. In *Judge Dredd*, co-writer William Wisher wondered 'What if the Lawmaster bikes could fly ...?' and the idea became so infectious that by the time it came to filming, the flying bike sequence had turned into an exciting three-minute chase produced entirely by the Visual Effects Department.

The state of technology has never been a major factor in turning the British cult comic character into a film, but it has made the result more spectacular. Had it been made in the early 1980s when Hollywood first acquired the rights, Mega-City One would have seemed a little more claustrophobic and its population would have been a little more ground-based. Ten years later and so many things have become possible, enabling the film to branch out in new and untried areas. *Judge Dredd* uses a combination of all the state-of-the-art effects that have emerged over the past few years, some of them so fresh that many people will probably think they are real.

That is when it works – when the vehicles on the road look as real as the vehicles in the sky, and when you don't notice that you are watching a digital Sylvester Stallone when just moments before it was the real person. Only afterwards is it rewarding to wonder how it was all done.

The workload on the Visual Effects Department kept increasing from the moment production on the film got underway. At first, the number of shots being talked about was 115. But with the lengthened flying bike chase, that escalated to 150. Steadily it went up to 160, then 170, and the number eventually ended up being around 180.

A huge team was assembled at Mass.Illusion in Lenox, Massachusetts, to work on the various stages of getting those shots together. The battle commander was Visual Effects Supervisor Joel Hynek and his woman on the field was Visual Effects Producer Diane Pearlman, who between them were

Mass.Illusion Director of Photography Dave Stewart, above right, *and Camera Operator David Hardberger go over the swimming pool shot for Fergie's taxi ride through Mega-City One*

Reference photos compiled by Mass.Illusion designers of an actual swimming pool for the Kachi Fitness Center (spotted by Fergie during his taxi ride), above and below

in charge of a previsualization department, a model building department, an art department, a computer graphics team, digital compositors and a camera department for filming the models.

The task was enormous. At the same time as work was ongoing on *Judge Dredd*, Mass.Illusion were working on two other films. In the case of *The Scarlet Letter*, they were involved in four shots, while *Die Hard With a Vengeance* only managed to notch up ten visual effects shots, despite trebling their original order. It puts the work required for *Judge Dredd* into perspective.

Cinergi's role was not only providing window dressing for the picture, it was creating sequences essential to the plot. Most of the time they were doing this on one side of the United States when the Director was in an editing room on the other side of the country, or in another country altogether. It was Joel Hynek's job to make sure what he was doing on the visual effects side matched up to what Danny Cannon was doing on the live-action side.

"A good visual effects supervisor will mold himself to and absorb the director's vision, his sense of style, and impart that vision and style to all the effects throughout the film. So that they all are of that style and blend together seamlessly and speak the same language," says Joel Hynek, a one-time optical printer who worked with *Dredd* Producer Beau Marks on *Predator*, and for Cinergi on the unmade film *Princess of Mars*.

One of the most vital steps in the process, according to Joel, is the previsualization. This,

essentially, is a rough animated video giving an idea of what the finished product will look like. It was useful in explaining the contents of an effects shot, especially when Danny Cannon was out of the country.

"A number of times on this show we've previsualized a move only to find out it's not what the director had in mind at all," says Joel. "And thank God we did, too, because then he was able to say 'That's not what I meant.' And I said, 'It's not?' And he said, 'No, no, no, this is what we want to do!' "

With the shots confirmed, the various departments were free to get started. The footage recorded in England was the raw material and included some specialized green screen shots that were overseen by Joel. Computer graphics and model shots were added on top of that and then digitally integrated together.

In the opening sequence of the shuttle approaching the wall of Mega-City, for example, the wall guard is the only "real" thing in the picture. The other main visual effects sequences for the film were when Fergie flies through Mega-City and sees an environment which was mostly created in the computer and on a model stage; the crash of the shuttle, which was compiled from elements filmed in Iceland and with models; Dredd's escape through Mega-City on the Lawmaster flying bike, which wouldn't have been possible without the input of Joel's team; and the final confrontation between Dredd and Rico on the Statue of Liberty, where the perilous drop beneath is all a cinematic trick.

Every wide shot of Mega City is a composite of sometimes more than half a dozen elements. One of the most ambitious shots to combine bits and pieces from different sources was the swimming pool.

As Fergie is flying over Mega-City, he spots the lofty heights of the richer sector and thinks his

Working on the gantry stage, above

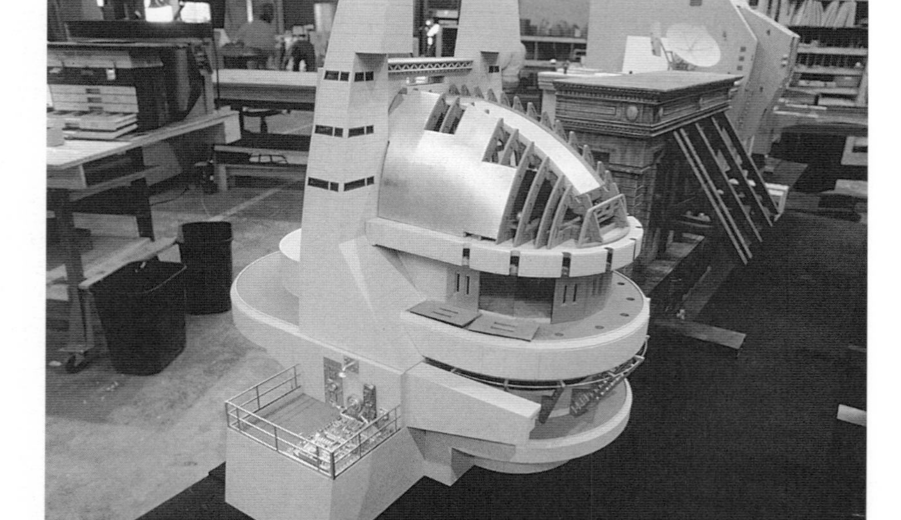

One of the Mega-City block buildings before completion in the model shop, right

Modelmaker Tony Whalen installs a sign on one of the add-on buildings, above

attractively named "Heavenly Haven" apartment block is bound to be nearby. What particularly catches his eye is the swimming pool on a building top adorned by beautiful women. This was a real-life swimming pool in Palm Springs which was filmed from overhead by a helicopter.

"It's hard to convince people that there are luxurious rich people someplace if you don't actually see them there," says Colin Green, who did the previsualization. "I did a series of animations, very simple, crude animations of what the motion path would be and what you would see of the pool and from what angles. That was approved by the director and we had that on video so that the helicopter pilot could see it and study it."

A lot of the people seen in that sequence are computer generated, people on top of surrounding buildings, and people guiding the taxi into land, but the women in the pool are genuine. They were filmed with a 24mm wide angle lens which ensured they look good, but is very unusual for an aerial shot. It meant the helicopter had to fly very close to the building. To help the pilot, the route was planned out meticulously beforehand with orange cones placed all over the Palm Springs hillside, forming a flight path.

"[The pilot] was able to have a real world reference to track," says Colin, "because we knew that it was very easy for the helicopter to shoot something that we couldn't match on our stage. We could get into trouble with having to blend in a pool that was gonna be really hard to match with our models."

In order to match up the shots, a special device was put on board the helicopter which monitored every move it made. A laser tracking device called a Sokkia, which is accurate to 20/1000th of an inch, recorded the flight path which had to be repeated exactly by the camera filming the miniature Mega-City buildings on the model stage.

"It was the first piece of equipment that we purchased on this particular job, it cost several tens of thousands of dollars," says Diane Pearlman, who watched over the visual effects budget. "The Sokkia allowed us to have points on the pool that we could measure from the helicopter and with

those exact measurements we're able to write software to match the movement of the camera in the helicopter to what our camera should move on the model stage."

"It's really one of the most difficult shots in the film," adds Colin Green. "That's because of the length of the shot and because the camera does almost a full 180° pan. The perspective on the pool is changing rather dramatically during the shot with no breaks, so we're not just adding subtleties to the camera or we're not just blending something that could almost be."

The film taken in Palm Springs was brought back to Mass.Illusion where the software to emulate the helicopter moves was written. It was then fed into the CGI (computer-generated imaging) equipment to create another rough video of the shot. This provided necessary information to the model builders for the miniature Mega-City. They used it to adjust the details to ensure the building and the swimming pool could be matted seamlessly together.

The Mega-City models were actually built in two sections. The first set of buildings for the foreground was one forty-eighth of the size it would have been in real life, reaching up to sixteen feet in height. But because the motion control camera has a limit of fourteen feet, the buildings were leant over at a 45 degree angle allowing the camera to film right up to the top with no problems. Another set of buildings was made at one-hundredth scale for the background and CGI was used for the buildings in the distance.

Probably the most important rule when building models which have to fool an audience is to avoid making them look like models. This was an issue addressed by Bob Taylor, Visual Effects Art Director at Mass.Illusion, who liaised with Nigel Phelps in England to make sure they got the look right. To make a futuristic movie they consulted a lot of books on modern architecture. There was one building in particular which demonstrated the design path to be avoided in *Judge Dredd*.

"The problem you have with the World Trade Center is it looks like two large Wheatie boxes!" says Bob. "As opposed to the Empire State Building, which looks huge, even though it's shorter, because of its use of detail and its own foreshortening as it works its way

Third stage set, above; *eighth-of-an-inch scale background buildings, tilted at an angle so the camera in the foreground can film them*

The Cinergi model shop, above. *Steel frames were needed to support the massive model buildings at an angle*

up. If that's the case and the windows on the World Trade Center look like a model even if they're not, how do we stop that from happening?"

When all was said and done, a hell of a lot of the construction work for the miniature buildings involved windows. It was one of the things Bob talked extensively to the Production Designer about as the drawings for the miniature Mega-City were being done.

"As you drew it you thought, 'Okay, so I'm starting to draw a window. Okay, now I've got a window, now what? Well, what kind of window is it? Well, it's futuristic. No, wait a minute! There's a guy across the street trying to blow a hole in my brains, so I've got to build a window that will prevent him from doing that.' So then I begin to get involved in armoring the windows and making them in such a way that you can't shoot at them."

All the buildings – windows included – came off the drawing board and were developed by CAD (computer-aided design). Bob was keen to get away from what he terms the "Captain Nemo effect" of lots of bolts and rivets. Instead he went for interesting shapes which became more sculptured as they went up the buildings and played with light and shadow to add depth. There are also a lot of "gizmos," like TV aerials and technically advanced transmitting devices, sticking out of the walls.

"But you can't just make it look cool, you've got to give it a reason to be there," says Bob. "Why is it there? You're not just building some damn thing! What's it for? What does it do? If you can tell me what it does, then you can build it. And if you can't, then don't, because I don't understand it."

The building chore was passed to Visual Effects Supervisor Eric Chamberlain, whose team had

Modelmaker Minamoto Yoshida touches up Lady Liberty, left

Laser-controlled smoke surrounds the model Mega-City and adds realistic atmosphere, below

Visual Effects Art Director Bob Taylor inspects window inserts, above, *and discusses a shot with Assistant Visual Effects Supervisor John Gaeta,* right

invaluable help from a laser cutter which allowed computer designs to be turned straight into highly detailed model kits that the builders then slotted together. "That machine was working twenty hours a day. We had two shifts on that machine. Without it this work would not have been possible," says Eric. The only inaccuracy in the final product was the variation in the thickness of the glue needed to stick the pieces together.

Eric's one big problem was how to get the largest

Kleiser-Walczak Lead Animator Eileen O'Neill working on the Hall of Justice, left

Working on the gantry stage, below

scale buildings to lean over at 45 degrees without falling over. It was a problem eventually solved by welding some sturdy steel frames to the bottom.

The models were filmed using a standard motion control camera, which is controlled by a computer. The camera's trajectory through the buildings is programmed in and can be repeated as many times as is necessary. And as with the swimming pool shot, it means the filming patterns for the foreground and background buildings match up.

One technical aspect of filming occasionally overlooked is the lighting. Models can only be

Above left to right: *Key Modelmaker Stephen Thurn, Model Shop Supervisor Eric Chamberlain, Key Modelmakers Daijiro Ban and David Merritt. The miniature Statue of Liberty is in the background*

convincing if they are lit to be convincing. In the case of Mega-City, the effect was enhanced by a puff of smoke which was regulated by a laser which kept it at a constant thickness.

"Whenever you're shooting models you need to put smoke into the air to make it look like real air does in the big city," says Joel Hynek. "There's always dust and dirt in it and as you look off into the distance it smogs them out a bit, makes them darker. It's something you're not always aware of, but when you shoot models you have to put smoke in there to give it a miniaturized atmosphere so that the models look real."

Computer graphics were added on top of that. The most noticeable computer-generated element is the flying traffic. In the case of Fergie's flying taxi, it was based on the design of the road-going Land Rover which was modified in the computer to turn it into a flying version. Others came straight out of the imaginations of the designers, onto paper and then into the computer, where various things like shadows and reflections were added for realism.

"We're working very hard to make our flying ships very realistic," says Joel. "You have to think that they are ships made out of Earth materials, with normal textures, and the way they catch light has to be exactly the same as a real physical object, which you don't see that much of in CGI these days."

Part and parcel of injecting that realism into an electronically created image comes from studying the idiosyncrasies of life, like the unpredictability of turbulence or a dented bumper. And in the case of a film, studying how a camera captures real life. This was one aspect tackled by Jeff Kleiser, a partner in the computer animation company Kleiser-Walczak Construction Company.

"A lot of these vehicles and motorcycles have lights on the front and we're simulating what happens when you photograph bright lights," he says. "There's a glow around the light and there's also lens flare, which is light that bounces around in the lens elements on a camera. You get those little repeating purple pentagons and so forth. Those lens flares are things that most DPs [Directors of Photography] try to avoid and we're breaking our butts trying to create them! It's pretty strange. But it does make a big difference to your willingness to accept that this is an image photographed at one time, if you see those little flares."

Jeff has also created little computer-generated people who appear all over Mega-City. The "synthespians" as he calls them are on the tops of buildings, guiding Fergie's taxi into land, peering out of windows and waving at passing traffic.

"Just to give the model a sense of realism," he explains. "It can be the most perfect model ever and if everything is just static in there something just doesn't seem right. You need some traffic of some sort, flying traffic or ground traffic or people in windows. I'm sure you remember in *2001*, the shot of the spaceship, it's gorgeous and it's gorgeous precisely because they've matted a little tiny window in there and some people walking around. And

Painter Perry Hall airbrushes a model, above

Camera Operator David Hardberger with the computer-controlled camera on the gantry stage, left

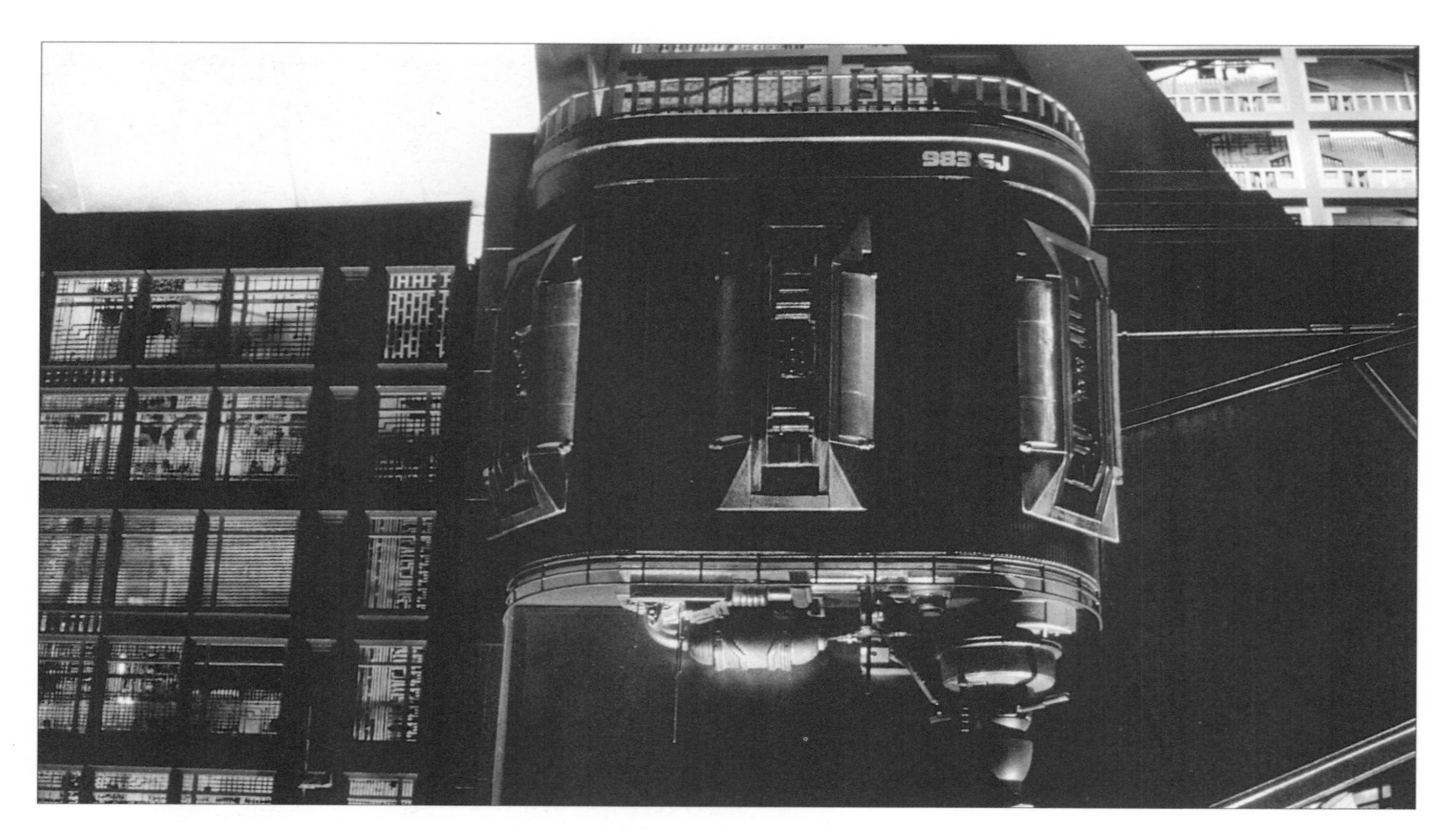

Detail on the top of the "Richard Boone" building in the Mega-City canyon set, above

Lab Supervisor and Projectionist Glenn Arnold, right

suddenly there's the scale, there's real people, without that little window it would have been 'Oh nice model.' Just the little sense of scale gave it everything."

The moment when the audience can really appreciate all the elements incorporated into Mega-City is in the shot unexcitedly titled "38/39." It is when Fergie finally walks onto the street and looks at the city ahead of him, moving his head from ground level right up into the sky.

In order to achieve the effect in one continuous shot, the life-size version of Mega-City had to match the model buildings. There is a point where Fergie's field of vision goes beyond the physical set built in England and has to join up with the tops of the buildings created at Mass.Illusion. Accurate measurements of the camera movement and the set were absolutely essential to make this possible. This shot was one of the reasons for buying the expensive Sokkia laser measuring tool.

"I think that back-lot set's probably the most surveyed set ever!" says Joel. "We accurately surveyed that set and then translated that survey in miniature to our set here. So that we could recreate the set in miniature, and then do the same

moves that the camera did in there in England."

"That's the type of shot that you probably couldn't have gotten very well twenty years ago," says Dave Stewart, who was in control of filming the models. "It would have been approached as maybe two, maybe three cuts if you wanted to go that far with it. You'd have basically static, locked-down cameras and then you could matte-paint the background or even match buildings and so forth. But the moving of the camera and changing perspective in adding buildings to the background, has been enhanced and actually made possible by things like motion control. And of course computers help in this a lot too."

The camera in England was mounted on an ascender rig, which began the shot at ground level and rose sixty feet up into the air. The record of the camera movement in England was transferred to the motion-control camera and the CGI equipment in the States and was then recreated for the many layers of effects that went on top of the live-action Mega-City. The final element to be put on was the sky. This wasn't the sky above the Shepperton back lot, but the sky in Lenox, Massachusetts. The information from the ascender rig was again used to repeat the original movement and get the right perspective on the sky. This was filmed in the last week of March 1995 when

Joel Hynek using the motion-control camera, above

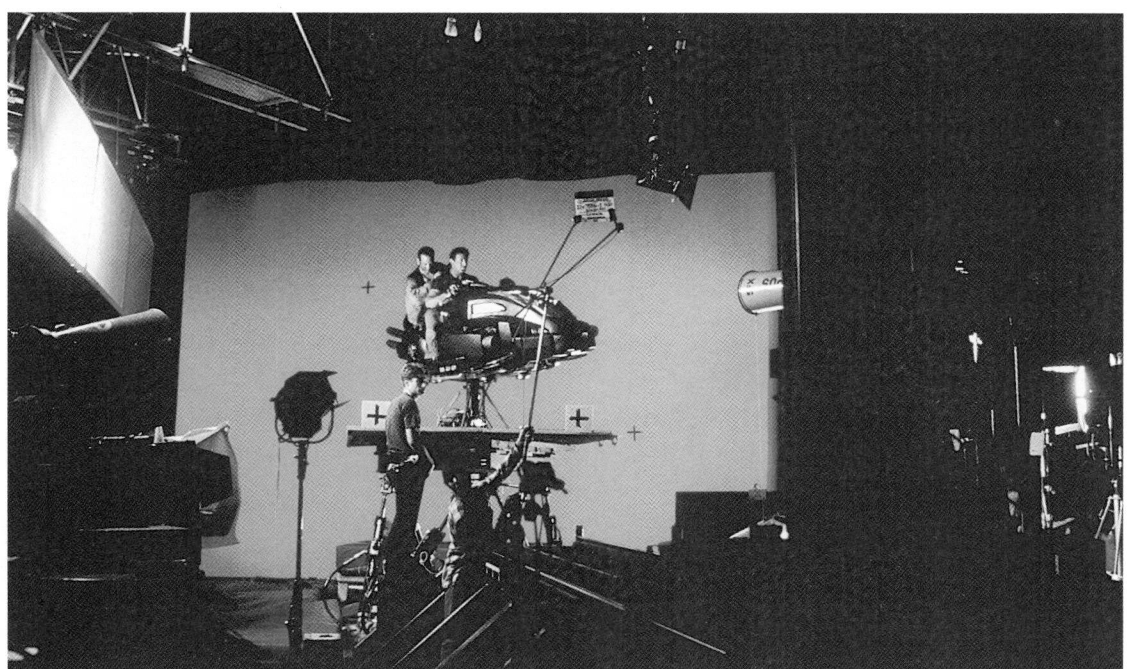

Shooting the green-screen footage at Shepperton for the aerial bike chase, left

Looking into the canyon set on the gantry stage; a great deal of time and effort would go into making Dredd "fly" through the city realistically

LEVEL
4

the visual effects team were keeping a constant eye on the weather forecast, waiting for the right mix of looming dark, dramatic clouds.

Without a doubt, the most impressive visual effects sequence in *Judge Dredd* is the Lawmaster flying bike chase. When FX Producer Diane Pearlman first took on the project it was a six-shot sequence where Dredd and Fergie blast out of the Hall of Justice, and begin plummeting to the ground until the last minute when the engine kicks in and they zoom back up into the sky. However, after Executive Producer Andy Vajna called for something with a little more"oomph," the chase became more like a futuristic version of *The French Connection* in the sky. Not unnaturally, Diane approached the new opportunity with a mixture of excitement and trepidation.

"We bit our nails off ... went away and drank a lot. No, I'm just kidding!" she jokes.

"It was always Joel's and my hope that we could have a sequence in the film that could stand alone, that we could make memorable, and I think this is the sequence we've been able to do it with. So it was scary in the beginning because it's virtually three minutes of visual effects that has to continue the storyline and continue the plot."

The brief was to create the most exciting chase possible with the available technology. Lots of ideas were put forward and were accepted and rejected as the sequence developed. Meeting after meeting and a string of video previsualisations saw the chase change right up until the last minute. The way in which the sequence took shape, allowed the visual effects team to put forward their own suggestions for stunts.

"You have the opportunity for a lot of the usual gags," says Supervisor Joel Hynek. "Yet it's in the future and it's in a different world and you're in the air, so you have to set up the gags differently and it's much harder to set them up. If you're doing a

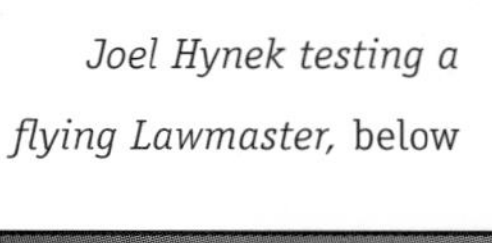

Visual Effects Supervisor Joel Hynek testing a flying Lawmaster, below

chase scene, everybody knows what an off ramp of a freeway is, and if you go the wrong way down it, everybody knows what can happen. But how do you do the same thing in an aerial bike chase? We've just come up with a few new things and one of them is the exact corollary to going down an off ramp the wrong way but in 3D ... It's been a real challenge to figure out how to do an interesting, involving chase in a future city. It's also been a real scheduling nightmare trying to figure out how to get it done in the time allotted because it just keeps getting bigger and bigger. But I guess that's a standard problem in most effects films."

The other question to address was how the sequence was going to be filmed. There were always three options: shooting the actors against a green screen and matting the background in afterwards; shooting model bikes and model actors in the miniature Mega-City; or generating everything on computer. The solution was always going to be a mixture of the three, it was just a matter of getting the right proportions of each.

"There was a great deal of discussion over what we were going to shoot of Sly [Dredd] and Rob [Fergie] green-screen, versus what we were going to make computer-generated," Diane Pearlman remembers. "We knew that there were only certain things we could do with Sly. We couldn't hang him upside down! We couldn't hang him at 45 degrees and make him go up a wall! We needed to work very closely with our computer-generated animators, Kleiser-Walczak, to make sure that they could make a bike that we were going to shoot green-screen and that they would be able to do the shots that we weren't allowed to do with Sly and Rob."

A green screen positioned behind an actor or an object allows a computer to put in a different background to the one that is actually in the studio. A computer can eliminate everything that is green in the shot and replace it with something else, whether that be a computer-generated city or another piece of live action footage. In the case of the Lawmaster chase, it gave the computer a clean image of Dredd, Fergie and the bike to

Above left to right: *Joel Hynek, Visual Effects Supervisor; Dave Stewart, Director of Photography; Byars Cole, First Assistant Director; David Merritt, Key Modelmaker and John Gaeta, Assistant Visual Effects Supervisor*

Set Modelmaker Nick Thielker puts finishing touches to the set using an overhead gantry rigging system dubbed "the magic carpet"

manipulate into the desired background.

Before the actors went in to film the green-screen scenes, around seventy shots were put down roughly on video within the space of two weeks to previsualize the sequence. It included all of the actors' movements, the positions of the bikes in relation to the background and foreground, and the camera moves.

"It was absolutely essential that all this was put in the computer," says Jeff Kleiser. "You have a mock-up of the motorcycle, a mock-up of the camera, and the background so 'Okay, we're going around like this,' look at it, cut all of these things together to see how the camera angles, how they cut, what the timing is. These are all aesthetic decisions that you can't make without some form of previsualization.

"In many cases the camera motions that we had programmed were sent down to the stage and they just took our data and the camera motion was plugged in. And in other instances they would program a certain move on the stage and send the data back up to us. We'd all be working with the same camera motion so we could choreograph our vehicles with precision so they would all look like they were in the same space, photographed from this one point of view ... If we hadn't done that, they would be down there on stage scratching their heads trying to figure out where to move the camera and the film would never get done!"

Not only did all the many elements have to fit together, the bikes had to look realistic, a problem which became more crucial as the Lawmasters' on-screen time lengthened. "We studied a lot of aeroplane tapes and motorcycle tapes and chase tapes and basically got our hands on all types of reference," says Diane. "How would a bike fly? What would that look like? How would that be real? ... It couldn't float, it couldn't be delicate, it had to be something that had some velocity to it. So there was all kinds of talk about what would that look like, would it slide, how does it go up the wall of the building? It slides right to left, but it can't go up and down like it's going up a hill. So there was a lot of testing in that regard."

The result of the tests was to put the bikes on top of a motion base which was programmed to simulate movements in the air. The fact that everything had been worked out beforehand meant it was possible to shoot around three shots a day, with little adjustments for the unexpected. The most difficult thing on the day turned out to be the lighting, which had to exactly match the part of Mega-City Dredd, Fergie and the Judge Hunters were flying through.

The traditional way to convince people the bikes are actually flying would be to intercut close-ups of the actors with model shots. Even in a film as recent and accomplished as *Raiders of the Lost Ark*, it is possible to spot which is the real Harrison Ford and which is the dummy. *Judge Dredd* didn't ignore this technique, but took it to the next dimension by introducing so-called "synthespians" which were digital stunt doubles of Sylvester Stallone and Rob Schneider made to step in when the moves got too dangerous.

Kleiser-Walczak recreated Stallone's face by taking two laser cyber scans. One laser measured the shape of his head and the other recorded the colours. When

Denny McHugh, Key Gaffer, adjusts lighting aspects on the gantry stage, below

combined, they produced an exact digital picture of Stallone's head inside the computer. The scanner wasn't big enough to do an entire body, and so the next step was for Diana Walczak to sculpt model bodies in a motorcycle-riding position.

"She made these sculptures which included the folds of the fabric and so forth," says her business partner Jeff Kleiser. "This is very difficult for a computer to do, a shirt with a sleeve with wrinkles

Visual Effects Editor Jennifer Wollan, above

Modelmaker Billy Messina puts finishing touches to a sign, right

in it, it's not obvious to a computer the physics that makes folds. So Diana can sculpt it, she can look at it and make it, then paint it to extenuate the highlights and the dark. And then this sculpture is scanned on the same device that we used to scan Stallone's head. Then we take off those pieces and put them back together and we have a realistic-looking body with Stallone's head on it."

So far so good, but as soon as this computer model of a human being starts to move, it becomes obvious it isn't real.

"The human eye is very sensitive to whether it's looking at something that is a real person or something that's a puppet. So we have a device that allows us to capture human motion, it's called 'a flock of birds.' It consists of a bunch of sensors that is attached to a person's body, to the shoulder, the elbow, the wrist, the legs and so forth. These sensors send their position in space to the computer sixty times per second."

By putting a real human being on a motorcycle, it's possible for the computer to register and recreate realistic movements. "We looked around in our company to find out whose body proportions matched Stallone's the closest and it turns out that it's my partner Diana!" says Jeff. "She's got the appropriate proportions. Not size, but proportions to match him. That's what we're interested in." Diana was put on a gimbal-mounted motorbike while a video of the chase sequence was played in front of her. The movements were then recreated with the help of six computer graphics students from a nearby college.

"They were holding this motorcycle, rocking it as they watched the playback on the monitor. So they would match the rotation of what Dredd is supposed to be doing. And Diana's watching too, she's leaning into the corners, capturing this motion for these sensors. So then we applied this motion to our sculpted digitized objects and we get a lifelike final result. We're hoping the shots where we're working with synthetic stunt doubles will be indistinguishable from the tighter shots. That's the whole idea. So you

Painter Perry Hall at work, left; below, *a detail of the same building*

won't be able to see this effect, it will just look like Stallone was somehow flying on a motorcycle down immense canyons."

All this ground-breaking technology hasn't entirely pushed model work out of the picture. All the spectacular Lawmaster crashes are actually models that were physically blown up on the model stage using pyrotechnics. Pyros were also used to create flak flying off the bikes when they are hit by gunfire or have a close shave with a building or another bike. The most spectacular crash is where the Judge Hunters fly into a huge holographic sign. It's become known as the "bug-zapper" sign, the physics of which are likely to get overshadowed by the excitement of the chase.

"It's a huge plasma ionization sign," explains Joel Hynek. "The idea is that air is being ionized in different colors – very much like a spark is blue – they've figured out how to ionize the air different colors and that creates a holographic image out of the air. It's very bright and very big and also very dangerous. The sign is opening and closing and Dredd times his approach ... but the third [Judge Hunter bike] which is disabled, can't time its approach and goes into the sign while it's on – just like a bug getting fried in a bug zapper."

This sequence is mostly created using model bikes flying through the miniature Mega-City, with close-ups of Dredd and Fergie cut in. The distant and medium-sized shots are computer-generated, as is the sign itself.

The speed of the chase is exhilarating. There are two almost invisible elements that help to create this illusion of fast movement. The first is motion blur. If you look at a single frame of a film of, say, a racing car going past, it will be blurred. Compare that with animation, which is usually made up of a series of sharp pictures. When they are joined together in a film they create the illusion of movement, but it just doesn't compare to the film of the racing car, partly because the blur is missing. In order to make *Judge Dredd* realistic, a smudge was artificially added by the computer.

"It turns out to be quite costly computing wise to

calculate what an image would look like during a fiftieth of a second," explains computer animator Jeff Kleiser. "If it's moving fast you have to blur the image digitally. For each frame you have to render ten or twenty frames and meld them in together to make an appropriately blurred image. The subtlety of it if you watch a blurred and a non-blurred image,

it's like night and day – one looks real, the other one looks like it's strobing."

Another trick is to add camera shake. The idea behind this is to simulate the effect that would be achieved if the camera was filming the sequence from another flying Lawmaster, instead of being mounted on a sturdy rig in the studio.

"We've come up with some methods for inducing a realistic shake," says Digital VFX Supervisor Serge Sretschinsky, who did the digital compositing for the movie. "It's funny because you don't actually control this entirely by hand. It's not like I take my hand and record a shakiness. We have all these mathematical tools and we'll generate some noise and then we'll take the noise and we'll smooth it out a little bit so that you get a shaking of a given frequency, but there's a bit of uncertainty to it because it starts out as noise."

Serge's job was essentially to pull all the various elements together for each shot. That's not an easy

task with some of the complex images being generated for *Judge Dredd*. "Some of them are up to a hundred megabytes a piece," says Serge. "A hundred megabytes is typically the size of a disk that you have on a personal computer and we have to deal with twenty-four frames a second and possibly several layers of that, so disk storage becomes very important.

"It's more than just putting one thing on top of another," he continues. "For example, they might shoot something like a miniature on a stage and there'll be a light beam that's going through the scene. Between the miniatures there's black and you might put some more distant miniatures or some other image behind that, but you want to capture some of that light coming across there ... Very early on in the film, these things were kicked around and then you go and you make all the pieces. When you get to us you decide where all the pieces belong and then you try to put them together. A lot of it is serendipity, some of the things that people thought

we might need ended up not being used, but other opportunities present themselves."

The end of the film has one last visual effects shot as Dredd and Rico fight in the Statue of Liberty and dangle perilously close to the edge. One of the

Key Modelmaker Daijiro Ban sculpted Liberty from clay, opposite left

Photos of the life-sized head filmed in England attached to the model in America, above

Close-up of the Statue of Liberty, left

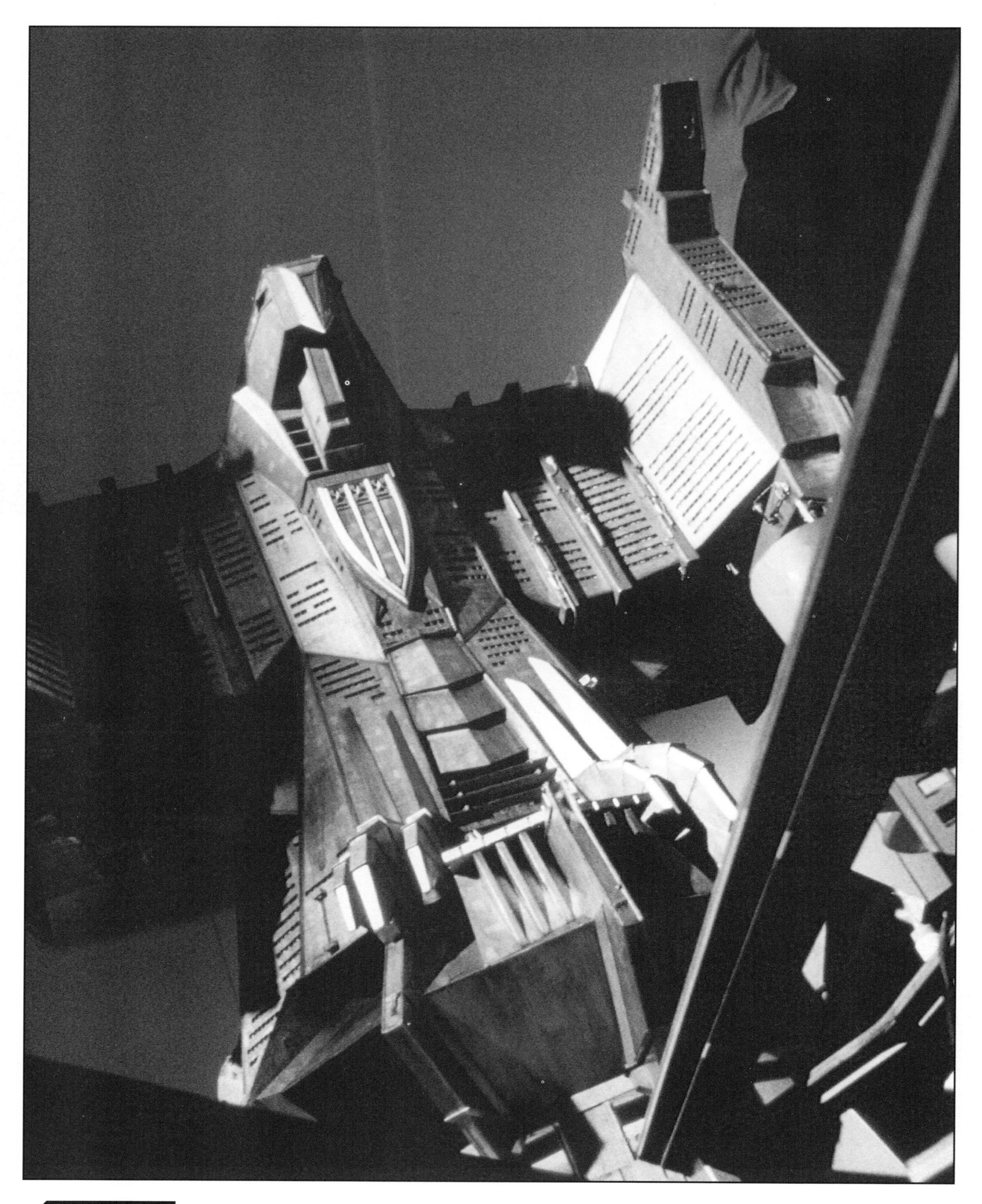

things to look out for is the rain, some of which was real water created on the sound stage at Shepperton, while the rest was computer-generated. The statue itself is one of Joel Hynek's favorite models, although at six feet high it's a little big to take home as a souvenir. "A lovely Statue of Liberty," the Visual Effects Supervisor enthuses. "Beautiful. The best Statue of Liberty model I've ever seen ... It's a motion controlled shot that starts tight on the head and pulls back. We did the live-action portion of that in England and then did the Statue of Liberty here in Lenox."

The scene brings to an end a visual feast that has become a trademark for blockbuster science fiction films. But as Joel Hynek so eloquently puts it, "There's always the question of how deftly you handle the whole visual effects pot, so that the soup that comes out is tasty and well suited for the meal."

At the time of writing, the soup is turning out just fine and hopes are high that the rest of the meal will go down well. So far there has been little time for digesting the contents of *Judge Dredd*, but there is already talk of a second helping.

"Let's get through this one and then we'll talk about the future of *Dredd*," says Executive Producer Andy Vajna cautiously. "Hopefully we'll be able to make several sequels and, I think, explore Mega-City and that sort of civilization. Those characters will be a lot of fun."

The Hall of Justice model, opposite, *dominates the Mega-City skyline*

Liberty, on the other hand, is decrepit and insignificant in comparison, left

STORYBOARDS DRAWING THE FUTURE

When a director walks onto a set in the morning he has to have his day's work planned out ahead. Very few people can work inspirationally on the set, and those that claim to, often upset the crew by being unprepared or upset the moneymen by spending hours of valuable filming time working out the shots. Some directors, like Alfred Hitchcock, were known to hold the entire visual contents of the film in their heads, while most rely on the preferred method of a storyboard.

In the case of *Judge Dredd*, Danny Cannon was closely involved with the storyboarding process, and even drew some of it himself. "He used to supply me with rough sketches, scribbles and things that I interpreted," recalls English storyboard artist John Greaves. "He'd have an action sequence followed by another action sequence and I'd put the bits in between that were needed."

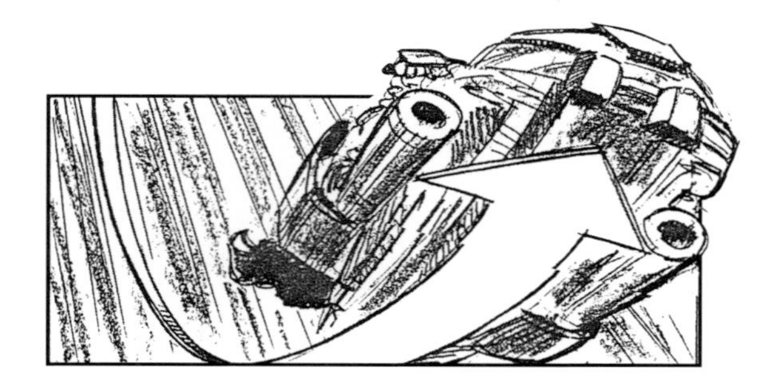

A storyboard provides a visual overview of a movie, a blueprint of all the elements that will be included in the final shot. As such it can help the director envisage the finished product and guide other members of the film crew in their preparations for a day's shooting. For *Judge Dredd* the storyboards for crucial scenes were photocopied and sent out to key people, while other copies were pinned up on a board on the set for easy reference.

Visual Effects Art Director Bob Taylor consults some storyboard artwork, below

Action sequences were drawn in detail. A line in a script can only hint at action, while a picture can visualize the moment simply and succinctly. And when it came to the effects shots, storyboards were essential. Very often a major element in a scene, like a flying vehicle, was just a glint in a computer animator's eye when the live action filming was taking place. The storyboard enabled everyone to see at a glance what would be added afterwards, and was necessary to set up the camera angle to ensure enough room was left in the frame for the computer-generated object.

The most closely and repeatedly drawn section of the film was the Lawmaster flying bike chase. Danny Cannon kept a constant eye on the development of this sequence by being in the office next door to the storyboard artist. "He'd sort of bring me piles of drawings and things and then I'd work on them and then we'd go through them and then paste them up on the wall," says John Greaves. "An action sequence like with flying motorbikes was pasted all the way round the room. I forget how many drawings there were, but there were a lot. And then we kept on adding bits in and taking bits out to make it more exciting."

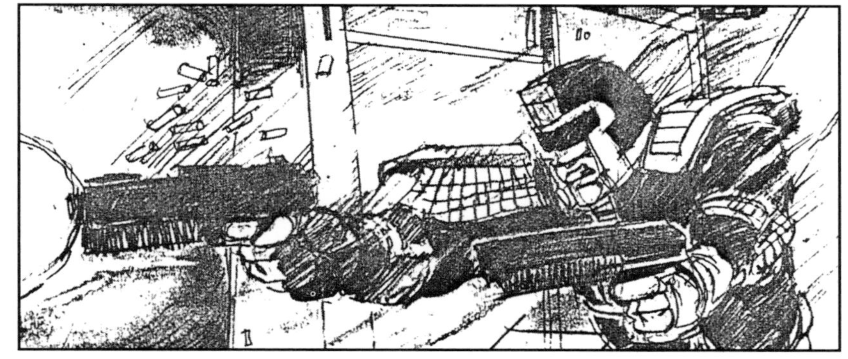

No one can deny the importance of getting a script right before filming. Films which have launched into production without a finished script have usually fought a losing battle to keep a coherent thread running through them. But film is also a visual medium, and in the case of a futuristic action movie like *Judge Dredd*, this is the dominant force. A production designer can bring a style, an architecture and a look to the future, but only a storyboard can bridge the gap between script and design.

The original drawings were done by Matthew Codd with a little help from Kevin Walker during preproduction in Los Angeles. Changes in the story were being made constantly up until the time of production, which meant almost half of it had to be redrawn in Britain. What follows is a collection of some of the storyboards drawn by Robbie Consing, John Greaves, Dennis Rich and Danny Cannon.

BLOCK WAR

Storyboards by Robbie Consing

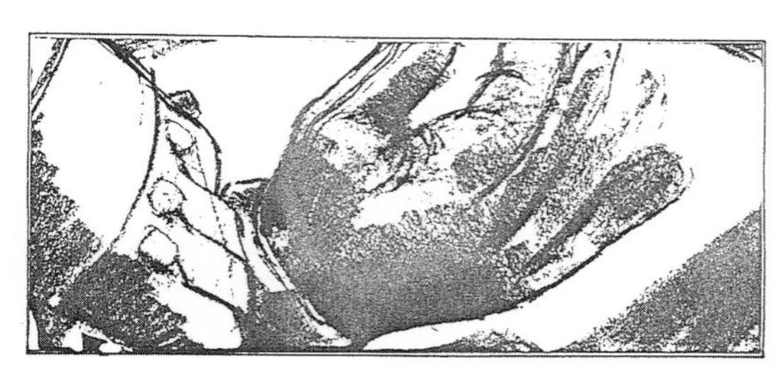

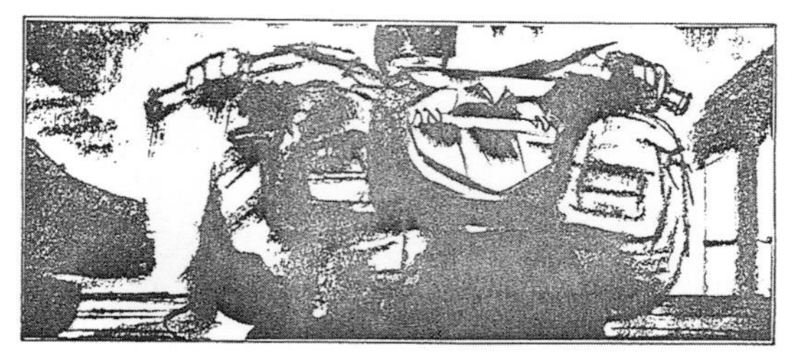

BLOCK WAR

by Robbie Consing

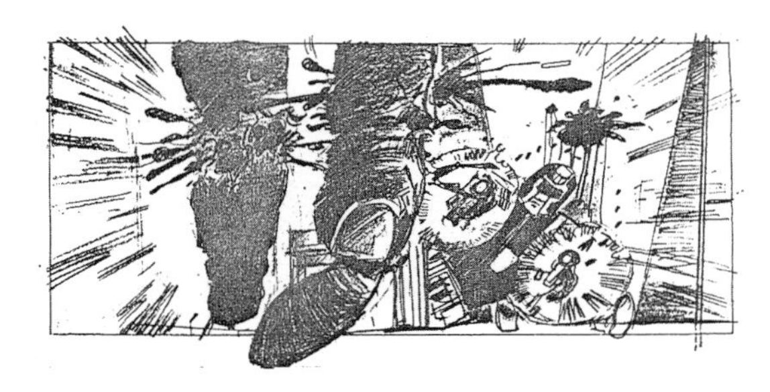

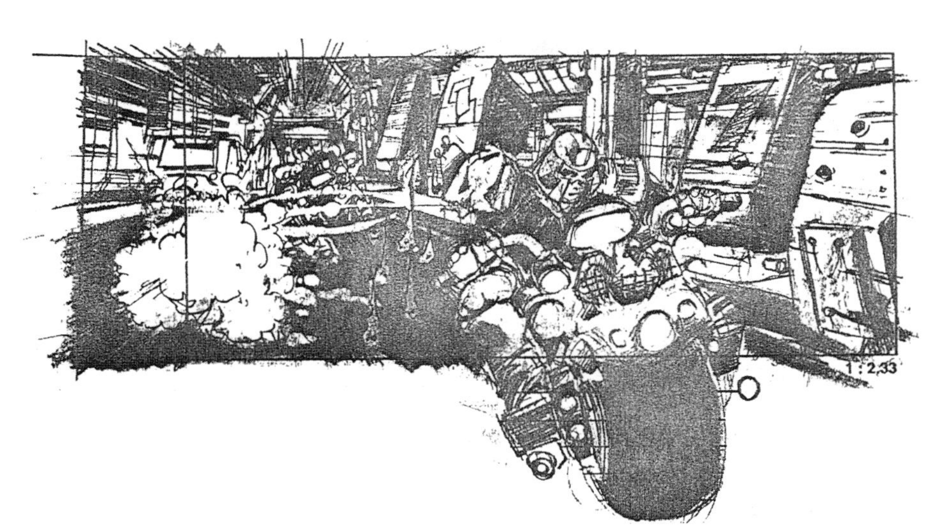

ASPEN PRISON

Storyboards by Robbie Consing

RICO ESCAPES

Storyboards by Robbie Consing

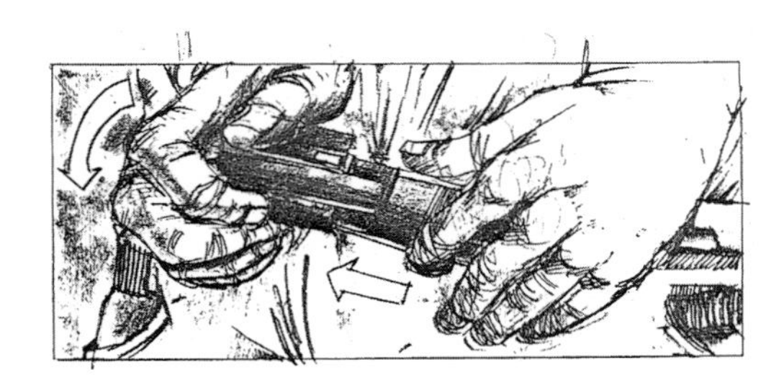

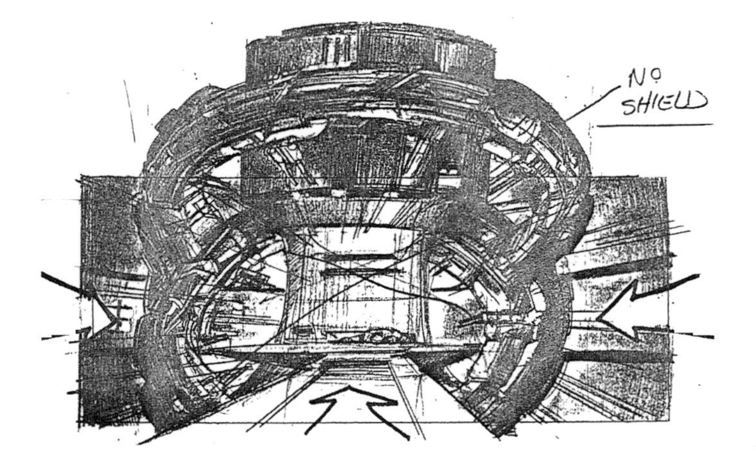

RED LIGHT DISTRICT

Storyboards by Robbie Consing

DREDD ON PATROL

Storyboards by John Greaves

ASPEN SHUTTLE IN THE CURSED EARTH

Storyboards by John Greaves

ASPEN SHUTTLE CRASH IN THE CURSED EARTH

by John Greaves

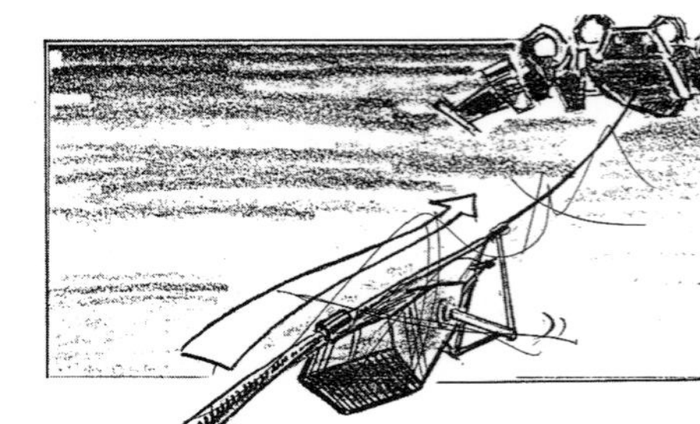

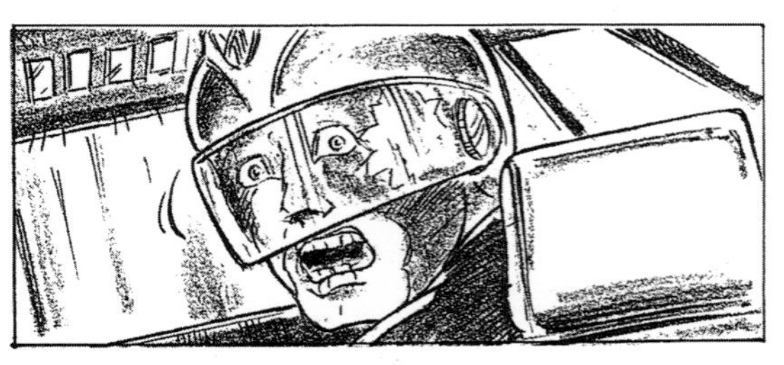

ANGEL GANG AND JUDGE HUNTERS IN THE CURSED EARTH

Storyboards by John Greaves

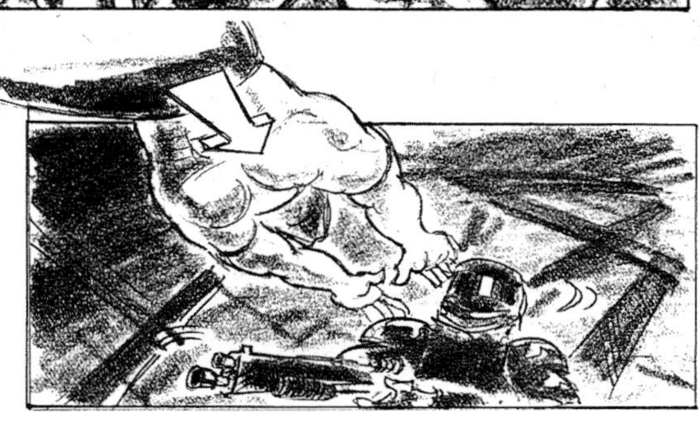

ANGEL GANG AND JUDGE HUNTERS

by John Greaves

HERSHEY ON PATROL

Storyboards by Dennis Rich

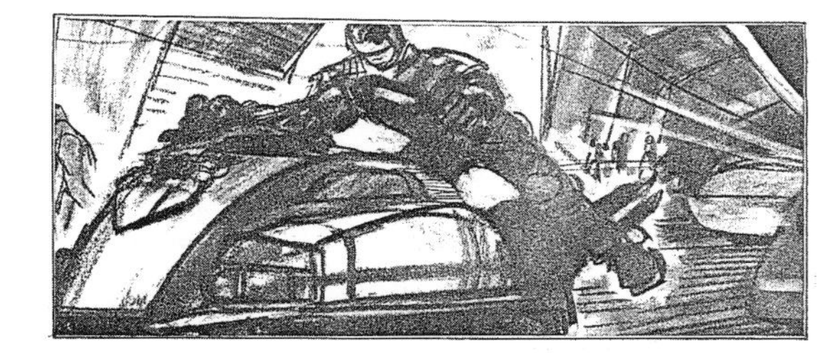

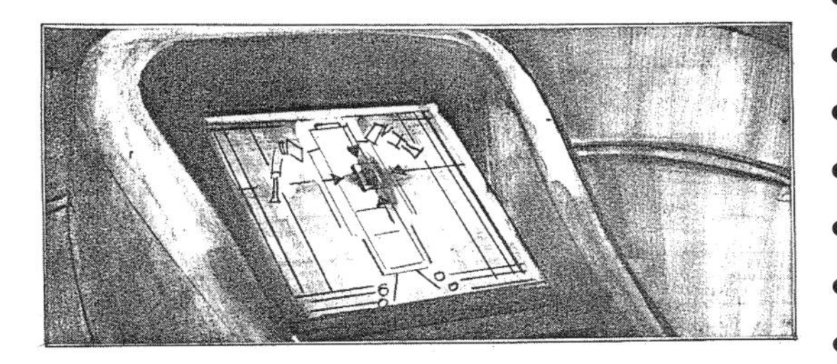

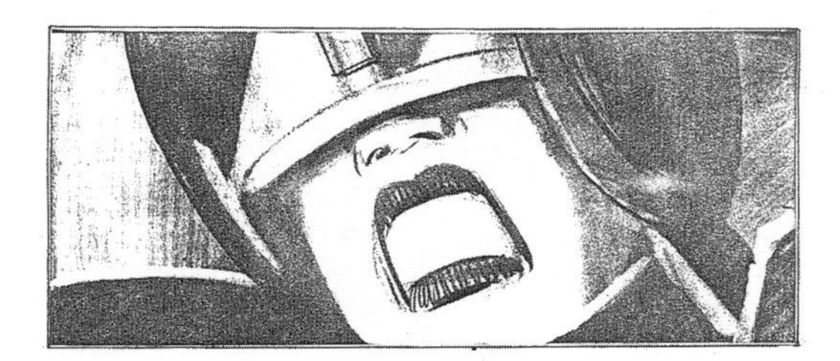

DREDD ESCAPES

Storyboards by John Greaves and Robbie Consing

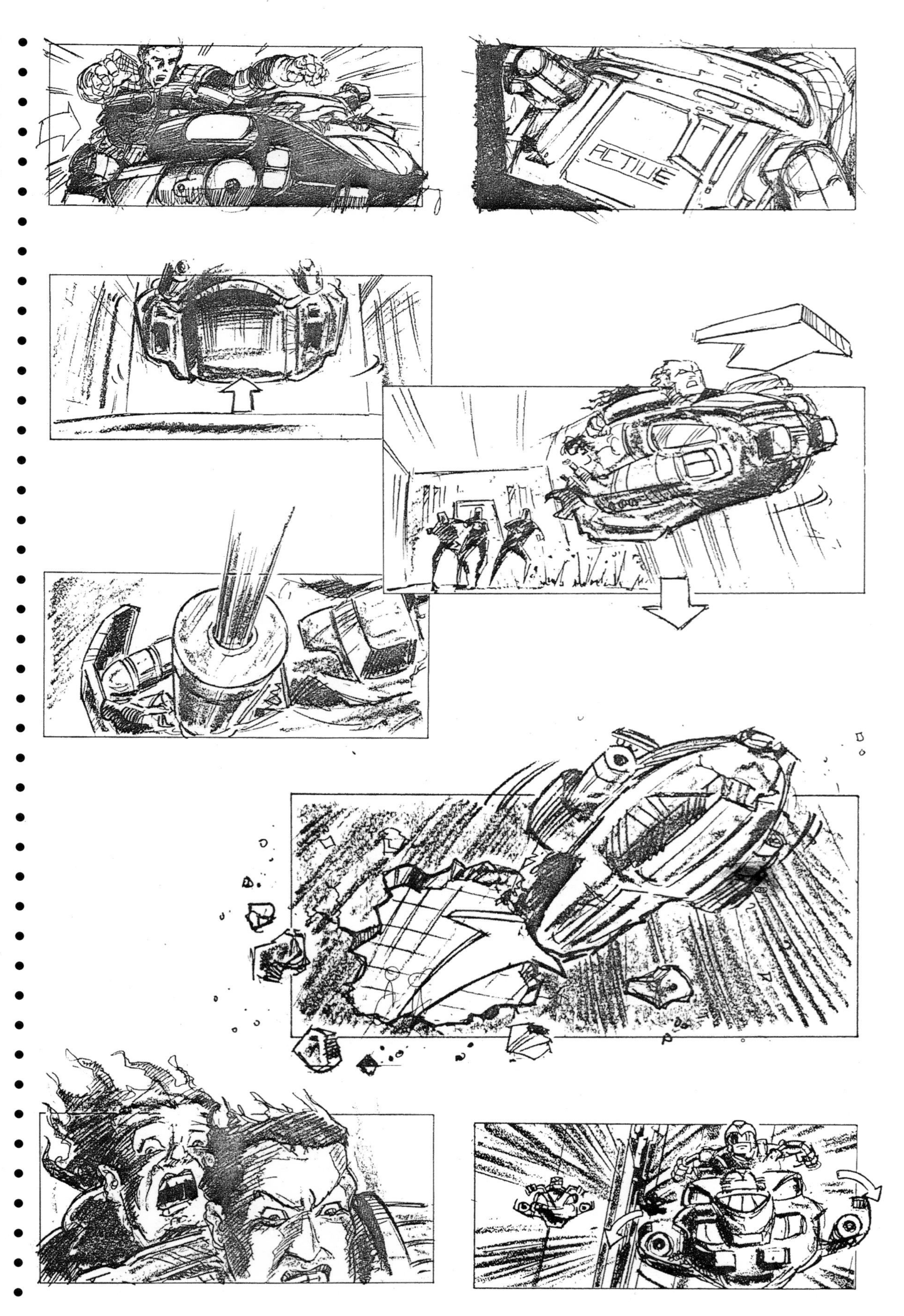

DREDD ESCAPES

by John Greaves and Robbie Consing

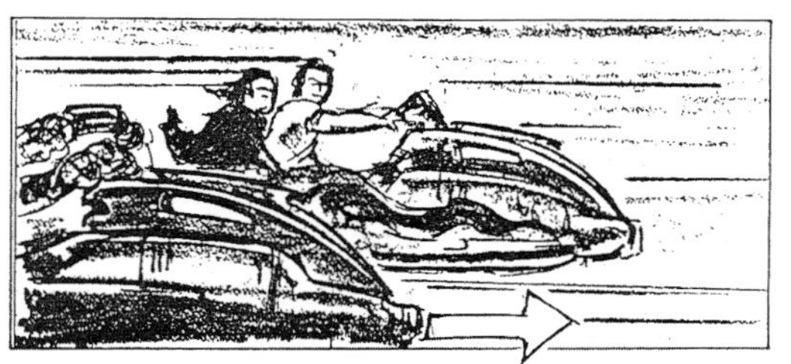

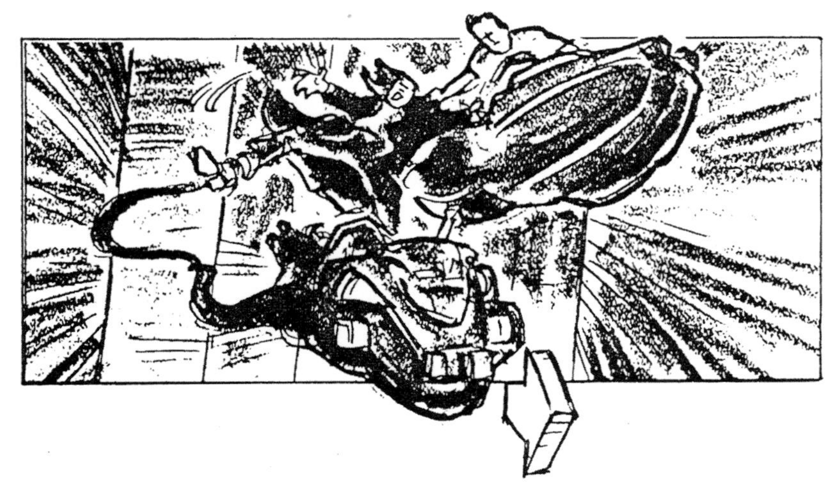

HERSHEY'S APARTMENT

Storyboards by John Greaves

HERSHEY'S APARTMENT

by John Greaves

JANUS LAB

Storyboards by Robbie Consing and John Greaves

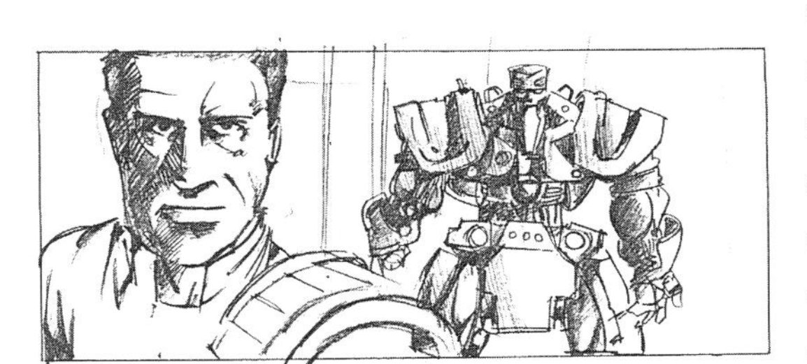

JANUS LAB

Storyboards by John Greaves

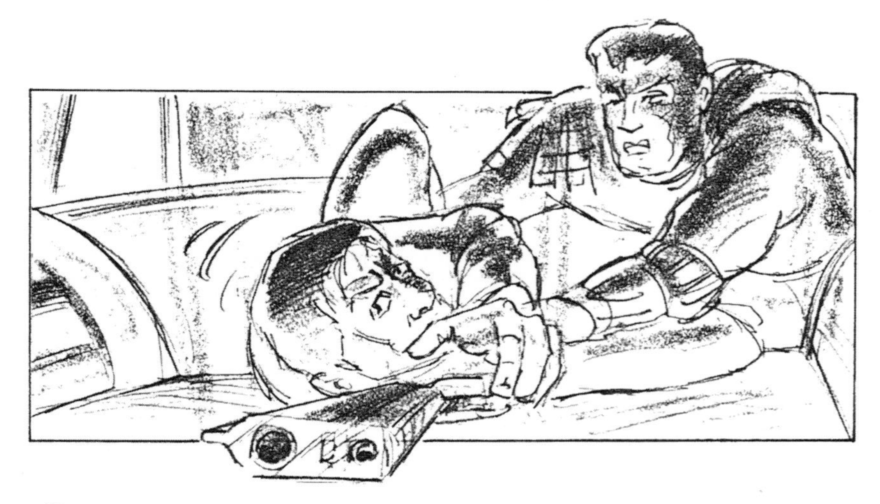

STATUE OF LIBERTY

Storyboards by John Greaves

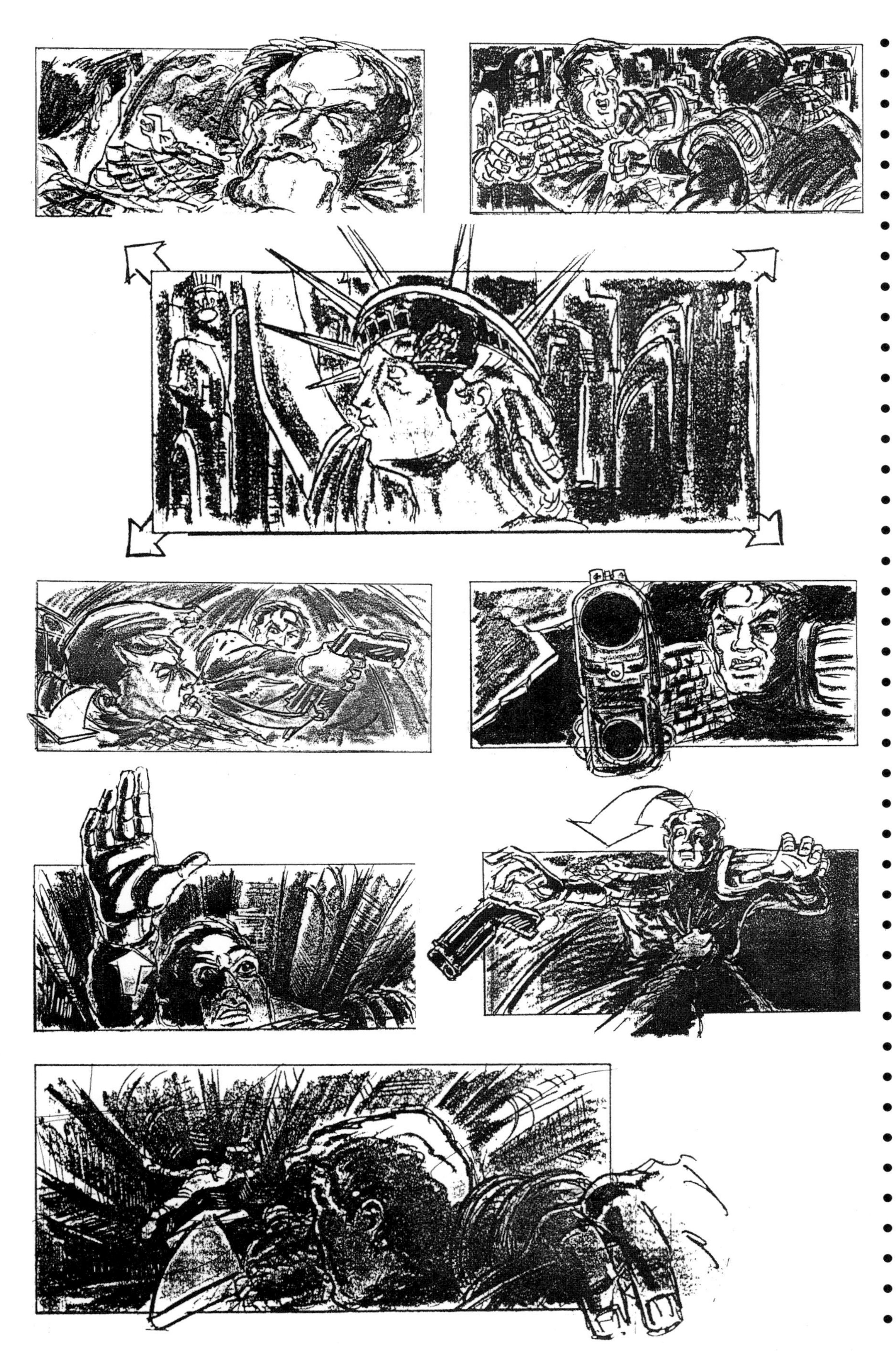

A JUDGE AGAIN

Storyboards by Dennis Rich

DREDD VERSUS RICO – AN ALTERNATIVE ENDING

Danny Cannon sketched this version in Fall 1993

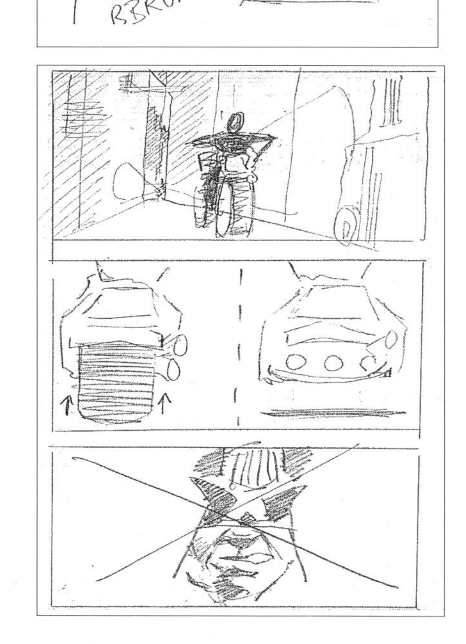

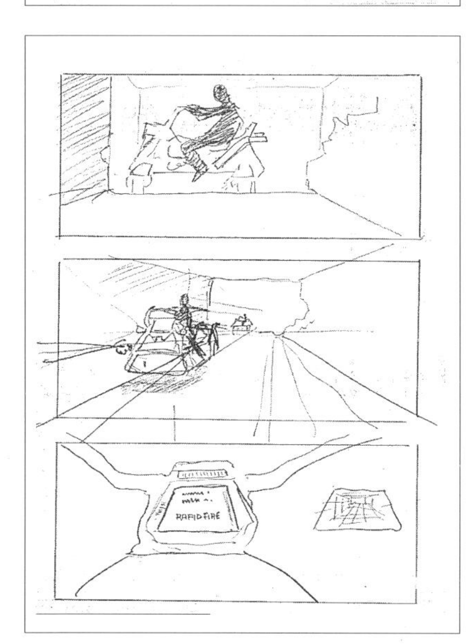

DREDD VERSUS RICO — AN ALTERNATIVE ENDING

by Danny Cannon

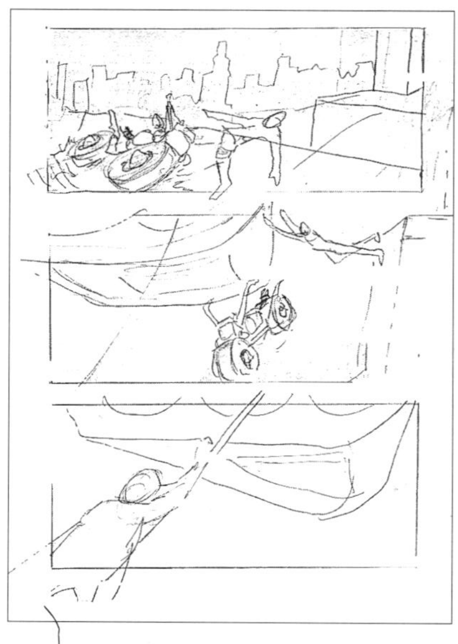

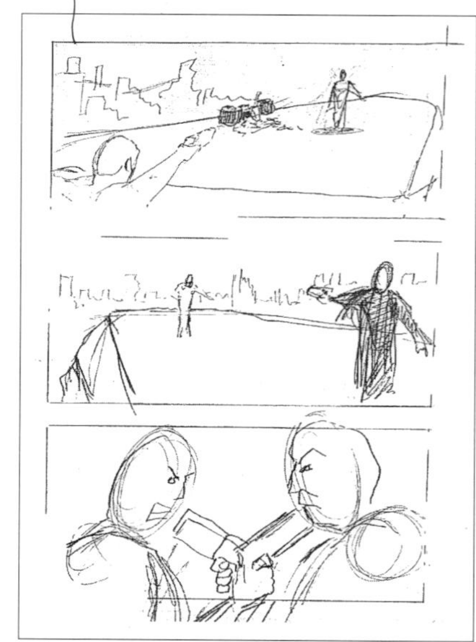

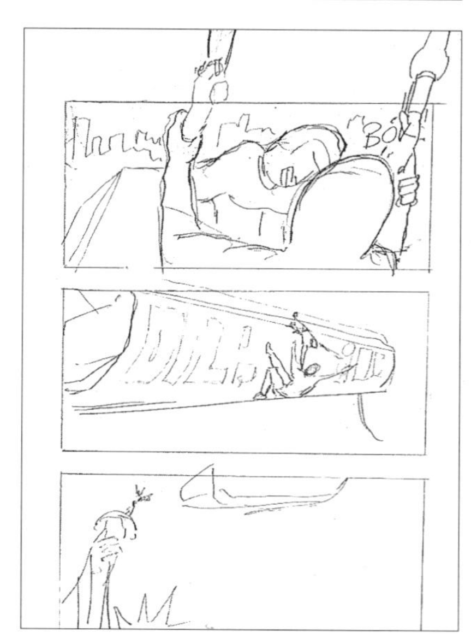

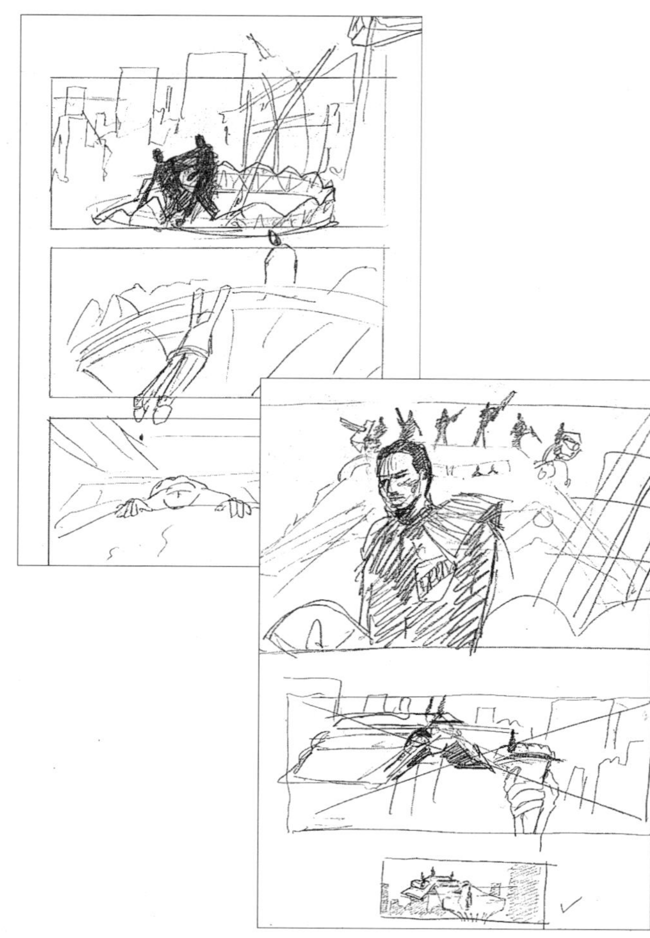

DREDD VERSUS RICO – ANOTHER ALTERNATIVE ENDING

This time sketched by Robbie Consing

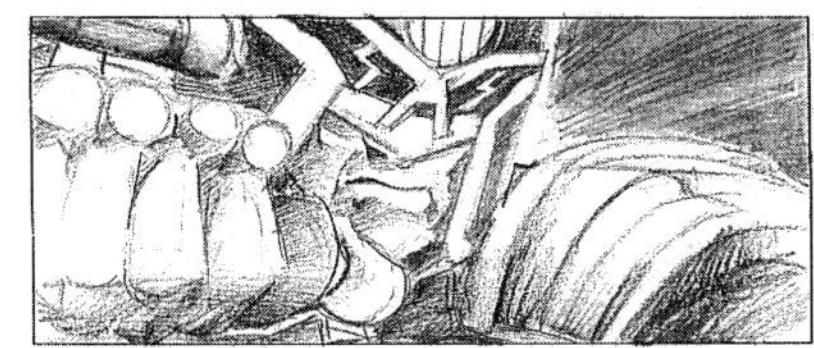

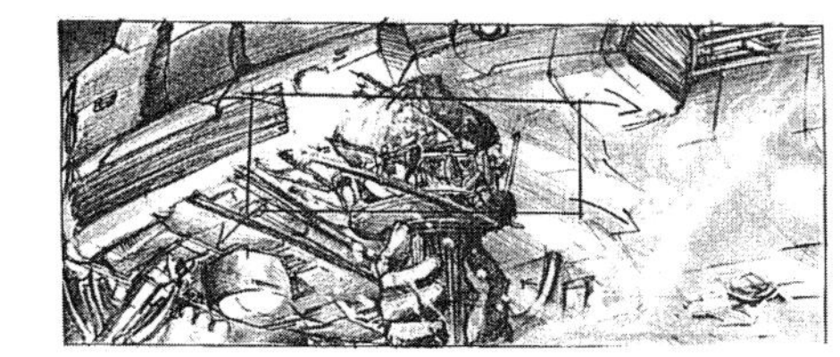

DREDD VERSUS RICO – AN OTHER ALTERNATIVE ENDING

by Robbie Consing

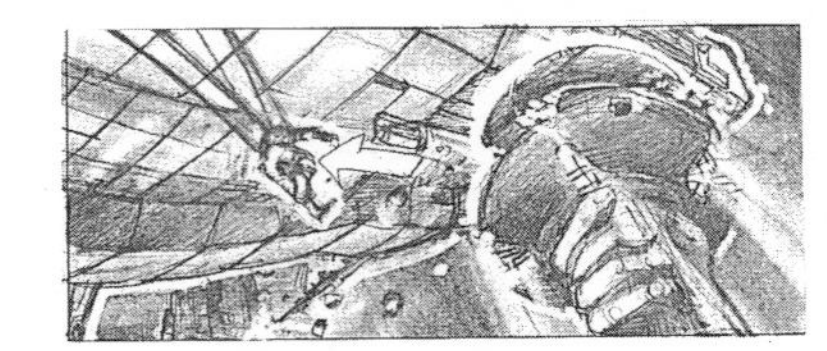

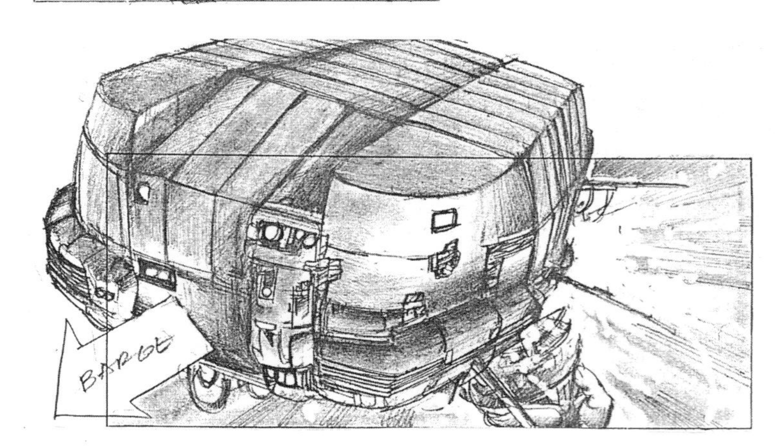

TEASER

TRAILER

Danny Cannon's concept, sketched Fall 1993 but never made

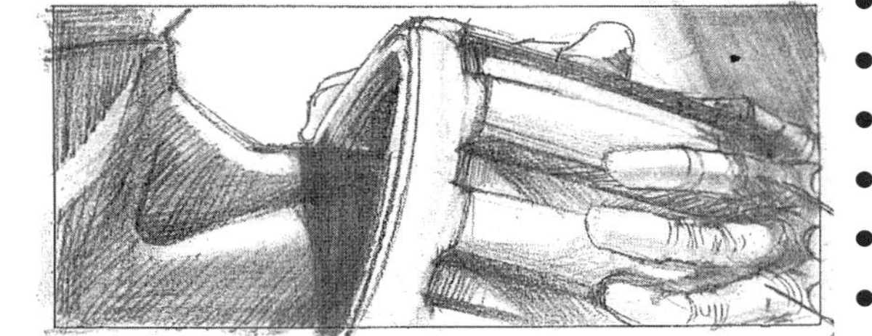

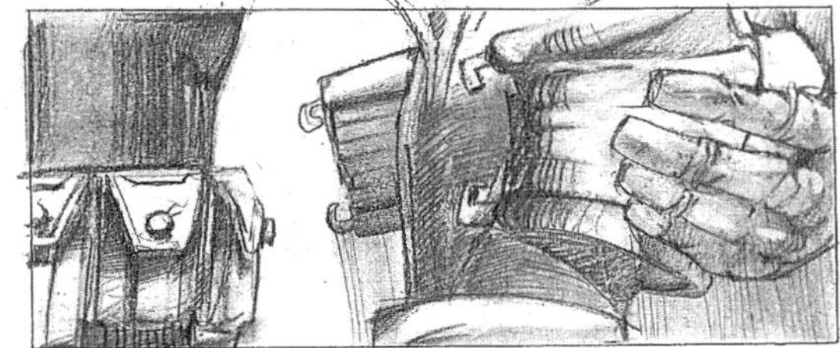

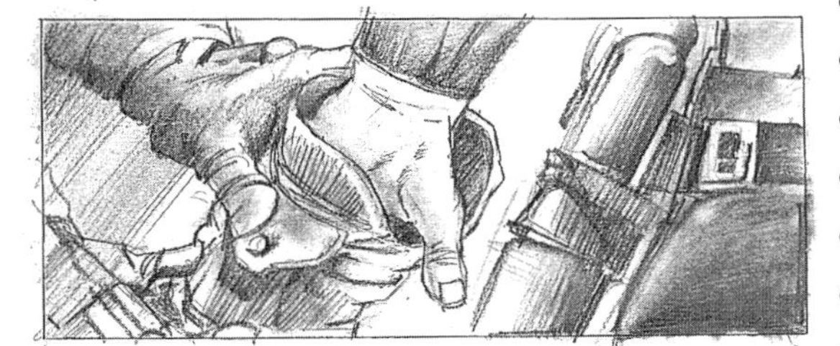

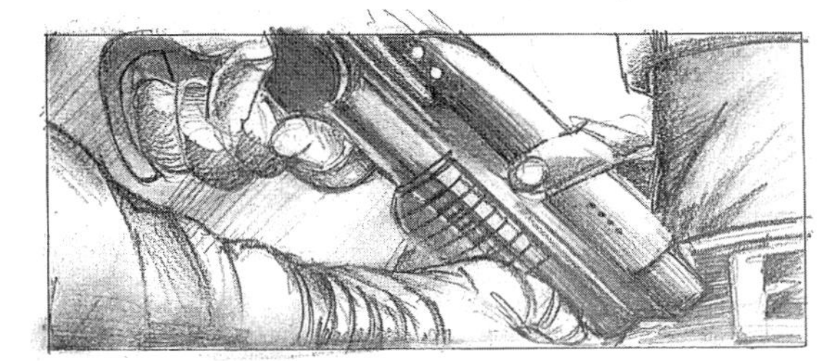

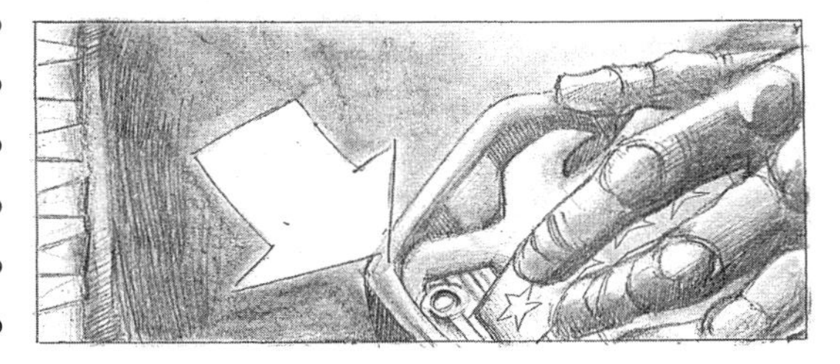

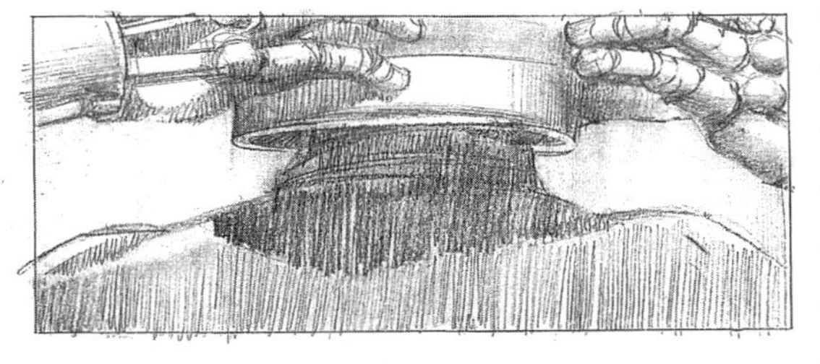

Film Credits

FROM HOLLYWOOD PICTURES

ANDREW G. VAJNA PRESENTS
AN EDWARD R. PRESSMAN/CINERGI PICTURES PRODUCTION
IN ASSOCIATION WITH CHARLES M. LIPPINCOTT

DIRECTOR....DANNY CANNON
PRODUCERS....CHARLES M. LIPPINCOTT
BEAU E. L. MARKS
EXECUTIVE PRODUCERS....ANDY G. VAJNA
EDWARD R. PRESSMAN
WRITTEN BY....WILLIAM WISHER AND STEVE E. de SOUZA
ASSOCIATE PRODUCERS....TONY MUNAFO
SUSAN NICOLETTI
DIRECTOR OF PHOTOGRAPHY....ADRIAN BIDDLE, B.S.C.
PRODUCTION DESIGNER....NIGEL PHELPS
EDITED BY....ALEX MACKIE
AND HARRY KERAMIDAS
VISUAL EFFECTS SUPERVISOR....JOEL HYNEK
VISUAL EFFECTS PRODUCER....DIANE PEARLMAN
VISUAL EFFECTS BY....MASS.ILLUSION
LENOX, MASSACHUSETTS
COSTUME DESIGNER....EMMA PORTEOUS
JUDGE DREDD ARMOUR COSTUME DESIGNED BY....GIANNI VERSACE
MUSIC COMPOSED AND CONDUCTED BY....ALAN SILVESTRI
CASTING BY....JACKIE BURCH

Cast

JUDGE DREDD....SYLVESTER STALLONE
RICO....ARMAND ASSANTE
FERGIE....ROB SCHNEIDER
JUDGE GRIFFIN....JURGEN PROCHNOW
JUDGE FARGO....MAX VON SYDOW
JUDGE HERSHEY....DIANE LANE
McGRUDER....JOANNA MILES
ILSA....JOAN CHEN
OLMEYER....BALTHAZAR GETTY
MILLER....MAURICE ROEVES
GEIGER....IAN DURY
MEAN MACHINE....CHRIS ADAMSON
JUNIOR ANGEL....EWEN BREMNER
JUDGE ESPOSITO....PETER MARINKER
JUDGE SILVER....ANGUS MacINNES
CLONE 1....IAN MILLS
CLONE 2....DALE TANNER
FEMALE CADET....ELLY FAIRMAN
CADET 1....CHARLIE CONDOU
CADET 2....AKBAR KURTHA
CADET 3....PATRICK PASI
CADET 4....SAM BARRISCALE
CADET 5....AMELIA CURTIS
CADET 6....HELENA HYKLUM
LOCKER JUDGE....LOUISE DELAMERE
FINK ANGEL....PHIL SMEETON
HUNTER SQUAD LEADER....STEVE TOUSSAINT
CHIEF JUDGE HUNTER....BRADLEY SAVELLE
JUDGE KILLED BY ROBOT....MARK MORGHAN
BARGE CREW MEMBER....ED STOBART
BRUTAL PRISONER....HUGGY LEVER
BRISCO....ALEXIS DANIEL
BORDER GUARD....JOHN BLAKEY
PILOT....HOWARD GRACE
REGGIE....DIG WAYNE
TWIST....MARTIN McDOUGALL
SQUATTER 1....ASHLEY ARTUS
SQUATTER 2....CHRISTOPHER GLOVER
SQUATTER 3....BRENDAN FLEMING
ZED SQUATTER 1....STEPHEN LORD
ZED SQUATTER 2....PHIL KINGSTON
ASPEN GUARD 1....EWAN BAILEY
CO-PILOT....STUART MULLEN
LILLIE HAMMOND....PAT STARR
FUPPIE....ADAM HENDERSON
HAMMOND....MITCHELL RYAN

Crew

PRODUCTION MANAGER....MARGARET ADAMS
FIRST ASSISTANT DIRECTOR....CHRIS NEWMAN
SECOND ASSISTANT DIRECTOR....BERNARD BELLEW
CO-SECOND ASSISTANT DIRECTOR....SALLIE ANN HARD
THIRD ASSISTANT DIRECTOR....BEN HOWARTH
SPECIAL EFFECTS and ABC ROBOT SUPERVISOR....JOSS WILLIAMS
MAKE-UP & PROSTHETICS SUPERVISOR....NICK DUDMAN
MEAN MACHINE SPECIAL MAKE-UP EFFECTS DESIGNED & BUILT BY
....CHRIS HALLS
SOUND DESIGNER....LESLIE SHATZ

Art Department

SUPERVISING ART DIRECTOR....LES TOMKINS
ART DIRECTORS....KEVIN PHIPPS
DON DOSSETT
ASST. ART DIRECTORS....MARTIN LAING
GARY TOMKINS
CONCEPTUAL ILLUSTRATORS....JULIAN CALDOW
CHRIS HALLS SIMON MURTON
KEVIN WALKER MATTHEW CODD
STORYBOARD ARTISTS....ROBBIE CONSING
JOHN GREAVES
SENIOR DRAUGHTSPERSON....PETER RUSSELL
DRAUGHTSPERSONS....STEPHEN DOBRIC
MIRANDA DIAMOND ADAM O'NEILL
JUNIOR DRAUGHTSPERSON....JON BILLINGTON
SCULPTORS....ALLAN MOSS
KEITH SHORT ROY RODGERS
GRAPHIC DESIGNER....ALEX RUTHERFORD
ART DEPT. ASSISTANT....ANDREA HEFFORD
ACTION VEHICLE ART DIRECTOR....DAVID ALLDAY
SARACEN ENGINEER....STEVE LAMONBY
FLOOR COORDINATOR....DARREN LITTON

BIKE DRESSING/STANDBY MODELLERS....OLIVER HODGE
PETER WATSON

LAND ROVER VEHICLES SUPPLIED AND DESIGNED BY
ROVER GROUP LIMITED

Camera

CAMERA OPERATORS....DAVID WORLEY
IAN FOSTER
FOCUS PULLERS....FRASER TAGGERT
JOHN FOSTER
CLAPPER LOADERS....RUPERT HORNSTEIN
ASHLEY BOND
CAMERA DEPT. TRAINEES....CHARLES GUARD
ROBERT NEILL
CAMERA GRIPS....JOHN FLEMMING
GARY POCOCK

Electrical

GAFFER.... KEVIN DAY
BEST BOY.... PETER GODDARD
ELECTRICIANS:....JIMMY WORLEY GARY COLKETT
GARY VARNEY VINCENT (BUGSY) CLARKE
GRAHAM DRISCOLL CHRISTOPHER DAY
RIGGING ELECTRICIANS:....GEORGE HUNT ALFRED EMMINS
JOHN ROBERTSON JOHN BARRY
LESLIE WEIGHELL ANTHONY RUBINI
PRACTICAL ELECTRICIANS:....ERIC MELVILLE EDDIE HACKETT
CHRIS DOWLING JAMES ROPER
GENNY OPERATOR....BRIAN McGIVERN
CHARGEHAND RIGGING GAFFER....JOHN CLARK

Special Effects

SPECIAL EFFECTS ADMINISTRATOR....MICHAEL DAWSON
SPECIAL EFFECTS SR DESIGN ENGINEER....BRIAN MORRISON
SPECIAL FLLOR COORDINATOR....CLIVE BEARD
SPECIAL EFFECTS WORKSHOP COORDINATOR....STEVE CULLANE
SPECIAL EFFECTS LEAD SENIOR TECHNICIAN....KEVIN DRAYCOTT
SPECIAL EFFECTS SENIOR TECHNICIANS....KEVIN HERD
BRIAN M. WARNER DAVE KNOWLES
ROBERT MALOS
SPFX LEAD TECHNICIAN....DARRELL GUYON
SPFX TECHNICIANS:....FRANK GUINEY DAVID HUNTER
MIKE DURKAN PAUL CLANCY
ALEX GUNN SHAUN RUTTER
FLYING WIRE SUPERVISOR....BOB WEISINGER
FLYING WIRE SR. TECHNICIAN....KEVIN MATHEWS
FLYING WIRE TECHNICIAN....NEIL CARR
ABC ROBOT SYSTEM DESIGN....BRIAN MORRISON
ABC ROBOT ELECTRONICS....ROB MALOS
ABC ROBOT ENGINEERS....PETER WHITE
PAUL TAYLOR MIKE DUNLEAVY
ROBBIE SCOTT

Wardrobe

WARDROBE SUPERVISOR....PATRICK WHEATLEY
WARDROBE MISTRESS....CYNTHEA DOWLING
COSTUMER TO MR. STALLONE....BRADLEY ANDERSON
WARDROBE ASSISTANTS....KERRY HOLMES
MICHAEL MOONEY ANTHONY GOFF

Make-up/Hair

PROSTHETICS ASSISTANT....REZA KARIM
PROSTHETIC WORSHOP TECHNICIAN....LAWRENCE SIMMONS
PROSTHETICS WORKSHOP ASSISTANT....COLIN SHULVER
PROSTHETICS TRAINEES....JAMES MORGAN
FAYE DE BREMAEKER
MEAN MACHINE SENIOR F/X ARTIST....PAUL CATLING
MEAN MACHINE MAKE-UP ASSISTANT....MICHELLE TAYLOR
MEAN MACHINE F/X TECHNICIAN....NEIL GORDON
MAKE-UP ASSISTANT TO MR. STALLONE....SCOTT EDDO
MAKE-UP ARTISTS....MELISSA LACKERSTEEN
JENI WALKER
MAKE-UP TRAINEES....HEATHER HARRIGAN
MICHELLE FREEBORN
CHIEF HAIRDRESSER....COLIN JAMISON
HAIR STYLIST TO MR. STALLONE....PAUL ABASCAL
ASST. HAIRDRESSER....JAN JAMISON

Set decoration & Property

SET DECORATOR....PETER YOUNG
PRODUCTION BUYER....JOHN LANZER
PROPERTY MASTER....TY TEIGER
CHARGEHAND STANDBY PROPS....MARK ALLETT
STANDBY PROPS....JONATHAN HURST
NICK TURNBULL
SUPERVISING PROPERTY STOREMAN....PAUL PURDY
CHARGEHAND DRESSING PROPERTY....MARTIN KINGSLEY
DRESSING PROPERTY....PETER LOOBY
PAUL CHEESMAN
MODELLERS....TOBY HAWKES
MARK J. WHITE EDWIN WRIGHT
ELIZABETH RICHARDS HOWARD MUNFORD
ARMOURER....CARL F. SCHMIDT

Sound/Video

SOUND MIXER....CHRIS MUNRO, C.A.S
SOUND MAINTENANCE....COLIN WOOD
SOUND ASSISTANT....ANDREW GRIFFITHS
VIDEO COORDINATOR....BOB BRIDGES

Production

2ND UNIT DIRECTOR....BEAU MARKS
PRODUCTION ASSOCIATE....MARY LOU DEVLIN
UNIT/LOCATION MANAGER....SIMON McNAIR SCOTT
PRODUCTION MANAGER – ICELAND....SNORRI ORISSON
PRODUCTION COORDINATORS....KATE GARBETT
CAROL REGAN
PRODUCTION COORDINATOR – ICELAND....ASTA H. STEFANSD
POST PRODUCTION COORDINATOR....REBECCA HILLIARD
PRODUCTION ACCOUNTANT – ENGLAND....GARY JONES
PRODUCTION ACCOUNTANT – ICELAND....SIGRUN OSK SIGURDARD
ASSISTANT PRODUCTION ACCOUNTANT....GARY NIXON
ACCOUNTS ASSISTANTS....CARMEL CASSIDY
MATT O'TOOLE
SCRIPT SUPERVISOR....SHEILA WILSON
2ND AD/CASTING – ICELAND....LEIFUR B. DAGFINNSSON
PRODUCTION RUNNER....PHIL STOOLE
FLOOR RUNNER....RICHARD GRAYSMARK
U.K. CASTING DIRECTOR....LUCY BOULTING
LA CASTING ASSISTANT....GAIL GOLDBERG
UK CASTING ASSISTANT....AMY ALLEN
STAND-INS....STEVE MORPHEW
STEVE PRICE
EMMA STOKES
DAVE GIBBONS
PUBLICIST....PETER J. SILBERMANN

STILLS PHOTOGRAPHY........RICHARD BLANSHARD
ASSISTANTS TO MR. VAJNA........JANE BULMER
........ANN MECEDA
ASSISTANT TO MR. STALLONE........KEVIN KING
BODYGUARD TO MR. STALLONE........GARY COMPTON

Stunts

STUNT COORDINATOR........MARC BOYLE
STUNT DOUBLE FOR MR. STALLONE........IGNACIO CARRENO
STUNT PERFORMERS........DEL BAKER, IAN JAY, STUART CLARK, VINCENT KEANE
STUNT PERFORMERS........RAY DE-HAAN, DEREK LEA, THERESE DONNELLY, GUY LIST, NIGEL FAN, NICHOLAS POWELL, NEIL FINNIGAN, LUISA SILVESTRE, NICK GILLARD, ANDY SMART

Editorial

EDITOR........JEREMY GIBBS
ASSOCIATE EDITOR........PETER ELLIOT
ASSISTANT EDITORS........HUMBERTO LUNA-GALLARDO, LIONEL JOHNSON, BAYLIS GLASCOCK, RUSS WOOLNOUGH, CHRISTOPHER KROLL, MARK SALE, MELISSA BRETHERTON
APPRENTICE EDITOR........KRISTIN EATON
POST PRODUCTION ASSISTANT........KATHLEEN TANNER
TITLE AND OPTICALS........BUENA VISTA IMAGING
NEGATIVE CUTTERS........D. BASSETT AND ASSOCIATES

Sound Effects

SOUND EFFECTS EDITORS........MALCOLM FIFE, KIM B. CHRISTENSEN, CHRIS GRIGGS, JIM McKEE, KRYSTEN MATE COMOGLIO
FOLEY EDITOR........E. JEANNE PUTMAN
FIRST ASSISTANT SOUND EDITOR........MARILYN S. ZALKAN
DIALOGUE EDITORS........PATRICK DODD
RICHARD QUINN
DIALOGUE ASSISTANT........LISA STORER
ADR EDITOR........DAVID A. COHEN
ADR ASSISTANT........NANCY JENCKS
LOOP GROUP COORDINATOR........BARNEY JONES
APPRENTICES........CHRISTOPHER E. BENNETT
KAREN ALANE RESTER
TEMP MIX SUPERVISOR........MARK LEVINSON
FOLEY ARTISTS........MARGIE O'MALLEY
JENNIFER MYERS
FOLEY RECORDISTS........RICHARD DUARTE
JIM PASQUE
RE-RECORDING MIXERS........LESLIE SHATZ
DAVID PARKER
DUBBING RECORDIST........PHILLIP ROGERS

POST PRODUCTION SOUND EDITING
AND MIXING DONE AT TWICKENHAM FILM STUDIOS

Visual Effects

DIRECTOR OF PHOTOGRAPHY........DAVID K. STEWART, A.S.C
VISUAL EFFECTS ART DIRECTOR........ROBERT U. TAYLOR
ASSISTANT VISUAL F/X SUPERVISOR........JOHN GAETA
ASSISTANT VISUAL F/X PRODUCER........CARRIE OWEN
2ND VISUAL F/X SUPERVISOR........DAVID GREEN
PRODUCTION MANAGER........MARIA CRISCUOLO
FIRST ASSISTANT DIRECTOR........BYARS COLE
POST-PRODUCTION COORDINATOR........JOAN COLLINS
PRODUCTION COORDINATOR........KEVIN ELAM
LONDON PRODUCTION COORDINATOR........MARA BRYAN
SHUTTLE CRASH/PYROTECHNIC PRODUCER........TIM GOLDBERG
MOTION CONTROL CAMERA OPERATORS........HARRY J. ALPERT
DAVID R. HARDBERGER
MOTION CONTROL ENGINEER/CAMERA OPERATOR........DWAYNE McCLINTOCK
LIVE ACTION MOTION CONTROL CAMERA OPERATOR........ERICK SWENSON
HIGH SPEED DIRECTOR OF PHOTOGRAPHY........WILLIAM NEIL
MOTION CONTROL/CAMERA ENGINEER........STEVEN KOSAKURA
FIRST ASSISTANT CAMERAPERSONS........ANTHONY BRAUN, LAURA E. KELLY, MARCO MALDONADO
SECOND ASSISTANT CAMERAPERSON........DANIEL KARP
KEY GAFFER........DENNIS McHUGH
BEST BOY ELECTRIC........RICK SANDS
3RD ELECTRICS........JACK W. POORE
MICHAEL JENKINS
KEY GRIP........MARC J. CATO
GRIPS........MARK C. ANDERSON, STEVE JEZEWSKI, DAN DENITTO
DIGITAL VFX SUPERVISOR/SOFTWARE DESIGNER....SERGE STRETSCHINSKY
SENIOR DIGITAL VFX ANIMATORS........NICHOLAS BROOKS
DEBORAH WILTMAN
DIGITAL VFX ANIMATORS........PAM AUDITORE
PETER PLEVRITIS
DIGITAL TECHNICAL ASSISTANT........PETER CHESLOFF
PREVISULAIZATION SUPERVISOR........COLIN GREEN
PHOTOSHOP ARTIST........WILLIAM McCOY
PREVISUALIZATION DESIGNERS........MICHAEL SCHMITT, PETER OBERDORFER, DANIEL LEUNG, DANIEL L. SMITH, JOHN VEGHER
MECHANICAL EFFECTS SUPERVISOR........KELLY KERBY
PRYOTECHNICIAN........THAINE MORRIS
MECHANICAL EFFECTS RIGGERS........DAVID NUNEZ
TOM QUINN
MOTION BASE ENGINEER........ROBIN LEYDEN
MECHANICAL EFFECTS MACHINISTS........YEZID O. GALLEGO
ROBERT KOHUT
MECHANICAL EFFECTS TECHNICIANS........MICHAEL KELLOUGH
MECHANICAL EFFECTS ASST. RIGGER........JEREMY BEADELL
MODEL DESIGNERS........KENT MIKALSEN
MARK MORGENSTEIN
ASSOCIATE ART DIRECTOR........MICHELLE QUIGLEY
MODEL SHOP SUPERVISOR........ERIC CHAMBERLAIN
KEY MODELMAKERS........DAIJIRO BAN
DAVID MERRITT
STEPHEN THURN
MODEL SHOP COORDINATOR........CRAIG CHAMBERLAIN
MODELMAKERS........JEN HOWARD, GARLAND M. BRANCH III, ROBB RUNYON, PAUL CLEMENTE, DANIEL KLEM, BARRETT SCHUMACHER, GARY CROSBY, PABLO MALDONADO, MARK J. SWIERAT, SHAUN CUSICK, BRIAN McGINLEY, STEWART VERRILLI, JOHN DODELSON, BILLY MESSINA, TONY WHALEN, JINNIE EDDLEMON, ED MIARECKI, CASH S. WILSON, FRANK GALLEGO, RINALDO RIVERA, MINAMOTO YOSHIDA
SET MODELMAKERS........JAMES SPIELER, NICK THIELKER, PAUL VALLERIE
PAINTERS........JOHN LESQUEREAUX
PERRY HALL

WELDER .... SANDY RHODES
SET DOCUMENTATION .... LARRY CURTIN
CAD DESIGNERS .... DAVE HARVEY
SCOT LANGE SUSAN THUM
LASERCAM OPERATOR .... AL AUMENTA
VISUAL EFFECTS EDITOR .... JENNIFER WOLLAN
LAYOUT SUPERVISOR .... LARRY PLASTRIK
ASSISTANT EDITORS .... ELIZABETH CASTRO
GORDON GRINBERG
PROJECTIONIST/LAB SUPERVISOR .... GLENN ARNOLD
E-6 LAB TECHNICIAN/EDITORIAL ASSISTANT .... ROY BERKOWITZ
EDITORIAL COORDINATOR .... HEATHER SANDS
DATABASE MANAGER .... LISA GOLDBERG
AUDITOR .... AMY COMSTOCK
PURCHASER .... THOMAS L. RINDGE
ASSISTANT PRODUCTION COORDINATOR .... SONJA REINHOLT
SYSTEMS ADMINISTRATOR .... RUSTY CASE
ELECTRONICS TECHNICIAN .... PETER LINDSTROM
ENGINEERING ASSISTANT .... RICHARD DUQUETTE
FACILITY MANAGER .... BOB PODOLSKI
RECEPTIONIST/OFFICE COORDINATOR .... LINDA ST. PIERRE
CRAFT SERVICE .... JAKE CHASKEY
OPERATIONS CONSULTANT .... LEE RUTTENBERG

COMPUTER GENERATED IMAGES & ELEMENTS BY
KLEISER-WALCZAK CONSTRUCTION COMPANY

COMPUTER GENERATED IMAGE SUPERVISORS
JEFF KLEISER & DIANA WALCZAK

COMPUTER GENERATED IMAGE EXECUTIVE PRODUCER
ANEZKA SEBEK

Kleiser-Walczak crew

HEAD OF SOFTWARE .... FRANK VITZ
LEAD ANIMATORS .... EILEEN O'NEILL
RANDY BAUER
SYSTEMS ADMINISTRATOR .... JOE HALL
ANIMATORS .... JEFFREY A. WILLIAMS
CHRISTINA HILLS
LIGHTING SUPERVISOR .... LUC GENEVRIEZ
LIGHTING AND TECHNICAL ASSISTANT .... RAE LONG
LIGHTING .... CHRISTIAN FOUCHER
XAVIER DUVAL PASCAL NICOT
PHILLIPPE LALOUETTE
SMOKE EFFECTS/PARTICLE SYSTEMS .... MIKE PERRY
ANIMATION ASSISTANTS .... TALMAGE WATSON
GREG JUBY
POST COORDINATOR .... MARY NELSON
DIGITAL ASSISTANTS .... ROBIN FRANCIS
MICHAEL MOORE
PRODUCTION MANAGER .... T. BAKER ROWELL
ASSISTANT TO EXECUTIVE PRODUCER .... KRISTIN COPPOLA
CHIEF FINANCIAL OFFICER .... JEFFREY M. TAGGART
BOOKKEEPER .... LORI FREDERICK
ADDITIONAL CGI GRAPHICS .... DIGITAL FAUXTOGRAPHY
EDITEL, NEW YORK
ASPEN PENAL COLONY MATTE PAINTING .... MAGIC CAMERA COMPANY
MATTE ARTIST .... DOUG FERRIS
MATTE CAMERMAN .... JOHN GRANT
WESCAM PROVIDED BY .... WESCAM, INC.
WESCAM OPERATOR .... STEVE KOSTER
WESCAM TECHNICIAN .... DAVE DAUNT

Transportation

UNIT CARS .... 'SPARROW' BROADWAY
BRIAN ESTABROOK LEN FURSSEDONN
MIKE BEAVEN
UNIT CAR MR. STALLONE .... STEVE HILL
TERRY REECE

Construction

CONSTRUCTION COORDINATOR .... MICHAEL REDDING
CONSTRUCTION MANAGER .... KEN PATTENDEN
CONSTRUCTION STOREMAN .... RICHARD LYON
HOD CARPENTER .... ALAN BROOKS
SUPERVISING CARPENTERS .... GEORGE COUSSINS
MICHAEL HAYWARD
CHARGEHAND CARPENTERS .... GEOFF HALL
DAVE PHILPOTT
CHARGEHAND WOOD MACHINIST .... JOHN LOWEN
HOD PAINTER .... KAVIN HALL
SUPERVISING PAINTERS .... BOB HARPER
PETER WESTERN
CHARGEHAND PAINTERS .... BRIAN SHELLEY
GRAHAM PEARCE
HOD PLASTERER .... DON TAYLOR
SUPERVISING PLASTERERS .... NEIL CLARK
ROY SEERS
CHARGEHAND PLASTERERS .... DAVE BAYNHAM
TONY BOXALL
CHARGEHAND PLASTERER'S LABOURER .... OTIS BELL
SUPERVISING RIGGER .... PETER WALLACE
CHARGEHAND RIGGER .... ALF NEWVELL
CHARGEHAND RIGGERS .... IAN PAPE
STEVE LAWRENCE
SUPERVISING STAGEHAND .... KEN WILSON
CHARGEHAND STAGEHANDS .... LEN SERPANT
TERRY NEWVELL
CARPENTERS .... JEFF REID DAVID WILLIAMSON
STEPHEN WHITWORTH PETER MURRAY
MICHAEL LUNNON NICK RUSSO
ALAN TILLEY MARK WILLIAMSON
DAVID GIBSON TREVOR NICOL
JASON PILFOLD JOHN BURN
JIM HACKETT DARREN CAEN
ARNOLD OKE DAVID RUSHMERE
DARREN PHILPOTT RICHARD MILLS
STEPHEN CLARK JOHN CASEY
LESLIE JONES KEVIN O'BYRNE
TONY MANSEY CHRISTOPHER CORKE
COLIN CLARKE WAYNE HAMMOND
STEPHEN MURRAY JOHN LAWRENCE
STEVEN CORKE KEVIN SWABEY
JOE McGURK PETER DE SOUZA
ALLAN WALSHAM STEVE ADLER
RICHARD DENYER PAUL HAYES
PATRICK O'LOUGHNANE
STANDBY CARPENTER .... STEPHEN EELS
WOOD MACHINISTS .... RICHARD ROWLANDS
BILL SOWER
PAINTERS .... GEOFF SHELTON JAMIE SHELLEY
ERNIE BELL EDWARD BRADLEY
JOHN HEDGER BRIAN ACASTER
JOHN WATTS GARY SMITH
BARRY CAHILL LEE SHELLEY

PAINTER'S LABOURERS .... GLYNN JONES
PAUL BUDD
DEAN BUDD
STANDBY PAINTER .... RAY CAMPBELL
PLASTERERS .... BRIAN PEGG, DANNY BOXALL
KEITH SHANNON, PAUL ROBERY
MAURICE STAFFORD, KEVIN TURNER
BILL CLAYTON, STEWART LITTLE
GEOFF BACON, MAURICE ANDREWS
JEREMY ROSE, FRED BEWLEY
GARY STOKES, STEVE POWELL
JOHN ROBERY, ALAN POWELL
ANTHONY TURNER, BOB BYRON
ANDY SANDBACH, IAN McFADYEN
MICK MELIA, PAUL JONES
WALLY BLANCHETT, JOHN WILLIS
PLASTERER'S LABOURERS .... JOHN BROWN
BILL THOMPSON, RICHARD STANELY
ASHLEY BELL, PETER DUNN
JIM DONOGHUE, GORDON WOODS
STANDBY PLASTERER .... JOHN MISTER
RIGGERS .... PAUL MILLS, JOHN PITT
JOE DOYLE, PETER FRAFFHAM
ROBERT DIEBELIUS, REG SMITH
JOSE ROMERO ABUIN, RON MILES
TRAINEE RIGGERS .... JASON CURTIS
JOE RUSSO
ANDREW THOMPSON
STANDBY RIGGER .... IAN ROLFE
STAGEHANDS .... FRED BROWN, MICHAEL COHEN
PETER STACHINI, NICKY WESTERN
PETER ANDREWS, CLIVE WHEELER
STANDBY STAGEHAND .... GEORGE CHAMBERS
CONSTRUCTION DRIVER .... BRUCE BEHRENS

Music

MUSIC SUPERVISORS .... BARRY LEVINE
.... ERIC HARRYMAN
ADDITIONAL MUSIC SERVICES .... STEVEN MACHAT
ORCHESTRATIONS BY .... WILLIAM ROSS
MUSIC SCORING MIXER .... DENNIS SANDS
SYNCLAVIER/AURICLE PROGRAMMING .... DAVID BIFANO
MUSIC EDITOR .... KENNETH KARMAN
ASSISTANT MUSIC EDITOR .... JACQUELINE TAGER
Soundtrack Album available on EPIC COMPACT DISCS AND CASSETTES

Judge Dredd comic character creators

CHARACTER	WRITER	ARTIST
Judge Dredd	John Wagner	Carlos Ezquerra
Judge Hershey	John Wagner	Brian Bolland
Rico	Pat Mills	Mike McMahon
Angel Gang/Mean Machine	John Wagner	Mike McMahon
Chief Justice Fargo	John Wagner	Carlos Ezquerra
ABC Warrior, Hammerstein	Pat Mills	Kevin O'Neill

Based on the Judge Dredd character owned by Egmont Foundation and created by John Wagner and Carlos Ezquerra

MADE AT SHEPPERTON STUDIOS
SHEPPERTON, LONDON, ENGLAND

Financing Arranged by .... CHEMICAL BANK, As Agent
Completion Guarantee Provided by
.... INTERNATIONAL FILM GUARANTORS, INC.
Production Insurance Arranged by .... MARC J. FEDERMAN
NEAR NORTH INSURANCE BROKERAGE, INC.

Cameras by .... PANAVISION
Lighting Equipment by .... LEE LIGHTING LIMITED
Colour by .... TECHNICOLOUR

Special Thanks to: .... JONATHAN BOREHAM & ASSOCIATES
BERETTA
AIR TREMBATH
REEBOK INTERNATIONAL LIMITED
CAMERA TRACKING COMPANY
MIKE LAKE
NICK LANDAU
MR. & MRS. CHARLES M. LIPPINCOTT
THE SAUL ZAENTZ FILM CENTER

A HOLLYWOOD PICTURES RELEASE

At the time of going to press the production credits had not all been finalised. The Publishers apologise for any incorrect credits and will be happy to amend them in the reprints.